EARLY INDIAN
JURISPRUDENCE

EARLY INDIAN JURISPRUDENCE

Precepts, Practice & Gender Status

Archana Mishra

PARTRIDGE

Print information available on the last page.

To order additional copies of this book, contact
Partridge India
000 800 10062 62
orders.india@partridgepublishing.com

www.partridgepublishing.com/india

CONTENTS

PREFACE

Law, in any society, represents the urge to establish order. It is a product of its intellectual thinking, legal scholarship and a sense of morality, aspired or existent within it, at a particular point in time. In the context of early India, the question engaging several scholars has been, whether Hindu Law in practice, was the same as or merely approximated to *Dharma,* which was essentially an ethical code. Though several scholars have acknowledged the antiquity of legal traditions in India and have extolled the Classical Hindu jurisprudence as put together in Dharmashastra texts, early India exhibits a distinct and unique tradition of law, which comprised of both, the metaphysical concept of righteousness called Dharma, as well as the rudiments of pure law. Even though Dharma embodied the elements of law, it was more of a moral code of conduct, propounded by the dominant section of the society, which specified the ways of rightful living along with the obligations of individuals and groups.

The idea of Dharma, drawn from the scholastic oral traditions and preserved in written form in the Dharmashastra texts, were in fact, dubbed by the English scholars as the first law codes of the country. Subsequently, the importance given to these texts during the colonial rule in streamlining the judicial system pertaining to Hindu civil law in a pluralist state, led to the coining of the term, "Hindu Law". Although historians, today, reject the idea that these Dharmashastras were purely legal texts or codes, one cannot deny that these texts exercised immense influence in legitimising various aspects of a deeply religious-minded society, into law. Law in the purely juristic sense was a later development, which evolved gradually through different stages adapting to the needs of a changed social milieu, symbolising an organic relationship between the legal system and the society.

Dharma laws continued to co-exist at all times in early India, evolving from one stage to another, depending upon the wisdom inculcated by its authors, in a complex society, where undercurrents of stratification and patronage were predominant. However, it was the State law, under the influence of reformist religions that seemed to have pioneered the idea of secular law in early India under exceptional kings such as Ashoka.

This work endeavours to explore the unique Indian concept of law, its origins and various aspects, as derived from the Dharmashastra texts and as gleaned from select epigraphic instances and secular sources. It attempts to study, how far Dharma and law shared a symbiotic or intertwined relationship and whether, Dharma constituted a source for constructing actual laws, along with the customs, usages and the king's edicts. The sources for this study cover a range of Dharmashastra works from Manusmrti to Katyayanasmrti and select secular works for understanding the lines of legal thinking. Among the epigraphic instances, prime study is based on the Vishnusena's Charter, which is of great relevance. The limitations of sources have been spelt out as well, so as to get an objective picture of law in Early India.

The study analyses the legitimisation of vested interests into various aspects of law– how it was explicitly or at times, subtly laid down in the Shastra, thereby creating a corpus of non-universal law in early India. Even though the concept of justice was emphasised repeatedly, ironically, the framework operated in the midst of patriarchy and a theologically sanctioned occupation-based caste hierarchy and hence, had its limitations as far as legal equality was concerned. These religious and secular texts put heavy emphasis on the role of the king, who was a pivot in the dispensation of justice, thus making the state accountable for justice and welfare of the people. They highlight the need to lay stress on the character and wisdom of judges as well, on whose shoulders rested the responsibility of ensuring justice. The work also highlights through an epigraphic instance, how popular aspirations in law were taken into account and could have been approved by the state.

Another subset of questions that are raised in this book is related to the gender status in law. Given the existent discourse of patriarchal Brahmanism and differential treatment, did gender factor in law in a substantial way? Do the heterogeneities in some Smrti texts, which sometimes talk of disabilities imposed on men, indicate the transitions in patriarchal mind-set or constitute isolated deviations in norms, set by various authors to the rescensionary texts? Gender aspect in law is a subchapter in the book that attempts to understand the vulnerabilities of women in society and therefore, also in law, along with an analysis of the limitations of legal privileges of men, although few and far between.

Law seems to be an institution that was used selectively as a tool of governance. Embedded in religion, and with factors like race, ethnicity and sexuality visible in law, the basic ideas of 'welfare of all' and 'legal equality' were left unaddressed in early India. Interestingly, legal scholarship was of high order in early India and several legal traditions may have worked in parallel, but what seemed to be lacking was the approach to legal universalism, cutting across the societal stratifications, which would have prepared the society for egalitarianism in law. This may have been difficult to achieve as first, political governance was varied in different regions and periods and second, different rulers brought different approaches to law, particularly when heterodox tendencies ushered in alternative thinking. The coexistence of Dharma precepts and elements of pure law underline a high order, aspirational thinking and a willingness to accommodate legal philosophy with practice, in order to achieve an ideal society. This ideal was, however, marred by social stratifications and varied governance in early India with only few exceptions.

Acknowledgements

This book would not have seen the light of the day without the immense support and inspiration of several people in my life. I owe my foremost gratitude to my husband, who not only inspired me to pursue PhD but also encouraged me to write this book. He went out of the way to analyse the content critically and resolved all the bottlenecks in this effort.

This effort would not have fructified had it not been for the inspiration, constant guidance, and blessings of my learned PhD Guide and Professor, Dr. K.K. Shah, a historian of repute, with several works to his credit, who retired as the Head of the PG Department of History, SNDT University, Mumbai. I acknowledge my deepest and sincere gratitude to him for all the knowledge that he imparted to me during my Post Graduation and especially while doing PhD under his meticulous guidance and this in spite of his worrisome health problems.

I would also like to extend my gratitude to my PG alma mater, the SNDT University, Mumbai, where I completed my PG and PhD, for providing me the right academic atmosphere and infrastructure. The University has a rich collection of primary and secondary works in the Library and I am extremely thankful to the library staff, as well as the office staff, for their constant support. I am particularly grateful to Ms. Kirti and Ms. Suvarna for their cooperation in obtaining permission for using my thesis for this book. I am also thankful to my alma mater, the Isabella Thoburn College, Lucknow, where I did my graduation, learning from worthy teachers, who shaped my academics and approach to learning.

I would like to express my gratitude to the Asiatic Society of Bombay for the Annual Fellowship extended to me while doing my PhD (the K.T. Telang Fellowship), as well as for being the source of majority of my source books.

I consider myself very fortunate that I had the support of both sides of my parents, who have always given their blessings, encouraged my love for learning and given me the strength to keep on moving ahead on the path of academics. My children, one of whom is in the Indian Institute of Technology, Bombay and the other in Class 8, have been a source of strength to me always and have always provided me the positive energy to complete this work. They showed keen interest while I was engaged in this endeavour and even made precious suggestions. The rest of the family too has always been supportive of my endeavour. I would like to acknowledge the good wishes of all my friends and colleagues at Jai Hind College, who made valuable suggestions in the Preface section and also whenever I needed to clarify.

My heartfelt gratitude to Prof. Dr. Naresh Chandra, ex Pro Vice Chancellor, Mumbai University, for his blessings and for providing the rightful support in the final stages of writing this book, without which this book would not have been possible. I would also like to thank Mr. Unmesh Kapadia, who designed the cover of this book with great enthusiasm. I appreciate the cooperation extended and the patience shown by Ms. Kathy and Ms. Sara from the Publishing team.

INTRODUCTION

Law, a vital element of any state and society, represents the standards of morality set up by the society at any given point of time. Rooted in the socio-cultural context of the time and place, law is an attempt to regulate human response in societal conditions; and as a hallmark of any civilised and visionary society, it sets the tone of normative behavior. Law and society are interlinked and law becomes a mirror to the value system or the aspirations of the society. However, it is at best indicative of the practised moralities, decided by a few rather than the manifestation of complete aspired morality. As between the wisest thoughts and actual laws is the governing elite who by virtue of the power that they wield in a given milieu is the main instrument of creation of laws. When normative law is talked about, it would exhibit the intent of the society, but it is the actual law and the praxis that can tell the quality of justice delivered. In other words to understand law of any society or community, one needs to understand the people and their way of thinking first. Societal set up reflects in law and laws or legal status have a bearing on people's access to resources, privileges and power enjoyed by them.

For understanding legal norms, legal systems or jurisprudence, there are various approaches, which have mainly developed from 18th century onwards. Jurisprudence forms an important area of study as it throws light on the purpose of laws and invites discussions on the philosophy of law. The word is derived from *'Juris'* meaning law and *'Prudentia'* meaning foresight, sagacity or knowledge. This would imply the science which studies law and its applications. There are various types of Jurisprudence depending on the core focus of investigations which can be broadly classified into two sets-such as school of Natural law (Aristotle or Aquinas) or Analytical schools such as Legal Positivist or the Command theory approach, Legal realist or Sociological jurisprudence or Critical legal studies. While Natural Law school believed in objective moral order, the analytical schools did away the connect between morality and law and studied law 'as it is' and not 'as ought to be'. Sociological Jurisprudence focuses more of a contextual analysis which treats law and justice as fundamental institutions of society and anayse law in the context of society than as an independent entity (works of Max Weber and Durkheim). The functional approach would look at the utility of law as an institution of society and would explain what purpose the law. Legal scholarship by Positivist approach could end up being more doctrinaire by approach as all laws may not originate through commands and there could be alternate sources of origin of legal precepts in some societies, including as in India.

Likewise, Friedrich Carl Von Savigny, one of the prominent German jurist in the first half of the 19th century and the founder of the historical school in German law emphasised on locus of law being located in the community's daily customs and practices than in state law and gave an approach of studying non- statist laws too. Geertz rejected the view that law was a dispute resolving mechanism and rather viewed law as constructive of social realities rather than merely reflecting them. The 'Constitutive Approach' was the consequence of growth of Cultural Studies movement. These thinkers looked at law as means to create meanings in the mind of individuals and constructing social relations. Many writers of school of Critical legal studies or Legal Feminism viewed law as constitutive of culture. Pierre Bourdieu expressed the essence of this approach by expressing the view that law was a form of symbolic power and means to create active discourse and a social world which also creates laws.

Compared to the Positivist school or Command - theory approach, which lays emphasis on state laws, Sociological Jurisprudence and the Constitutive approach hold greater relevance in the study of India as we see in early India elements of Natural Law combined with laws originating from wise men, community and usage but laiden with vested interests. Here, the sociological approach can be blended with the functional approach to gather a perspective based on the origins and functions. Indian law here, is treated more by the historico-functional approach to understand the objectives with which it was created and to ascertain to what extent it achieved the ends, which were envisioned by different seers at varied times. From sociological perspective, studying the sources of law, analysing the role of society and religion and taking into account institutional and non-institutional inputs would enable us to understand the kind of precepts and laws prevailing in any society and the quality of justice delivered. The Constitutive approach would endeavour to analyse how through laws a symbolism was created and contestations in power in society were attempted.

An additional approach would even be to look at how the laws or principles of Dharma, a moral code containing laws too in the Indian context, affected the different sets of people, especially in society and in matters of legal status. This would entail a sophisticated analysis of how an emphasis on a moral code combined with coercive institutional power could determine individual status of people through a cross-section of categories of analysis. This juxtaposition of the normative and the actual aspects of early Indian law offer a unique area to study very different from Western conception.

The problem with any study on ancient Indian law pertaining to Hindus is that the study becomes even more complex owing to the comprehensiveness and varied gamut of source texts in the treatment of law and in subjects, intertwined with law. The chronology, structure, and authenticity of the texts themselves are a struggle for any researcher, more so owing to the void of a purely legal text, which would spell out laws in a straightforward way, as seen in compilations in the West. The uniqueness of Hindu law, however, lies in the fact that its a huge corpus of legal scholarship derived through works of various scholars at different times that survived independent of the political authority and as part of the larger sociolegal, ethical system of Dharma, prevalent in the Hindu tradition.

Here, the most ancient lore and traditions in the society were utilised by the governing Brahmana preceptors to create legal ideas and make them enforceable by attaching divine sanctions. These texts provided the ideological basis of the evolution of legal precepts in India. But how far this legal thought was retained on the hard rock of reality is one of the most important aspects to be ascertained, for that alone would help in measuring the proportion of adherence to, or deviations from, the norm. Embedded deep into its base were the considerations of caste and gender, alien to the post-enlightenment ideal of human equality but governing prescriptions and sanctions of every *smritikara* (writers of Dharmashastra), thus imparting a unique character to ancient Indian legal philosophy. Deviations from the norms laid down within this framework are but few and far between among available sources.

The task of sifting the ideal from the reality that might have existed becomes even more complicated when the period under study is considerably much earlier to the present times. Voluminous studies have been done on the theoretical content and various enunciations made by the Hindu law writers. However, an endeavour to correlate it with actual application of law in the societal framework is somewhat missing in the academic purview. The task becomes challenging also in view of the fact that even within a single tradition, there could be numerous or divergent attitudes at various levels.

In the early Indian society, where certain societal laws were embedded within the larger concept of Dharma or righteous conduct and where existence was defined by a particular world view, normative legal theory was built on the conception of right and wrong derived from the ways of existent intellectual traditions, tracing examples from the earliest Sacred texts. The subjective freedom in the conception of right and wrong were, however, substantially restrained at any given point, as the power elite—symbolised in the Brahmanical class, conscious of the threats to their position attempted to create a deliberate order and maintain it. The implementation of such moral laws was attempted to be accomplished by consciously attaching divine sanctions to several Dharma laws enunciated, projecting the outcomes for non-adherence in both the material and in the spiritual world.

However, these norms were at most of the times according to the layers of the institution of caste, and hence, the intellectualising of laws may have differed according to different levels of education and understanding. In other words, in practice, the normative legal perceptions were further intricated by existent hierarchical societal frameworks with situated interests of group or groups. Ancient Hindu law, hence to this extent was an outcome and a by-product of Dharma scholastic traditions. These normative laws and the customary law stand in contrast to the Western pure law which had a concrete single source origin in the command of the sovereign, under the positivist Austinian conception.

What is remarkable and fascinating is that there is noticed a continuous evolution of these ideas and progressive elements in the Dharmashastras, reflecting and imbibing changes in socio-political scenario. However, though the Dharmashastras cannot be called purely legal texts as the scholars have rightly pointed out, their importance cannot be undermined as they precede the somewhat purely legal thought that is culled out from later commentaries such as *Dayabhaga* (by Jimutavahana) and *Mitakshara* (byVijnaneshwara*)*, which, as rightly pointed out by Rocher, represent the interpretation of ancient texts rather than a stage in evolution of legal precepts. The terms such as *achara* (customary law) and *vyavahara* (legal suit) indicate that norms and practice may not have approximated exactly but may have been based on intellectual application.

The more important aspects of laws as extracted from Dharmashastras are indicative of the presence of legal consciousness among the scholars amidst the urge for spelling out ways of rightful living. The application of these injunctions, if any, required sifting the laws from the larger corpus of ethics, layered enunciations, as well as a meticulous interpretation of the same. While doing this, the legal traditions of India exhibit a high level of sensitiveness towards multiple issues, though same cannot be exalted to say that it was the ingredient of a perfect society. The larger goal towards establishing a moral society and public welfare is consciously inbuilt into the later Smrtis or Dharmashastra texts, which mirror the outcome of constant thinking over the issues pertaining to defining the norms and standardisation.

As law was linked to the way of thinking and the rules for rightful living, its objectives were broad and several. Like any normative law, it was welfare oriented for the self and the society. The ordering principle and adopting a righteous approach was at its core while the outcome expected was to gain happiness by correct administration of justice. In the Indian thinking, *varna* (caste) and a gender bias in favour of men as well as *purushartha* (fourfold goals of life) are constantly the intralayers to any such normative enunciations. The approach in various Smrtis is consequentialist towards achieving the designated ideal society but at the cost of universalism. However, the uniqueness of the gamut of Dharma laws is the voluntariness of its application dependent on individual consciousness. Aim was to prevent the moral lapse or disorder and create deterrence while focusing on justice.

In the present study, an effort has been made to see laws as innate in Dharma in both the theory and practice as it evolved over time as available in both the textual and the epigraphic sources. Neither the texts nor the inscriptions alone can provide a complete picture of law that might have existed in early India under study. A correlative study of both kinds of data is important. Law in its various aspects—procedural, civil, and criminal—seems to have been inherent in the Hindu system of jurisprudence; and it is worthy to take note of its subtleties. The focus is also on the gender aspect, which implies the analysis of legal injunctions or customary laws with respect to both men and women as categories of composite social existence.

The period chosen for the study is from 200 BC to 600 AD. The period from 200 BC onwards is of crucial importance and invites attention; for it saw, as Dr. Basham says, the crystallisation of certain cardinal ideas in the sociocultural fabric of India, which, in many ways, has continued in large measure till date. It marks the beginning of a definite period in History for which direct source material is available in the form of textual and epigraphical heritage. From the point of view of law especially, this period saw the codification of Hindu law (which may be debatable among scholars) and the flowering of such works, which gave rise to the commentaries that formed the basis of the two prominent law schools that emerged in India: the *Mitakshara* and the *Dayabhaga* in the later Hindu law. The period, hence, represents not only a period of ups and downs in history and construction and deconstruction of political empires but a simultaneous evolution of legal, political, social, and ethical and gender frameworks and philosophies in early India.

The theory and practice of law can be studied for this period with respect to the then-existing social actualities wherein lie the insecurities, which explain the rigidity and orthodoxy in the political and legal thought that emerged therefrom. It is this period that saw the unique institution of caste system adopt and assimilate the foreign elements, even though, theoretically, remaining severe on all occasions. The period witnessed definite ideas with respect to both sexes emerge with references to various functions and parameters such as the contract of marriage, the duties of husband and wife, property, divorce, widowhood, sati, and monetary transactions such as debt, ownership, title, possession, etc. Procedural law, which is more a locus of analytical jurisprudence, seems to have evolved from rudiments to refinement by the sixth century AD. Hence, any study on law for the period that would draw its components of actuality from various inscriptions would be meaningful as it would enable us to get somewhat a better, if not a holistic, understanding about law as also in reaching the historical reality, which is the very purpose of any such exercise.

The methodology selected for this research was first to identify the major Dharmashastra texts as the sources of thoughts on theoretical law, through study of the various enunciations made by *Manu, Yajnavalkya, Narada, Brhaspati,* and *Katyayana.* At the same time, references with respect to pure law, if any, were searched for and located in the available epigraphy. For this purpose, volumes of *Epigraphia Indica* and *Corpus Inscriptionum Indicarum* have been scanned through and studied. Apart from this, references pertaining to civil, criminal, and procedural laws were located in the plays of *Kalidasa, Shudraka, and Vishakhadatta* as also in *Bana's Harshacharita and Kadambari and Dashakumaracharita.* One must admit that references pertaining to the practice of law or to the legal thought are meagre. Whatever references are there are incidental by nature and had to be corroborated with other references. An effort has been made to avoid drawing any simplistic parallels between the theoretical and the epigraphic evidences, for such comparisons may be unwarranted given the dynamic nature of history and the debate whether Dharma laws could be called laws as such. It is also true that the Smrti law, which was in large part the law of *Aryavarta,* (historic name of present day Indian subcontinent) did not apply to the whole of India. Legal variations might have existed within and outside the larger tradition given the extent of the Indian subcontinent and political differences. Law has been studied with respect to its various aspects such as civil, criminal, or procedural rather than as existing in different regions. Even with respect to gender, no generalisation for the whole of the sub-continent is possible.

CHAPTER I

Conception of Law and its Relation with Dharma

In making an exhaustive study of the history and precepts of law in early India, it is of primary importance to ascertain the theory of law that was prevalent and could be adopted in the process of study. A student of legal history is, however, faced with many alternatives about defining "Law", some in strictly Western sense, and others as prevalent in the indigeneous traditions such as in India or in other countries, where the school of Natural Law and religion based laws were important.

By laws, we mean today the rules imposed by the supreme political authority or legislature of a country and more specifically as laid in the Constitution of a country or designed by the legislature and accepted as statute. However, in the western conception there has been a debate between the schools of natural law, positivist law or the empiricist laws. In the Western conception and more so in the Austinian sense, law is presumed to have originated and been promulgated under the auspices of the supreme political sovereign or authority, as he calls it command of the sovereign state, and implemented with the coercive power of the state. Eminent historian Radha Binod Pal has analysed that in its earliest form, this authority is that of divinely ordained or divinely dictated body of rules; in its latest form, it is a dogma that law is the command of the sovereign in a politically organised society. In both these situations, the emphasis is on single unchallengeable will, divine or temporal. However, this is not wholly true. Universal law or law of nature existed prior to the creation of a politically organised state. Even in primitive society, some kind of law or its element seems to have existed without any political sanction.

1

Essentially, positivist theories came up in opposition to the Natural law theory. Hart, who went beyond the Austin's conception, explained that laws could go beyond the conception of command of sovereign as it would apply even on those who would enact them. Besides, laws could be contrary to coercive orders as these could even confer certain powers. He refers to laws imposing obligations as the primary rules on individuals while those which would support it, as the secondary, including rules of recognition, change or adjudication on public functionaries. Hart who denies any logical relation between law and morality, however felt that rules of recognition could consider compatibility with values as the basis of legal validity. He even says that by changing the indeterminate laws, judges may actually create new laws.

In early India, law did not mean a sum total of chronological statement of king's shasanas (royal orders) or enunciations by any legislative authority and court orders. There was no statutory law but a prevalence largely of customary law. It was more a comprehensive concept based on intellectual interpretation of Dharmashastra tradition and usage, than being merely a set of legal injunctions to be implemented verbatim. The study of this jurisprudence belongs largely to the school of historical jurisprudence whose fathers were German jurist, Savigny and the British jurist, Sir Henry Maine. The quality noticed in these injunctions is the appeal embedded to an individual conscience to adhere or feel obligated to follow certain rules based on the stated wisdom of it and religious sanction. This was the normative quality which overruled the descriptive or positivist aspects

Early Jurisprudence seems to have a deeper connect with the concept of Dharma, which was largely the code of ethical behavior or code of righteousness pertaining to various situations one could face in life. Law and Dharma occurred as simultaneous terms but Dharma, was not pure law though it had elements of law in it. Laws were supposed to uphold the aims of Dharma, which was to achieve justice. In other words, the dividing line between the legal injunctions and moral injunctions was very less. Mahamahopadhyaya, P.V. Kane, an authority on study of Dharmashastra rightly commented that there is no term in English that corresponds to the meaning of Dharma. Dharma can only be explained as a cosmic theory of cardinal importance that prescribed the norms of social and political behavior, according to the four-fold aims of Hindu living. It was predominantly conceived by the Brahmana intellectual elite who reigned supreme in a hierarchic society fortified by attaching divine sanctions.

Law itself did not have a fixed connotation. Its definition underwent change in emphasis over the whole period of evolution. Dharma is primarily propounded in the smrtis, but elements of law are often traced from Vedas itself. One distinction that must be emphasised is that Vedas only talk about cosmic laws and not substantive or procedural laws.

The Vedic concept of law had *rta* as the central concept. '*Rta*', which was supposed to be the eternal law, was believed to be firm and immutable (*rtasya drdha dharunani santi*). Transgression of such rules was not merely a violation of human laws to be enforced by divine sanctions but was supposed to be punished in this life and hereafter by supernatural forces.[1] *Rta* becomes the antecedent of the later conception of law embedded in Dharma. Dharma, as one of the aspects of *rta*, refers specifically to the moral function of rewarding the good and punishing evil.[2] This was the nodal point, where from the idea of cosmic law developed the conception of rightful duties; and this idea was larger in concept than law in juridical sense, which can be accredited more to the Dharmashastra than the Vedas.

The Samavedic conception of law is similar to that of the Rigveda considering *rta* as an eternal and immutable code. However, till the Upanishadic period, little thought was given to what was the end of law. The Brahmanas and the Upanishads declared the end of law to be the preservation of social status quo.[3] Henceforth, we see a degree of liberalisation in law and a more humane approach.

Dharmashastra, on the other hand, was a comprehensive code that spelt rules to regulate human conduct in society in accordance with the scheme of creation. Dharma had so many definitions that no single definition could be ascribed to it. Dharma came to stand for nature, intrinsic quality, civil and moral law, justice, virtue, merit, duty, and morality.[4] A recent definition would restrict it to the actions or duties conforming to four *ashramas* and *varnas* in relation to the ends of life (*purushartha-fourfold*). It encompassed various types of dharma like that relating to caste (*varnadharma*) that relating to stage of life (*ashramadharma*) that dealing with both the two families (*varnashramadharma*), that related to function (*gunadharma*), and that related to occasion (*naimittikadharma*).

In the codes of Manu and Yajnavalkya, the concept of law evolved to a new stage where the monarch was seen as the upholder or fountain head of justice. The king's relation to law was considered primary, where the king was supposed to protect the subjects to maintain the status quo of *varnashrama*, punish the wicked, and dispense justice to those wronged. Customary laws may have existed separately and did play an important role. It is only in the works of later Smrti writers that law emerges in its procedural form and a systematic attempt is made to distinguish various aspects of law and judicial procedure.

In other words, Dharma was the composite of social existence that formed the basis of the emergence of legal precepts in India. Three unique features of Hindu concept of law could be probably seen as the following:

1. Law existed in some form or the other (as *rta or cosmic law*, truth, morality, or Dharma) from the earliest times, independent of the political authority. There is a systematic evolution of these legal precepts from rudiments to somewhat refined jurisprudence.
2. Law had both the legal and metaphysical aspects of Dharma that came to be accepted by society at large even though carrying forward with caste distinctions or without egalitarian notions.
3. The Hindu theory did not recognise the human role in the creation of law. Law was deemed to be perfect, divine, and immutable. Law was found, not made.

Human beings could only interpret, codify, or classify it by the study of judicial concepts associated with Dharma. India seemed to enjoy the security afforded by divine law (by wide interpretations of sources and meaning of Dharma). Hence, the Hindu theory of law cannot be studied in isolation from the theory of Dharma. Varadachariar correctly remarked that there is probably no term in Sanskrit language that could convey the legal meaning dissociated from the ethical sense.

The Hindu tradition speaks of salvation being achieved by a proper coordination of the three pursuits of human existence—Dharma (Laws of social existence), Artha (prosperity), and *Kama* (pleasure)—Dharma, of course, being the most important.[5] (The fourth *purushartha* was Moksha or salvation which was the crux of all existence and goal of the rest of the *purusharthas*). To maintain the Dharma, was the king's foremost duty, and every individual of the Hindu society was expected to serve it. To act according to Dharma would then imply that the man accepts his position and role ascribed on the basis of caste to which he was born and follow the norms or rules enunciated by the Smrti writers. Duties implied that there was a greater emphasis on obligations than legally permitted rights. What is observed here is the fact that religious discourse decided the duties as well legal commitments of the people in different strata till pure law emerged under different social milieu.

Dharma was indispensable to the scheme of law, for it promoted social welfare as well as provided individual securities, which are also the objectives of any state and laws. As the *Satapatha Brahmana* puts it, Dharma was the foundation of individual and collective security, for a state of nature without law was equivalent to anarchy (*Matsyanyaya*). It was above the king and the political authority and existed independently. It was deemed to be supreme and divine. The King was supposed to uphold this law by means of '*Danda*' or punishment. The Mahabharata through a conversation between Yudhisthira and Bhishma highlights that it was not easy to define Dharma, but one thing was certain that Dharma must ensure welfare of all human beings. It was an instrument to sustain order and would lead to common upliftment. This would probably imply that the true aim of Dharma was welfare of all, but in the process of enunciation and linking it with actual practice, it seems that caste and vested interests deterred it from its the true path. The moral code was at all times more important than just investment in law making.

These principles of Dharma were embodied in the Dharmashastra texts or law books, which later drew a distinct picture of the legal framework for the society. In other words, moral injunctions were intertwined with the legal rudiments. These law books were considered to be elaborate codes of law, but to rely only on them as a source of study of law without considering or corroborating with the epigraphical evidence would be not without dangers. These law books, which originated verily from the Brahmana class, represented aspirations at creating a perfect social system (although with hierarchy as its basis). It also reflected the early Indian society as conceived by the Brahmana elite. Hence, actual validity of these enunciations needs to be ascertained by correlating with other historical evidences and references pertaining to these laws.

Moreover, since these laws originated from the highest caste of Brahmanas, caste remained the keynote of such laws or regulations. Every law or enunciation that was made was laid with the aim to maintain and perpetuate the caste-based social order. The primary aim of such law writers was to ensure the superior position and status of Brahmanas through these codes. Social and legal privileges lessened with every step down in the social hierarchy. Brahmanas enjoyed legal privileges and protection but were on occasions regarded as above law.

As a result, law rooted in Dharma and based on caste was neither egalitarian nor recognised equality of all before law. The irony being that though Dharma was essentially a moral code, yet in law it was not applied equitably owing to being captive of vested interests. Caste was the undercurrent in deciding duties, rights as well as the judicial punishments. The higher orders were shielded and were the beneficiaries of extreme privileges while the burden of obligations largely fell on lower orders. This was the space where reformist religions stepped in the context of society and law. Noted scholar Romila Thapar, who has compared the Buddhist and Hindu traditions with reference to law says that the Buddhist tradition was a protest against against caste, "they recognised that in practical working of the society, there could be social distinctions but these ought not to be taken to a point to reject the concept of equality of all human beings.[6] Buddha considered all castes as equally pure and, hence, was in favour of equality before law.[7] In one such instance, it is mentioned that an offender brought before justice must be judged and punished according to his offence and without any concession to immunities or privileges relating to caste.[8]

In fact, the heterodox traditions moved to recognising the opposite of Hindu Law as envisioned in Dharmashastras. It talked of equality of all humans and equality before law, abrogation of slavery, and better status for women. It de-emphasised the intellectual formalism in the Hindu traditions. In fact, their opposition to the brahmanical setup suggests that the imposition of brahmanical thoughts on society and law in totality was not a historical reality, although it may have been the predominant system.

Moreover, in the Hindu tradition, there is a greater semblance of duties and obligations than legally permitted rights. Rights and powers were more the prerogatives of the upper echelons while misery and subordination was spelled out for lower orders and also for women. Within the localised groups too, there was limited conception of rights. As Thapar puts it, the functioning of each small unit was controlled by its own mechanism and within this unit the individual member could claim rights of equality and self-expression.[9] Similarly, a member of the sub-caste could claim social and economic security or the right to equality provided he observed the rules of a particular group. This was the key to the functioning of the Hindu tradition where it was the group that claimed rights and not the individual. It was the adherence to the group that could ensure freedom in society and a degree of legal protection. The idea of Dharma was initiated as means to secure individual conscientiousness for duties to facilitate both the individual and group rights, inorder that everybody would emjoy security and there would be harmony in the society. It aimed to avoid chaos in society by seeking everybody's conscious participation in ensuring social stability. However, owing to the fact that it emanated from the elite class, the concept saw the vested interests and fortification of the rights of these classes embedded in it.

These legal codes, hence, which highlight the somewhat theoretical aspects of the ancient Indian law, conform to the world view taken by the reigning Brahmana elite and not much is known about the co-existence of any alternative or parallel societal or legal codes that held sway as the larger tradition or over large section of people. The challenge to it came from heterodox traditions as and when individuals or groups could provide alternative discourse towards achieving salvation which remained more or less the prime objective of all religious groups. There prevails a great degree of confusion regarding the authorship of these legal texts as well, whether these were written by single authors or were compiled over a period of time with different authors. The rescensionary character and the heterogeneity of thoughts in a single text make it difficult to take these texts on their face value. They are neither well-articulated legalistic compendiums nor a manual of historical realities. They are at best a reflection of the aspirations of the ruling elite: incorporating the metaphysical thoughts from the Hindu oral traditions into the stream of legal and social thinking although very selectively. At some moments, the metaphysical ideal of human rights are extended to legal realms too, but as Prof. Thapar correctly sums up, "even in such moments, the rights were extended only to the elite groups; the slaves, the shudras, the serfs were all beyond the pale".[10]

Here, the dangers of selective presentation of certain maxims may be a danger that historians could face. The selective highlighting of a text could be a way of legitimising the past. Seen in this perspective, a few chosen maxims of a text can be made to convey any intended meaning or may be twisted to prove or disprove a premise at the expense of objective history. The *Arthashastra*, which is a text advocating the maximisation of remarks and the authority of monarchy, can thus be seen as a treatise on socialism for a welfare state (H.C. Ray wrote on it), the *Bhagavadgita* as a text of desire less action, and the *Manusmrti*, an epitome of Brahmanical patriarch, as a text upholding the dignity of women. The present-day dilemma of historian is to work with the discrepancies and inconsistencies in the texts. Probably, it was these dichotomous constructions or a different interpretation of Manu's maxims, for example, that led V. Raghavan to comment favourably on *Manusmriti*. Scepticism to such level is justified and welcome in the sense that it provokes thinking and lifts history from the age-old quagmire of continued interpretation on the same lines.

In approaching the historical reality, the plays that cover the life and times they represent reflect on the supposed working of law if these injunctions are taken as semblance of laws. In *Kalidasa*, we come across references pertaining to the administration of civil law, description regarding courts (even prison architecture), role of king with respect to justice, and officials associated with the administration of law on crime, punishment, and death penalty. In *Dashakumaracharita*, there are laws relating to judges' mentality. The *Mrcchakatika* brings forth that legal procedure was known by the term *Vyavahara* (as also in the smrtis) and points of law are called *Vyavaharapada*. How it was possible to lodge a complaint and file a suit in the court, cross-examining of witness or the evidence legally entered and judged, and other points of trial all came up in this play. It even mentions the types of legal crimes such as non-payment of gambling debt, murder of a woman, or other political offences. For political offences, punishment related could be anything from lashing to imprisonment. The play also talks of ordeals and suggests that punishments were probably out of proportion from modern humanistic point of view. The *Mudrarakshasa* by Visakhadatta describes a society where the king could announce corporal punishment on his ministers, although theirs might have been sparingly practised.[11]

It is historical evidence in the form of inscriptions that brings us closer to the historical reality. The Ashokan edicts, which embody the philosophy of Emperor Ashoka on his professing of *ahimsa* or non-violence, depict him functioning as the fountainhead of justice. His edicts are meaningful in the context of this study as they come forth as attempts of a ruler at resolving the problems of human beings in a complex society. His exhortations to his periodical officials and certain innovative enunciations like the uniformity of law (*vyavaharasamata*, uniformity of procedural law, and *dandasamata*, uniformity of punishment), permission of re-appeal in the capital punishment bears considerably on his clarity towards law and society and the role of king in legal matters. The norm of conduct suggested by him depicts his conviction or faith in humanity within the framework of existing social relations. Ashoka's edicts are a plea for dignity and justice based on a sense of tolerance of one another in societal relations. However, one must note that this is an effort under the influence on king from alternate religious tradition, whose primary teaching of universalism matches the Upanishadic philosophy within the ambit of Hinduism that emphasised unity as essence of existence.

Another very important window to the functioning of legal aspects in society is available from the *achara-sthiti-patra* of Vishnusena. The document dated on 5th day of bright half of the *shravana* (month according to Hindu Calendar) in the year 649 can be referred to the Vikrama era and taken as corresponding to 592 AD.[12] It enlists seventy-two *acharas*, of which some throw light upon the principles of procedural law, same on aspects of civil law, and others on matters pertaining to crime. It even comments on woman's position if her husband has committed crime and thereby throws light on the legal status of wife in early India.

The inscription is a description that a King Vishnusena was approached by the community of merchants, apparently of Lohata as suggested by the endorsement with the request of being favoured with the ruler's *achara-stithi-patra* which they they could utilise in their usage for protecting their own people (*loka-samgrah-anugrahartham*). It tells that merchants were actually favoured with ruler's *achara-stithi-patra* used in the protection and settlement of people of his dominions.[13]

This document appears to be in the nature of a compilation of prevalent customary laws. In this case, it was actually granted to the community of people. Vishnusena acts in the nature of modern-day legal functionary, from whom it was expected that this body of customary laws be taken in for incorporation into the written law. This document is of immense value to a researcher on customary law in early India and contains several technical words, related to law, some of which are very difficult to interpret. The seventy-two acharas quoted in this document provide a window to understanding or comparing how far the Dharmashastra law were adhered to or deviated or modified.

This Charter is indicative that, to a large extent, the oral traditions and customary law were written into these texts and documents and in practice, wisdom of those exercising the discretion or debating the dilemmas were carriers of the intellectual traditions of the country and not lawyers in strict sense of the term.

Overall, the legal consciousness and debate was the spirit which was seen in the changing norms of later Dharmashastra as well as an ability to keep itself growing or evolving.

NOTES AND REFERENCES

1.   N.C. Sengupta, *Evolution of Ancient Indian Law*, p.3.
2.   P.V. Kane, *History of Dharmashastra*, 3.295.
3.   R.B. Pal, *History of Hindu Law*, p. 177.
4.   K.V. Rangaswami Aiyangar, *Some Aspects of the Hindu View of Life according to Dharmashastra*, p.63.
5.   Manu, VII, 151-2, Vashistha-1, 4-5, Gautama, XI, 19.
6.   Romila Thapar, *Ancient Indian Social History, Chapter on Society and Law*, p.29.
7.   Buddhist legal ideals were never codified in a single source; legal ideals are found in Buddhist Canon in Vinaya Pitaka.
8.   Quoted from Majjhima Nikaya, II, 128–30, II, 148–54, II 88.
9.   Romila Thapar, *op cit.*, p.31.
10.   Thapar, *op cit*, p.33.
11.   *dushkaleapi kavisarupau pranae param rakshatam nitam yena yashasvinati laghutamaushinariyam yashah*
12.   Justice M Rama Jois, *Legal and Constitutional History of India, Ancient Legal, Judicial and Constitutional System*, p.695, Apendix II
13.   Ibid

CHAPTER II

A Survey of Textual and Epigraphic Sources
Extracting From the Dharmashastras, the Inscriptions, and the Secular Literature

Laws in any society at any time have served as a parameter for assessing the welfare of people as well as a tool for efficient administration of justice. In the Indian tradition, the unity and conformity in the web of Indian culture has been strongly permeated with Hindu ideals of life and a legal tradition, which has imbibed changes as well as retained its core to serve as legacy to the present generation.

The concept of law in the legal philosophy has almost never been the same. As discussed in the introductory chapter, whether derived from the Vedic concept of *rta* or considered synonymous with Dharma, it was Dharma that served as the basis of the evolution of later Hindu law. It would, therefore, be appropriate to survey the development of Hindu Law right from the ancient Vedic texts into the literature of the times in order to arrive at an understanding of Hindu law formation.

Sources of laws for our purpose of studying the theory and practice of law encompass the entire range of textual and epigraphic sources within the period of study (i.e., 200 B.C.–650 AD), although it is difficult to have a hard-and-fast chronological sequence of early sources. The theoretical component of Hindu law predominantly emerged from the earliest stages in the *Rigveda* and developed through the post-Vedic and Smrti epochs of Hindu law. The origin of Hindu law is probably to be found in vague traces in some earliest records of the people known as Aryan, who came as settlers on the Indian soil since 4,000 or 5,000 years ago. There is also a pre-Vedic stage of law as expressed in the Dharmashastra; but it was the Rigvedic conception of law, in which *rta* predominated as the ordering principle of cosmos, that gradually took into its fold law and religion, characterised as Dharma, and from which even the most advanced law-givers could not dissociate.

The textual sources include the Vedas, the post-Vedic literature, the Dharrnashastra, and the Epics. The Epics—the Mahabharata, the Ramayana, the Shrimad Bhagavadgita, the Dharmashashtras (that is, the smrtis of Manu, Yajnavalkya, Narada, Brhaspati, and Katyayana), the Arthashastra of Kautilya and the Kamasutra of Vatsyayana, and the Mahakavyas—and the Sanskrit Classical literature, prominently from the pen of Bhasa, Kalidasa, Shudraka, and Vishakhadatta.

The study on gender status is based on the cross-examining of injunctions in law with regard to men or women, and this needs an understanding of epigraphic data as well getting a complete picture pertaining to both men and women. For instance, in approaching the historical reality, the plays that cover the life and times they represent reflect on the supposed working of law. In Kalidasa, we come across references for women, but the second and the other important half of this study constitutes the evaluation of actual legal practices that could possibly be prepared from the available historical evidence i.e., the inscriptions. Hence, epigraphic records of the period published in the well-known Epigraphia Indica Volumes and the Corpus Inscriptionum Indicarum series have been thoroughly scanned. Among the secondary sources on inscriptions, works of D.C. Sircar, Diskalkar, Devasthali, and some other works have been taken into account.

For analysing the issues pertaining to gender, for instance, as historian Dr. K.K. Shah has rightly put it in his book that whether of Dharmashastra tradition of orthodox Brahmanism or canonical type of heterodox faiths or even the epic variety, is of normative nature in respect of women. What inscriptions offer us are variations of, and even deviations from, the norm. It will be seen that no norm has been followed strictly or uniformly all over the country. In fact, in certain areas, variations and deviations so dominate the pattern that they render the norm itself as variation. However, by and large, the scenario is one of interplay between the ideal and the real. At times, one overshadows the other while gets overshadowed at other times.[1]

Both the sources pertaining to the ideal and the real become pertinent in a study as this as one can appreciate that any civilisation is ultimately embedded in a tradition. If tradition means the handing down of knowledge from the past to the present, it must be realistic in order to be correct. The normative texts represent the formalised *Great Tradition*, but there are also numerous *Little Traditions*, the study of the interplay of which is a must to arrive at a composite understanding of the historical evolution. Redfield used these terms to contrast the formal literate tradition exhibited in the urban elite with the largely oral and informal tradition of folks or masses.

To Redfield, the Great and Little Traditions complement each other in portraying a single civilisation. But to rely on these norms alone—which are often a product of particular circumstances, milieu and mind-set—would be undesirable. The historical reality is much more complex and multidimensional for which the epigraphic component must be incorporated to arrive at a holistic understanding. The inscriptions moreover provide the variations from the norm that might have existed and, hence, are indispensable in search of historical reality.

There has always existed a dichotomy between the normative literature and the inscriptions. D.C. Sircar, the great epigraphist of our times, recognised this dichotomy as also the existence of countless local traditions side by side with the great overarching tradition. In clear terms, he stated the state of society suggested by the Dharmashastra, Arthashastra, and Kamasutra works is theoretical to a considerable extent and that this seems to be admitted in the passage *sastrarthan vyapino vidyat prayogams tv ekadesikan*, speaking of the wide scope of the Shastra and the limited nature of its application.[2]

In early India, rocks and lithic, metallic, earthen, or wooden pillars, tablets, plates, pots, bowls, and other objects were often used for engraving inscriptions. There are also found legends on coins, seals, or wooden tablets, which, Sircar explains, are not truly engraved. They differ in nature and type, varying from first a mark or word to somewhat longer dedications. It may contain eulogies in kavya form or in drama or mere charters indicating the grants or donations.

In the preface to the Epigraphia Indica, Volume 1, James Burgess, its great Indologist editor, thus stressed the value of epigraphic records for reconstructing the life and times of early India. "Indian Inscriptions—more so even those of any other country are the real archives of the annals of its ancient history, the contemporaneous witnesses of the events and of the men whose deeds they handed down, and their authenticity renders them most valuable for the historian and deserving of careful record. They supply important data bearing on the chronology, geography, and religious system affiliations of families and dynasties, taxes, land tenures, magistrates, customs, manners, organisation of societies, language, and systems of writing of ancient times."

However, as Sircar rightly opines, "no doubt many of them deal with historical events and passages, but history is often shadowed in them by poetical, eulogistic and conventional, elements. 'Most records' therefore, give the impression that references to historical events in them are incidental."[3] He remarks that their evidence is often indirect and leaves things to be surmised and inferred. This is very true in the case of this study too. Inscriptions pertaining to direct laws or ordinances are rare, except for the Edicts of Ashoka or the Charter of Vishnusena, which is an *achara sthitipatra* (a sample of law in practice). In those that can be studied, legal implications have to be inferred or searched for, wherever possible.

These inscriptions are very useful in ascertaining the chronology of the early events. They are also remarkable in that they were "generally free from variant readings as they were not usually liable to modification, like those of literary works which were copied and recopied by people in later times".[4] At times, they have mentioned the names of Smrti writers.[5] Those inscriptions issued by the ruling authority themselves are more useful than the record of private donations; for the former depicts the position of state vis-à-vis law, the status of law in the society, and the nature of ordinances or laws that were laid down in society with the legitimation from the state authority. The whole range of available inscriptions from Ashoka to the post-Gupta times has been studied for the purpose. Ashoka's inscriptions are named edicts, but they are hardly so in the strict sense of the term, signifying commands of a legal overlord breach of which would entail penalties. They are properly speaking summons and exhortations to people at large. But such proclamations, at once, direct us to the legal and social norm that might have formed the background to such enunciations. They also hint at the prevailing areas of legal concern, or areas, which needed some sort of social and legal legislation or governmental regulation.

The traditional approaches on studies on law have relied heavily on textual sources and their varied interpretations. Rarely have they been compared or contrasted with the inscriptions available because probably there are fewer references available and those that are there are incidental references. In this work, a humble attempt has been made to incorporate those inscriptions, which hold relevance from the viewpoint of law.

In the field of law, Ashokan edicts stand out as they talk of justice, its administration and expectations from judicial officers, the need for impartiality in justice, existence of death penalty, stringent criminal law, and place of mercy in justice. They also depict the reality that the king was the fountainhead of justice and state had a responsibility to ensure the proper administration of justice. Similarly, the Allahabad Pillar Queen's Gift Edict throws light on the identity and status of Queen Karuvaki and also the legal implications of such a donation, especially women's right over property.

There is an instance of drafting of a document by a female officer.[6] In another inscription, there is mention of the five sins that bring with them immediate retribution.[7] The Nalanda Spurious Copper Plate Inscription mentions *Akshapatala* as the court of law or as the repository of legal documents. Those of the Gupta period talk of officers like the *Dandika, Dandapasika, Mahadandanayaka,* and *Chauroddharanika.* Finally, the Charter referred earlier too, the charter of Vishnusena, mentioned in last chapter, which is in the nature of an order issued by a modern-day Legal Remembrancer, seeking the incorporation of the customary laws in the actual practices relating to law.

These inscriptions provide the source material for whatever could be gathered about the practical law prevalent at different times. It is ironical, however, that despite law being an integral part of the politically organised state, there are hardly any manuals or codes available to us that could have been promulgated as laws by different kings. It might also imply that such laws were not given much importance and the textual sources themselves served as law codes to be inculcated in practice. It could also be indicative of the great oral tradition of preserving wisdom. Instances of such civil and criminal cases being practised might have actually used the Smrti laws in a court of law, citing these as the actual law texts within the precincts of court of law are hardly any.

Textual Sources

Regarding the interchangeability of the terms law and Dharma in early India and importance of Dharmashastras, noted scholar Jolly puts it, "many Dharmashastra give nothing at all about law proper and only a few later compilations such as the Naradasmrti may be called purely judicial works".[8] These law books regarded the Vedas as the foremost source of Dharma, which are frequently quoted in the Dharmashastra. The Vedas, however, provide the maxims of large social and religious existence; and even in peripheral concerns for Dharma, they contain occasional references on legal matters. The Dharmasutras[9] somewhat provide a judicial interpretation of some Vedic utterances; and in them there are visible law of inheritance, government, and legal procedure in their rudiments. However, these philosophical sutras that form a part of greater collection of sutra works mention law as on secondary basis, their primary concerns being to treat the Vedic maxims for Dharma. Thus, an exhaustive treatment of law by itself was needed. But since the Dharmasutra literature treated it in a stepmotherly fashion,[10] these were provided by the Dharmashastra.

The Sutras represent the last phase of the Vedic literature divided into the (1) *Srautasutras*, (2) *Grhyasutras*, and (3) *Dharmashastra*. The earlier two are of not much importance to the study of Hindu Law. *Srautasutra* dealt with the regulation of rituals, *Grihyasutra* with matters pertaining to family, and *Dharmashastra* with aspects of civil and criminal law.

Although these Dharmashastra are not exclusive legal codes, law, civil or criminal, as enforceable by the supreme political authority, i.e., the king, makes its appearance in the Dharmashastra. A whole range of topics of law in its concrete form emerges from these texts to be administered and enforced by the king. These Dharmashastra texts embody the injunctions on ideal living and are also repositories of jurisprudence developed by indigeneous scholastic traditions. The term "Dharma "means rightful duty in conformity with the cosmic law or order while "Shastra" signifies an Indic branch of learning. The

Dharmashastras deal primarily with three sections-1.*Achara*- which explains the ideal behavioural norms expected to be practiced by individuals while following the *"Varna"* system (4-fold classification of society according to hierarchy prescribed in a RigVedic verse and occupation based hierarchy-*Brahman, Kshatriya, Vaishya and Shudra*) and *"Ashrama"* system (which specified the four stages in an individual's life starting from *Brahmacharya* or student life based on celibacy, discipline and learning to *Grhastha*, the householder to *Vanaprastha*, detaching oneself and handing over responsibilities to next generation and proceeding to live in forest and lastly, *Sanyasa* which signifies *renunciation of worldly life in search of spiritual pursuits)* 2.*Vyavahara*- or legal procedure which removes or resolves situations arising from violating Dharma (which means substantive law) and 3.*Prayaschitta* or rules about penances resorted to expiate from violations of Dharma.

These Dharmashastra differ from Vedas as Vedas is considered in Indian tradition as "Shruti", based on what was enunciated by divine intervention, authorless and carried forward or preserved through oral traditions (4 Vedas -the Rigveda, Samaveda, Yajurveda, & Atharvaveda) while Dharmashastra texts are classified as "Smrtis", which implies that which is derived by memory or as preserved in oral traiditions. These are compendiums of enunciations for rightful living written by wise men through recollections and are derivative secondary works. They are considered to be less authoritative than the Shrutis (these also include Vedangas and Puranas and other branches of knowledge)

These topics contained in the metrical smrtis or Dharmashastra were classified into approximately following heads, as gleaned from the text of P.V. Kane's study: (1) Sources of Dharma (2) Varna or caste, (3) Samskaras or rites especially marriage (4) Orders of life (5) Five great sacrifices (mahayajnas) (6) Rules for eating (7) Religious gifts (8) Rules for renunciation (9) Duties of a king (10) Legal procedure, (11) 18 titles of law (12) Categories of Sin, (13) Expiations and penances (14) *Karma* or action (15) Funerary and Ancestral rights (16) Pilgrimage (17) Vows (18) Festivals(19) Propitiatory rites. Substantive law, however, had 18 titles of law.[11]

Manu and Yajnavalkya are looked upon as authorities on early Hindu legal system, with the classical Hindu jurisprudence laid down in these. However, in spite of being codes of civil law, they concentrated more on sacerdotal matter such as *achara* or the rules of good conduct for all persons of all castes in various stages of life. Pure judicial law code is traceable only in the works of Narada, Brhaspati, and Katyayana who made systematic attempts to lay down *vyavahara* or procedural law in detail.

Mm. Dr. Kane rightly addressed them as the triumvirate in the realm of the ancient Hindu law and composition of the Hindu Legal literature.[12] All these three jurists exhibit an excellent analytical insight and the most perfect legal acumen in elaborating and explaining the juristic principles and philosophy.[13] The law codes of these authors belong to the latest production of the Smrti epoch of Hindu law, and their legal character and their judicial content are definitely more advanced than those of Manu or Yajnavalkya Smrti.

	DHARMASHASTRAS 600 BCE to 500 CE	CHRONOLOGICAL ESTIMATE	UNIQUE FEATURES	STRUCTURE AND CHARACTER OF THE TEXT	COMMENTARIES AND TRANSLATIONS (SELECT)
1.	Manusmrti	Friedrich Schlegel 1250 BCE to 1000 CE Recent scholarship 200 BCE to 200 CE	Earliest law book treated as Law code of Hindu Jurisprudence, earliest text in Dharmashastras tradition. Even though the text seems to have come to existence much before (1250 BCE), in its present form, it was compiled by Bhrigu. Most studied ancient legal text. Its the most controversial text as it upheld the caste system rigourously. India's constitution maker, Dr.B R Ambedkar burnt the copies of it rejecting caste based inequalities.	1034 verses, speaks on law and polity; dialogue between Manu's disciple Bhrgu and his students. Not a homogeneous text, written by several persons called Manu, resulting in incongruities, It's a metrical text in Sanskrit. There are several contradictions within the text which makes it difficult to treat it as an authoritative text on law	Bharrucchi (10th or early 11th century, according to Kane) Medhatithi First translated by Sir William Jones(1794) Translation by G. Buhler, The Laws of Manu (1886)

2.	Yajnavalkyasmrti	Dates to Gupta period between third and fifth century	More systematic than Manusmrti, succinct arrangement of shlokas: According to Olivelle Patrick Yajnavalkya is the best-composed and most homogeneous text. Sages of Mithila approach Yajnavalkya and ask him to teach Dharma: speaks on evidence, documents, witnesses and five types of ordeals; a distinction n between courts appointed by king and those formed by communities.	Organised into three sections: achara, vyavahara, and prayaschitta. Beginning of substantive or procedural law, eighteen Hindu titles of law.	Sacred Books of Hindus, Vol 22, Robert Lingat wrote *Classical Law of India* translated from French by JDM Derrett.
	Naradasmrti	Came in three rescensions: 1st rescension - 879 verses; 2nd rescension - 550 verses; Jolly added from minor rescension to 1028 verses.	Focuses purely on substantive and Procedural law: deals with 18 titles of law.	According to, Patrick Olivelle it is the only text that does not speak about rightful conduct or penance.	Max Muller (1907), Introduction to Narada The Sacred Books of the East, Vol. 33, London "The Naradasmrti By Richard W. Lariviere (tr.)"

	Date	Features	Borrows	Availability
Brhaspatismrti	6th century AD assigned by Jolly while Kane does not place him later than 4th century AD Mulla says this text would be between AD 200 and 400 AD	First to distinguish between civil and criminal suits. It's a valuable relic in the list of legal literature, as its treatment of topics of law is not mixed with other subjects. He gives details about juridical law in great measure.	Borrows heavily from Manusmrti and reiterates the authority of Manu.	Available in reconstructed form, which has been edited by K.V. Rangaswami Aiyangar.
Katyayanasmrti	Kane places the text between 300 – 600 AD	Highest point in the evolution of Hindu Law in the list of smrtis. Deals with Civil Law in detail. Limited material on criminal law. He is known for his verses on women's property. He devoted 27 verses on the topic of Stridhana. Kane says Katyayana's treatment of Stridhana attained classical rank. He also mentions judicial personages such as *Stobhaka* and *Suchaka*.	Karyayana is profusely quoted by the Mitakshara (Commentary). Karyayana looks upon Brhaspati as the authority.	
		Two main branches of vvavahara, according to him come from Dharmashastra and Arthashastra (An Introduction to legal theories, Gokulesh Sharma p. 258).		

Table 1.1 Major Smrtis considered in this study with chronology and features.

It is Smrtis that dealt in detail about the concept of justice, role of king, gradation of courts, aspects of law, appointment of judges, etc., as well as the substantive and procedural law. The other smrtis that are relevant to the study on legal system are Narada smrti, Parashara smrti, Vishnu smrti, Brhaspati smrti, and the Katyayana smrti. Mimansa (one of six orthodox schools of Hinduism which talks about theories on nature of Dharma), played a significant role in ushering in the art of interpretation in order to reach to the real meanings of the legal injunctions stated. Purva Mimansa of Jaimini and well-known commentary on it by Sabaraswami as well as the work of Kumarila Bhatt (700 AD) constitute as valuable sources to any study on legal aspects of ancient India.

The Manusmrti

The Manusmrti remains one of the finest embodiments of Classical Hindu law and of fundamental importance in any study on law in India. Buhler designates Manusmrti as 'Bhrigu's version of the Institutes of Sacred law proclaimed by Manu'.[14] Its opening verses describe how Manu, the descendent of the self-existent Brahmana, was approached by the great sages to explain the sacred law. Buhler further explains that if the versions given by commentators like Govindraja, Narayana, and Raghavananda as well as the Kashmir copy and others MSS are accepted, "we have therefore, a triple exordium instead of a double one and Manusmrti does not contain the original words of Bhrigu but a rescension of his rescension such as it had been handed down among his pupils".[15] Most scholars have presumed *Manavadharmashastra* to be the origin of Manusmrti, including Buhler.

However, the layers of interpolations of an earlier and later date bring us to conclude that Manusmrti is not a work of single author as such, but a heterogeneous texts consisting of floating are proverbial wisdom surrounded by various rescensions at different times, separated by two to three centuries. Mm P.V. Kane was convinced that the text did not undergo any changes since the second or third century of the Christian era. However, there is some evidence of changes in its form and content before the third century AD in the commentaries on Manusmrti and other Smrti texts too. Professor Kane believes that most authors of Dharmashastras starting with the second century AD gave credence to Manu's views; the Manusmrti, hence, must have existed by that time.[16] Most of the scholars have placed the text between 200 BC and AD 200.[17]

The present version of Manusmrti contains a total of 2,485 verses divided into twelve chapters (Buhler totaled it to 2,734 verses).[18] Buhler has grouped the verses as laid down by Manu under different heads. In chapter 1, Manusmrti lays down a summary of contents of laws as enunciated by Manu. He lays down eighteen titles of civil and criminal law, which ought to be taken up by a just king. Manusmrti dwells at length on the duties of women as well as duties of husband and wife.[19] It is the first systematic exposition on categories of civil and criminal law. It somewhat laid the ground for advanced legal thoughts by other later writers.

From the fourth century AD, Hindu scholars and invaders carried their traditions of life and imposed them in the kingdoms, which they provided in Malaya and Eastern Archipelago. For ten centuries, these kingdoms enjoyed remarkable prosperity and continued to cherish the ideals imported by their founders.[20] The Common law of Burma is well-known as based upon Manusmrti.[21] However, to presume that the Manusmrti and other Dharmashastra have not undergone any changes would be wrong. Sivaswamy Aiyar in *The Evolution in Hindu Moral Ideals* says it would be incorrect to presume that the rules contained in the Dharmashastra have undergone no changes or evolution in the course of ages. On the contrary, he contends that Hindu ethical ideals have undergone changes from time to time in accordance the exigencies of the times.[22]

Sir Henry Maine considered Manusmrti to be an idealist fiction of law as conceived or imagined by the Brahmanas. To him, this Hindu code called the laws of Manu, which he accepts as a Brahmin composition, undoubtedly enshrined several genuine observances of the Hindus; but the opinion of the best contemporary Orientalist is that it does not, as a whole, represent a set of rules ever actually administered in the country. It is in great part an ideal picture of that, which in view of the Brahmins ought to be the law.[23] However, J.D. Mayne has refuted the view of Maine and maintained that Smrtis were partly based upon contemporary and anterior usages and in part on rules framed by the Hindu jurists and rulers of the country. In 1910, he wrote that Classical Hindu law has the oldest pedigree of any known system of jurisprudence. Smrtis and digests were not as much private law books as recognised authorities in the courts and tribunals of the country and that the Smrti rules were concerned with the practical administration of justice.

Although law in its concrete shape as in civil and criminal category found its rudiments in Manusmrti, judicial procedure was not as much advanced as seen in later Smrtis. They originally concerned themselves more with ceremonial and religious conduct, with infliction of penance and spiritual rather than legal aspects as much.

About a dozen commentaries are learnt to have been written on Manusmrti besides the numerous unknown ones. Of these, seven have been published by V.N. Mandalik while five others have been mentioned by him.[24] Das has mentioned that Manusmrti was probably "written in a period of great transition when old ideas were yielding place to new".[25] However, his analysis that Manu tried to blend the opposite tendencies into a grand synthesis does not seem convincing. He has cited a number of authors like K. P. Jayaswal, Annie Besant, Bhagwan Das, and Jolly and Ganganath Jha, all of whom have extolled the unique place of Manusmrti in the legal history of India and its value as a code of complete social conduct.

The text of Manusmrti has relevance to the point that it is one of those finer expositions of Hindu law, which had great impact on the minds of society of Manu's times and much later. Aiyangar quotes D.S. Sharma, who has made good study of Hindu scriptures, as stating that rules of Dharmashastra are obsolete and "our trying to follow the laws of Manu now would be as ridiculous as if a modern Englishman tries to follow the Laws of Alfred".[26] Quite truly, the major portion of the text have no practical use for our times except that they throw a beacon light on our legal heritage. In the modern context, blind reverence has been replaced by a questioning attitude. In 1927, Ambedkar ceremoniously cremated the text at Mahad in Maharashtra. The debating intellectual traditions post colonial awakening ultimately had accentuated the demands for egalitarianism in law which were reflected in the spirit of the Indian Constitution that came following the independence.

However, to a student of Hindu law, Manusmrti as a source book will continue to be relevant, even though its paradoxes and heterogeneities may have to be explained. In this context, study of Narhar Kurundkar seems interesting, who points out that although it is clear that not all the references in the ancient literature of Manu could possibly be attributed to one and the same person, 'the commonality of the names and a great confusion about the date of their time adds an additional degree of veneration to the author of Manusmrti. It does not matter that the book probably was not compiled by one individual. The name of Manu tends to place a protective cover even around the basest of verses in the book.'[27] Hence, it would be a grave mistake to consider the text as a homogeneous one or composed by a single author and base our conclusions on it.

Several commentaries such as *Manubhasya* by Bhatta Medhatithi, *Manutika* by Govindraja, and *Manvartha Chandrika* by Raghavnandana Saraswati have been written on Manusmrti as well as some others.

Yajnavalkya Smrti

The Smrti of Yajnavalkya occupies the next important place after the Manusmrti among the legal texts in India. It contains 1,010 slokas or stanzas and is divided into three Adhyayas or books namely *Achara* or ecclesiastical and moral code, *Vyavahara* or the judicial procedure, and *Prayascitta* or the penance. Each part or *adhyaya* contains the following stanzas:[28]

Achara—368 stanzas
Vyavahara—307 stanzas
Prayaschitta—335 stanzas

There are several well-known commentaries on Yajnavalkya's Institutes such as by Apararka, Vishvarupa, and Vijnaneshvara, Mitra Mishra, and Sulapani. There are also the *Bhagvantabhaskara* by Bhatta Nilkantha and seven others.[29]

The commentary of Vijnaneshvara has superseded the others, and under the name of Mitakshara, it is accepted as authoritative in most parts of India. The full name of the commentary of Vijnaneshvara is Ritu-Mitakshara. But the name of Mitakshara is known, more so by its brevity. The whole of Yajnavalkyasmrti was translated by Mr. Mandlik into English in 1880 AD, leaving the commentary and the gloss of Balambhatta. The first chapter of Yajnavalkysmrti speaks of the sources of law, the second on Brahmachari Prakarana. The second chapter contains the famous *law of adoption* by Baudhayana. Other chapters deal with marriage, castes, purification, *shraddha*, etc.

With the exception of Manu, Yajnavalkya, and few others, writes Vidarnava, the Smrti as a rule do not treat of Vyavahara or what may be called Legal Procedure or Positive Law. Yajnavalkya I mentions fourteen sources of law. Monier Williams considered the Dharmashastra of Yajnavalkya, along with its celebrated commentary the Mitakshara by Vijnneshvara, as the most important law book next to Manu and declared him to be the principal authority of the school of Benaras and Middle India. According to Williams, Acharya Vidarnava quotes, it seems originally to have emanated from the school of the White Yajurveda in Mithila, or North Behar, just as the code of the Manavas did from a school of the Black Yajurveda in the neighborhood of Delhi.[30] Williams also remarks that Yajnavalkya's work is more concise, comprising of three books instead of twelve. As to the date of the smrti, it is placed in the 'middle of the first century of our era', says Williams. Its present redaction is supposed to be much more recent than that of Manu's law book.[31]

Acharya Vidarnava has analysed that since it has not been critically studied, great ambiguity exists about its age. No other Smrti is perhaps deemed to be so comprehensive. It is more a compilation than an original work.[32] Some of the verses have been taken from Manu.[33] Jolly too has shown its indebtedness to Vishnu and Naradasmrti for some verses.[34] It is also believed to have borrowed from Matsya, Vishnu, and Markandeya Puranas.[35] Vijnaneshvara flourished in the 11th century AD, according to G. Buhler.[36] Mitakshara is the law of Hindus, in large portion of India, even though the whole of the text has not been translated in English.

Naradasmrti

Narada reflects the higher end in the evolution of thoughts on Hindu law. He comes next to Yajnavalkya and Manu. Naradasmrti does not mention Yajnavalkyasmrti by name, which shows it may have not reached the stage of authoritative work in law. Dr. Jolly has studied that there was considerable gap between Manu and Narada. Buhler, who placed Manu between 200 BC–200

AD it would follow that Naradasmrti could hardly belong to a period before the fourth or fifth century AD.[37] Kane has, however, rejected Jolly's views for assigning Narada a date later than 300 AD and held that Narada flourished in the first centuries of the Christian era between 100 and 300 AD.[38] Naradasmrti is available in two rescensions (some scholars say three), which deal exclusively with *Vyavahara* topics of Dharmashastra. It is here that it differs from Manu and Yajnavalkya, which deal with *Vyavahara* as well as *Achara* and *Prayaschitta* aspects of Dharma. Narada covers the entire gamut of secular law, both civil and criminal.

Narada merely professes to be a compiler of the traditional law, which he derived from the *Manavdharmashastra*.[39] In the introduction, Narada refers to it as an abridgement of the larger work of Manu and refers to four successive versions of Manusmrti.[40] The extant Naradasmrti constituted the ninth chapter of the original code which was headed, judicial procedure. This part of the Narada's abridgement of the ninth chapter of Manu's code is designated as *Matrka* or *Vyavaharamatrka*, containing a summary of proceedings at Law or General Rules of Procedure.[41]

Narada has dwelt on the administration of justice, the objects, and the eighteen titles of law and underlines the importance of judicial procedure. In other words, it has two divisions: one deals with the procedural law, and the other enumerates the titles of law with a remarkable clarity of thought. He has discussed the "mutual duties of husband and wife" as the twelfth topic of law.

Narada has dealt law in a systematic manner even though not without certain drawbacks. He is more exhaustive and advanced in treatment on topic of law but at the same time more conservative than his predecessors.[42] Narada was well-known as a legal author as gathered from the later smrti texts and digests. Professor Jolly has rightly remarked, "The repute of Narada as a legal writer appears to have been so great that upwards of half of his work has been embodied in the authoritative composition of the medieval and modern writers in the province of Sanskrit Law."[43]

Among the three law codes hence, i.e., Manusmrti, Yajnavalkyasmrti, and Narada, Narada is considered as the leading code with respect to enunciations in law. Regarding its importance, Dr. Mulla has observed "it affords a great help in deriving a reliable knowledge of the line of evolution Law and Jurisprudence had pursued during the era of the Dharmashastra. There is intrinsic as well as other evidence to show that the work had been compiled after there has been remarkable political, economic, and social progress in the country, when the highest intellectual capacity of the people had already produced the philosophy of the Upanishads out of which had been developed the doctrine of *Karmayoga* and when considerable advancement had been made in Hindu Jurisprudence.[44]

Vishnusmrti

The Vishnusmrti or the Vaishnava Dharmashastra is in the main a collection of ancient aphorisms on the sacred laws of India and is ranked along with other ancient works of this class.

According to Jolly, the size of the Vishnusutra and the great variety of subjects treated in it would suffice to entitle it to conspicuous place among the existing Dharmashastra, but it possesses a peculiar claim to interest, which is founded on its close connection with one of the oldest Vedic schools, the *kathas* one hand and with the famous code of Manu and other ancient law codes on the other hand. Tradition leaves us entirely in the dark as to its real author.

The fiction that laws in the chapters II-XCVII were communicated by God Vishnu to the goddess of the earth is vague. Jolly considers it utterly worthless for historical purposes and all that it can be made to show is that those parts of this work in which it is stated or kept up cannot rival the laws themselves in antiquity.

Vishnu's rules have supposedly a less archaic character than the corresponding precepts of Manu, not only in the shlokas but in the Sutra parts as well. Jolly cites in introduction that written documents and ordeals are barely mentioned in the code of Manu (VIII, 114, 115, 168; IX, 232); Vishnu, on the other hand—besides referring in diverse places to royal grants and edicts, to written precepts and other private documents—dwells on them at length.

Brhaspatismrti

Brhaspati is believed to be later to Narada. Jolly assigned him to the sixth century AD[45] while Kane, taking into consideration all evidences and especially the fact that Katyayana looked upon Brhaspati as an authority remarks, "Brhaspati must have flourished several centuries before and therefore, cannot be placed later than the 4th century A.D." According to him, it must have been compiled one or two centuries after Narada and at a time when in many branches of it the law had made further strides in its line of development.[46] Mulla in his study argues that since Brhaspati was well acquainted with extant Manusmrti and Yajnavalkyasmrti, and also probably the code of Narada, and that he must have flourished between 200 and 400 AD.[47]

Brhaspati's work is available in a reconstructed form, which has been edited by Prof. K.V. Rangaswamy Aiyangar, basing it on citations from the Brhaspatismrti in medieval and later works on Hindu Law. The edition referred is divided into seven sections of which the *Vyavaharakhanda* is the major portion Patkar studies that out of the total number of 2,300 shlokas collected by Aiyangar from numerous works, 1,271 verses deal with the subject matter of law proper.[48]

Brhaspati looks upon Manu as the supreme authority. Whatever is contrary to the dictates of Manu is according to Brhaspati unacceptable and fit to be discarded.[49] Brhaspati has explained the terms more elaborately because of which Kane styles him as a Varttikara of Manu.[50]

Brhaspati was the first lawgiver to make a specific distinction between civil and criminal suits. He gives the following technical terms for lawsuits:

1. *Arthasamudbhava* or civil
2. *Himsasamudbhava* or criminal

The former originates in demands regarding wealth while the latter in injuries. Further, those originating in money are of fourteen kinds and those from injury are of four kinds.[51]

Brhaspati's work is a valuable relic of Hindu law. In its treatment of topics of law and by its clarity in not mixing law with other subjects, he not only is superlative but also decidedly advanced over his predecessors.

He has given details not only on courts but also on everything pertaining to juridical law from the filing of complaint to the passing of decree, which makes him fit to be compared with modern jurists.

Katyayanasmrti

Katyayana represents the high watermark in the evolution of Hindu Law. In his work is found a place for pure positive law. According to Dr. Kane, he occupies a very prominent place among the smrti writers on law and procedure. Next to Narada and Brhaspati, he is cited more frequently than any other smrtikara in such commentaries and digests as the Mitakshara, Smrtichandrika, the Viramitrodaya, and the Vyavaharamayukha.[52]

Katyayana is later than Kautilya, Yajnavalkya, Narada, and Brhaspati. In his treatment of ordeals, believes Kane, he is less elaborate than Pitamaha. Pitamaha quotes Brhaspati, so Katyayana is later than Brhaspati and earlier than Pitamaha. Katyayana is profusely quoted by the Mitaksara and other writers of 11th and 12th centuries as equal authority with Yajnavalkya, Narada, and Brhaspati.

Kane cites that in the Valipatana plate of the Silahara king Rattaraja dated Saka 932 (1010–11 AD), in which one verse of Katyayana about the requisites of a valid royal edict is quoted as from smrti. Kane has placed the Smrti between 300 and 600 AD as it is later than Yajnavalkya, Narada, and Brhaspati.[53]

The compiler of Katyayana smrti has freely borrowed from other authorities wherever they suited his purpose. As a result, we have a number of verses ascribed to Narada, a dozen are to be found in Manu, couples of them are from Kautilya's Arthashastra, and verses 326–327 are from Vishnusmrti while some are from the Yajnavalkyasmrti (11, 113, and 183).[54]

Katyayana, in his treatment of topics, starts with the characteristics of the king and his duties followed by rules and characteristics of Vyavahara. He follows the earlier writers in legal phraseology and in technique.[55] Kane has listed the special feature of Katyayana in a section. Katyayana is known for his views on women's property.

For his exposition on the topic of *stridhana*, to which he has devoted twenty-seven verses, Dr. Kane observes Katyayana's treatment of *stridhana* has attained classical rank. It appears that he was probably the first to define carefully the several kinds of *stridhana* (such as *adhyagni, adhyavahanika, pritidatta, sulka, anvadheya, and saudayika*) to lay down woman's power of disposal over the several varieties of stridhana and to prescribe lines of devolution to *stridhana*.[56]

In the Katyayanasmrti, we come across two new terms with regard to judicial personages: *stobhaka* and *suchaka*. These are two persons who bring to the notice of the king certain offences, but there is a slight distinction between the two.[57]

No doubt a wealth of commentarial literature exists on the Smrtis. It can hardly be treated as direct source for the purposes of present study, having been penned down in periods subsequent to the period of our interest. In all likelihood, commentators must have inserted modifications in the meaning of the original provisions to accommodate changes in socioeconomic conditions of their times and regions. Many Dharmashastra works were, in fact, rejuvenated by the commentators that would otherwise have been completely lost. Numerous citations from the codes of Brhaspati and Katyayana, which were otherwise lost, could be retrieved to a reasonable extent from these citations alone. The *Smrtichandrika*, for example, an early digest compiled in South India, contains as many as 600 verses from the Katyayana smrti and an equal number from the code of Brhaspati.[58]

The Sanskrit dramas had seen full flowering by the time of epics and Dharmshastras. That dramas always reflect the life and times that they represent can scarcely be doubted. Bharata himself described 'it is the art of reproduction by imitation'.

Dramas are supposed to depict the world as mirror. Ratnmayidevi Dikshit remarked, "The good or evil in society, the good or evil in man and its consequences are to be presented on the stage."[59] Whether it is the plays of Kalidasa or the *Mudrarakhsasa* of Vishakhadatta or the *Mrcchakatika* of Sudraka, references relating to law, their practical translations in civil and criminal proceedings, have been incorporated in this study. In the absence of eyewitness or first-person accounts, these incidental and rare references are the only available holes through which we can glimpse court proceedings and actual application of law. They throw valuable light on the practical aspects of law and hence constitute an important source for study.

The Arthashastra

Kautilya's Arthashastra is also one of the sources of Hindu Law. Acharya Vidarnava has stated in the introduction of the Yajnavalkyasmrti, "With the exception of Manu, Yajnavalkya and a few others, the smrtis as a rule do not treat of *Vyavahara* or what may be called legal procedure or positive law. This formed the subject matter of Arthashastra, which treated of statecraft, International, Municipal and Positive Laws. Sovereigns administered Civil and Criminal Laws according to Arthashastra."[60]

Rangarajan, writing on the origin of Arthashastra, rightly remarks that Kautilya was not the originator of the science. He (Kautilya) himself acknowledges that his work is based on similar treatises in the past. There are 112 places in the text where a number of earlier authorities have been mentioned. Five different schools of thought—those of Brhaspati, Ushana, Prachetasa, Manu, Parashara, and Ambhi are referred to—often because Kautilya disagrees with the advice given by them.[61]

The Arthashastra existed prior to the Yajnavalkyasmrti. In the latter Smrti and later Sanskrit texts, compound words greatly prevail, which indicates that Yajnavalkya was aware of Kautilya's Arthashastra.

The Arthashastra contains fifteen *adhikaranas* or books. The first chapter of book 1 is a detailed table of contents and, in one verse, states that the text has 150 chapters, 180 prakarnas, and 6,000 verses in all.[62] The text is in the prose or the sutra form with 380 shlokas.[63] Book 3 is concerning the law and the administration of justice. It reproduces, as Rangarajan says, a complete code of law. Book 4 deals with the suppression of crime and includes sections on detection of crime, control over merchants and artisans, torture, and capital punishment.

Shamashastry's translation of the Kautilyan Arthashastra was published about five decades ago. In later editions, he incorporated notes from

Bhattasvamin's commentary as well as the Malayalam commentary. Kangle's three volumes is a translation of text in English, incorporating the studies made by large number of scholars.

Rangarajan is of the view that several areas covered by the Arthashastra are overlapping with those in the Dharmashastra. "There is however a crucial difference between the two, the Dharmashastra address themselves to the individual teaching him his Dharma and regard deviations from it as sins to be expiated by ritual. The Arthashastra is addressed to the rulers and regard transgressions of law as crimes to be punished by the state."[64]

The Arthashastra, hence, serves as the source to study laws enunciated as punishable by the state. The Dharmashastra treated men at the spiritual, metaphysical, and theoretical level. The Arthashastra talks of the practical learning of the laws and their application in the lives of men the failure of which would invite penalty or punishment in this world.

This presupposes an evidently crucial role to be played by the State in maintaining the welfare of its people. Rangarajan states it implies two things: "maintenance of law and order and adequate administrative machinery. In this context, maintaining law and order involves not only the detection and punishment of criminals (as in Book IV of the text on the removal of thorns, i.e., antisocial elements), but also upholding the fabric of society."[65] The state has a responsibility for ensuring the observance of laws concerning relations between husband and wives, inheritance, the rights of women, servants and slaves, contracts, and similar civil matters. "Further, there have to be laws to avoid losses and misuse of power by servants of the state. Therefore, an integral part of Arthashastra is *dandaniti*, the enforcement of laws by a voluminous and comprehensive set of fines and punishments.[66]

The treatment of the topic of administration of justice in a special adhikarana shows not only the level of legal acumen at the time of its writing but also its superiority to the Dharmashastra in several respects. The Arthashastra gave the name of *Dharmasthas*, a name that refers to Dharma or Law, while the Smrti writers used the word *pradvivaka* for a judge. In the first adhikarana, it describes the king as the final arbiter of justice, both in appellate and revisionary capacity. His judgement in any legal matter is supposed to be unquestioned.

The text does not refer to *sabhyas* or *sabhasads* in the codes, which the smitis often refer. Law of procedure and law of evidence were framed for trials concerning nonpayment of debts. The concept of witness has been dealt with at length. For perjury, different schools of Arthashastra recommended various kinds of punishments. The text knows about documentary evidence but does not attach much importance to it compared to the testimony of witness. This can be considered as the rudiment of evolution of law of evidence. The necessity of judges to be impartial is brought about by prescribing punishment for any dereliction of duty.

A remarkable provision even entails the judges to be fined or punished for errors in pronouncing judgements and for making an innocent persons suffer corporal punishment. They themselves are to undergo the same punishment. They are also to make good any loss suffered by a party through a wrong judgement eight times over.[67]

The Arthashastra attaches much value to *rajashasana* (edicts of king) when it declares it as the highest authority on the basis of which a case is decided. This, however, does not deem the king as the lawmaker as historian K.A. Nilakanta Shastry presumed.[68] There is no evidence that the king had the power of legislation as such. Likewise, K.P. Jayaswal made distinction between what he calls 'artha laws and *dharma*' laws, the former meaning king's laws or rajashasana and latter implying laws as laid down in the Dharmashastra texts. He argued that the authority of king's decree was higher than other laws, a fact shown by a remark in the Mahabhasya—*naiveshvara ajnapayati napi dharmasutrakarah pathanati*—where, according to Sanskrit syntax, the order of the king is given preference over the teaching of Dharmasutras.[69]

There is no evidence to prove the existence of separate class of 'artha' laws and 'dharma' laws. Laws in the Arthashastra are the same laws, which are there in the Dharmashastras; the difference is no greater than between the smrtis themselves. Jayaswal also talked of Dharma law—that is, sacerdotal law and the Vyavahara law, which is secular law. He believed that the three sets of laws—*dharma, artha,* and *vyavahara* was combined for the first time by Sumati, the supposed author of Manusmrti in the Sunga times. However, there is no evidence of existence of separate Vyavahara set of laws. Achara and Vyavahara formed part of the Dharma law itself. The absence of ordeals from

Vyavahara law is cited as the point of distinction between the two, but several other early sutras hardly mention of ordeals. Manu has mentioned it with hardly much emphasis.[70] Only `Yajnavalkya onwards, it is given importance.

However, the Arthashastra did not receive as much importance as the Dharmashastra as the source of study of law, even though the Arthashastra is much more systematic and rational in arranging the topics relating to law. The early Dharmashastra hardly compared well with the text in matters of law for their treatment or detail. Manusmrti could be considered worth comparison; but when compared, the former is found lacking rules on various topics like *dasas*, *Karmakaras*, *Vastuka*, *dandaparushya*, (the lower orders). Its author's strong bias in favour of Brahmanas has given rise to differences within the rules laid down. It is possible, as argued by several authors, that Arthashastra or text like this could have been the source of Manu and other smrti writers probably circumscribed those body of customary laws.[71]

Srisa Chandra Vidarnava has somewhat rightly remarked, "It appears that originally Smrti texts were codes of Ecclesiastical Law, but on the revival of Hinduism, the Brahmanas were not slow in incorporating Positive Law in Smrtis, ignoring altogether the existence and importance of the Arthashastra. It is the misfortune of India that in the early days of British rule, Arthashastra was not discovered for this would have prevented the codification of personal law of Hindus on the present lines."[72] In fact, the Smrtis can hardly be called legal codes whereas the *dharmashathiya* section of the Arthashastra has all the components to be taken as a code of law in the actual sense of the term. This work is, however no less rooted in tradition than the Dharmashastra.

THE HISTORICAL IMPORTANCE OF EPICS: THE RAMAYANA, THE MAHABHARATA, AND THE BHAGVADGITA

Mahabharata

Although the efforts at creating an "Epic age" in the history of India have proved unconvincing, it is true that the Epics form a part of the later Vedic literature available to us, containing in parts legal lore as well. Between the composition of the Rigveda and the age of Buddha, a period of four or five centuries, the source of reconstructing history is limited to the later Vedas,

Brahmanas, and Upanishads. The Aryans at this time had pushed their way down the Ganges in the east.[73] The social conditions were in transition, but it is hardly represented in the sources available for the period. A.L. Basham says about the Epics and Puranas that "these are so overlaid by the accretions of later centuries that no attempt at interpreting them historically has so far won general acceptance, and it may never be possible to sift the fact from the fiction".[74]

It is the Bharata war, the great battle of Kurukshetra, magnified to titanic proportions that formed the basic core of Mahabharata. Around these legends, the lores and rescensions were laid down. However, Basham rightly remarked that "it is futile to try to reconstruct the political and social history of India in the 10th century B.C. from the Mahabharata as it would be to write the history of Britain immediately after the evacuation of the Romans from Malory's Mode de Arthur."[75]

However, from the legal point of view, the epic Mahabharata has relevance in that it helps in ascertaining or eliminating the elements of theoretical law, which were derived from the Shruti and Smrti texts. Mahabharata, which is a self styled *Itihasa - Purana* (historical narration) tells that the Veda should be studied, with the help of *Itihasa-Purana*.[76] Its twelfth book, known as Shanti Parvan, is a collection of many disparate passages on statecraft and human conduct. It was probably an insertion in the epic in the early centuries of the Christian era.[77]

These interpolations were mostly religious and legal injunctions. The most sacred of these interpolations was the Bhagvad Gita, which by itself appears to be a compilation from various sources. In these additions, probably, legal literature from the smrtis and other religious legends made way into the epic; and today, they serve some kind of a compendium or encyclopedia of early Hinduism. The Mahabharata was thus transformed from secular literature into sacred literature, with its various sermons serving as the contents of Hindu philosophy, if not history as such.

E.W. Hopkins says history fails us, and who can trust Hindu tradition?[78] He feels the epic Mahabharata to be of obscure origin as well as inwardly inconsistent. The poem is mentioned in the sutra of Ashvalayana; the poem, he says, is also known to the Mahabhashya, but Panini's evidence is negative.[79] He has analysed the writing over of the poem and remarked, "Its introductory part states it to have had different beginnings and lengths—8,800 couplets, 24,000 and 100,000—but as aside from other proofs of the recent time, it is evident that the last length could not have been noted till the work had been completed. This whole statement can only be regarded as one of comparatively later origin, belonging to the final development of the Epic—a time when the writers knew little in regard to the writing over of their inherited verses. At present, the text is overburdened with extraneous matter, tales, laws, moral codes, theologies, metaphysics, quite stifling the original body of living poetry."[80]

The inversion theory, which says Pandavas do wrong, is reproached, excused, and the poem was rewritten to make them appear good as advanced by Schroeder is rejected by Ludwig. However, what comes forth in Hopkins analysis is that the didactic morality cultivated in the epic inculcated at last was superior to that recognised at first. As Hopkins puts it, "consider how penetrated the epic is by this later morality, how ethical need imposes long sermons on us (not religion) at every turn, how it has added chapter after chapter at variance with earlier feeling and custom . . . how it imposes, its new law on the daily acts of life, how it has composed a formal 'code of fighting' that inculcates law more humane than was possibly consistent with the practices of the older times". Although Hopkins is questioning the intention of priests that might have been playing in handling the heroes of the epic, in excusing their sons, it comes out that the Epic has different reproaches, which need to be analysed in the background of the times and morality that existed at that time, especially among the priests who wrote it as the text is interpolatory by nature.

Its nucleus being the war tale, it is the later moral and didactic interpolations in Mahabharata that could be used for as source for studying the morality and theory of law that might have existed in the later Vedic period. Its use in legal history is limited by the fact that its own historicity is questioned. It nonetheless serves good use in contributing to the legal philosophy of the times it represents.

The Ramayana

In any society, offence is met with punishment, but is it possible to bring the guilt to the mind of the offender by forgiving? Valmiki says, "No one should return evil for evil but should try to maintain one's moral excellence. This is what good men do. It is proper to show compassion even to those who are criminal and worthy to be slain. Who is there who doth not commit a crime?"[81]

A text that describes the 'ideal' of every relationship, the ideal man, the ideal ruler, the ideal son, the ideal husband and wife, the ideal brother definitely has much to teach of law and dharma. The concept of dharma and law or righteousness is at its supreme high in the Ramayana. It says, "The virtue of the administrators consists in humbly and freely dispensing justice and administrative discipline favor and punishment. They should not follow their whims and passions."[82]

The text with Rama as its hero belongs to a period when Aryans pressed into the east, setting up janapadas in Kosala and Kashi, near Banaras. It is the second great epic revered till date, for the ideals it put up to shape an ordered society. It is believed to have received its final form around the beginning of the Christian era.

The contents of Uttarakhanda describing Rama's life and career are said to have been certified by no less an elite of ancient India than Kalidasa in his semi-epic, the Raghuvamsa.

Rama is depicted as a military hero in never-to-be-defeated warrior style.[83] As Ghurye says, "accordingly, we find as early as before the first century B.C., the BhagavadGita recording this phenomenon. For in it, Lord Krshna dilating on his universal form and identifying himself with the highest, best or the perfect specimen of a whole category of objects, ideas and values chose Rama as the highest or most perfect specimen of those who bear arms, i.e., of warriors (B.G. X. 31)."[84] The Valmikian Ramayana discusses the ideal duties of a husband and wife among other ideals. It presents a glorious illustration of ideal womanhood in the character of Sita. He identifies an obedient wife with complete Dharrna in which and Artha and kama fully participate.[85] He is seen as a paragon of virtues.

"The Ramayana condemns *Strihatya* (the killing of a woman) for instance, as a great sin. Rama himself tells a *nahyenamutsahe hantum strisvabhavena rakshitam*. Being by her feminine nature, I have no heart to kill her."[86]

Similarly, Bharata tells Shatrughna-woman ought not to be slain by any creature.

Hanuman too refers to a special hell reserved for the slayer of woman

Ye ca strighatinam lokavadhyaisca kutsitah [87]

Khan studies that "despite these ideals, the text tells how Rama, at the behest of Vishwamitra killed Tattaka, a woman." He interprets it in the light of relatively pragmatic Valmikian principle by three arguments.[88]

First, Tattaka had murdered a number of holy priests (Bala Kanda 25-16, 19), and Vishwamitra tells Rama that it is the duty of to protect his subjects; second, Vishwamitra tells Rarna under similar circumstances, Indra killed woman and he must follow his example, putting aside all notions of pity and for a woman who is a murderess.[89] Third, Rama must obey at the behest of his father as Parashurama killed his mother, obeying his father. Khan concludes that Rama did it for self-defence ultimately when violently attacked by her.

Valmiki's Dharma is not just an ideal. It is to be interpreted with pragmatism. It has not as much significance as the purely law texts on our topic. But its concept of Dharma, which shows not only an awareness of the ideal of law and justice but an ideal one, too is important. Its approach is not wholly unrealistic although at times it is pure rhetoric. It depicts a social melodrama where Dharma, Artha, and Kama dictated the course of life. Variations and deviations from this course were looked upon as sins. Transgressions of norms had to be penalised and purified. Hence, legal components are visible scattered here and there within the text although not without a definite course.

As T.R. Venkatarama Sastri wrote, "The author of the Ramayana puts in the mouth of his Divine hero the words *"atmanam manusham manye"*, suggesting that, according to himself, his conduct was that of a human being desirous of acting conformably to the highest ideals of Dharma or the best traditions of his time.[90] However, lessons of life, he says, are available as much to those who do not accept his Divinity as to those who accept him as such.[91]

Notwithstanding the limitations and doubts about the historicity of the text, we can hardly put it aside as unimportant in any study pertaining to law and dharma or of norms pertaining to man and woman living in a society. Srinivasa Shastri has thus estimated the epic hero, Sri Ramchandra that he is no better as husband, as son, as king, as man, we see him growing up as a character. That is the beauty of the Ramayana. The man who reads the Ramayana thinking that from the beginning he is dealing with God will get nothing out first. You must read the story as a human story, lived among human beings by a human being, and then, oh, what rich treasures there are of wisdom in it.[92]

The Bhagvadgita

The Bhagvadgita is like the Bible of India. As a Christian has to take oath by touching the Bible, a Hindu touches the Gita before taking such oath in the Court of law. A fragment of the great epic of Manbharata, Gita is a religious poem that teaches a theory of devotion, the philosophy of *ekayana*, and the doctrine of *Karma*. As Basham puts it, it "teaches a full fledged theism and is part of the more recent Hinduism, rather than of the old Brahmanism which slowly changed from a religion of sacrifice to one of devotion."[93]

The text forms a part of the present Mahabharata (chapters 23–49 of the Bhishmaparva). The book is supposed to be a philosophical dialogue between Arjuna of the Pandavas and Krshna, the incarnation of Vishnu who was acting the charioteer of Arjuna. As Shakuntala Rao Shastri puts it, "its official designation, as indicated by the Colophon is Upanishad and along with Upanishad and Brahamana it is one of the triple canons—*prasthanatraya*."[94] It is, however, hard to believe that such a discourse could have been held in the midst of two armies waiting for the battle. Shastri remarks that the battle of Kurukshetra, if it be a historical fact, must have taken place some centuries before the birth of Buddha. But we do not find any trace of the fundamental teachings of Gita in the Buddhist period. The book bears traces of a post-Buddhistic age. The reputed author Sri Krishna, if he be a historic figure at all, is not known to be a great philosopher except in the Bhagavadgita.[95]

The ideas spelt out in the text appear to be of the later Vedic origin. It's innate with the doctrine of incarnation and also the doctrine of Karma.[96] Krishna sermonises not only righteousness but also the value of fulfilling one's karma or duties without thinking of the end result. The whole discourse appears in the nature of an evaluation of what is correct and what is riot, what one should do and what one should not do, regardless of fruits. He reconciles the path of knowledge and the path of action, i.e., the Sankhya and the Karma Yogas, ultimately giving way to the conception of salvation. This doctrine is dangerously near to the doctrine of determinism, although he attaches much value to detachment, which frees one from the consequences. Shastri quotes that the Upanishads are the cow, Arjuna is the calf, Sri Krshna is the milkman, the Bhagvadgita is the milk, and the wise are the drinkers.

Sarvapanishado gavo dogdha gopalanandanah
Partho vatsah sudhirbhokta dugdham gitamritam mahat[97]

The Bhagvadgita does not speak on law as much as it does on the concept of salvation. However, to develop an understanding on law and dharma, one cannot ignore the concept of dharma innate in the text. Unlike the Mahabharata and the Ramayana, Gita teaches the practical philosophy of life and is much more rooted into reality than its other companions. It not only depicts a society of Varna distinctions and said superiority of Brahrnanas but also emphasises on maintaining these rigidities of caste. It talks of intermixing of castes and the impurity it brings with it and so on.

SOURCES AND BASIS OF LAW

(As specified in these texts)

For a proper understanding of the Hindu Law, it is necessary to examine the institutional or other sources from which these laws emanated, how far these laws were legal by implication, the role of the king, and whether popular and customary law as a body existed or was visible or not. *Vyavahara* or law being an integral part of religion and ethics (Dharma), the Dharmashastra offer the verdict and overwhelming data on religious and social obligations, philosophy, and manner of living in the society. However, the amount of literature on Hindu law is vast and conflicting, for it represents an evolution though different strata of civilisation pertaining to the changing social milieu. As Mayne observed in the first edition of Hindu Law published in 1878, "Hindu Law has the oldest pedigree of any known system of jurisprudence and even now it shows no sign of decrepitude".[98]

What is important to analyse is what formed the basis of these laws. Most authors have clearly spelt *shruti* and *smrti* as the main source points of law and Vedas as the primary core from where the concept of Dharma emanated in the form of *rta*. Nearly all the *smrti* texts have relied on the intellectual capacity of Brahmanas in fulfilling the role of creating and upholding law. Manu, in chapter 1, speaking on creation says, 'The very birth of a Brahmana is an eternal incarnation of the sacred law, for he learns to (fulfill) the, sacred law and becomes one with Brahman.'[99]

Clearly, caste as a factor was the overwhelming over principles of law and morality. The hegemony of Brahmans in society was mooted through these repeated assertions as he is seen as a repository of wisdom who would fulfill the sacred law. The exclusivity over wisdom in such a belief society was seen as the basis for asserting that this alone could do so.

Manu says the Brahman as not just a seer of law but as an important class in upholding divinely ordained law. It becomes his moral duty to fulfill this law told to him by the Gods, and he is answerable to Gods alone for this task. The text of Manu declares Brahrnanas superior position vis-à-vis laws in society. He becomes an upholder of sacred laws and thereby, is raised to a sacrosanct status. The hierarchically stratified Brahmana superior status society is what is reflected in this verse of Manu. The text, hence was not accepted by large sections of society in modern times owing to these biases.

In one verse, Manu says, "In order to settle his duties and those of the other (castes) according to their order, wise Manu sprung from the self-reliant, composed these Institutes (of the sacred law)."[100] It believes that the laws were spelt by the wise Manu who originated from the self-existence, and his primary object was to maintain the framework of caste duties and obligations. Sacred law was ordained probably to keep the four Varna or orders in place, and this was the primary law ordained for the Brahmanas. That is why he emphasises on good conduct of those superior born, which he believes to be the transcendent law.[101]

In the second chapter, Manu has enumerated the sources of law: "The whole Veda is the (first) source of the sacred law, next the tradition and the virtuous conduct of those who know the (Veda), further, also the customs of holy men and (finally) self satisfaction."[102] The Manusmrti regards the Veda as the supreme repository of laws ordained divinely.[103] By Shruti (revelation) Manusmrti explains, is meant the Veda, the Smrti (tradition) represents the Institutes of Sacred Law. These two should never be disputed or called with question as the sacred laws are believed to have originated in them.[104]

In the text of Manu, the basis of origin of laws is spelt out as the Veda while tradition is represented by the Dharmashastra or the Institutes of Sacred law, and what is difficult to understand is the so-called "virtuous conduct" (*sadhunam acara*) of Brahmanas (or those who know Vedas) their customs, as well as self-satisfaction. Manu interprets it as custom handed down in succession.[105] Traditionally, virtuous conduct would imply a specimen of conduct that entail fewer sins and explicit virtues, but this appears to be subjective and judgemental. Who would determine that a particular conduct was appropriate to be deemed virtuous? In these, the text of Manu does not interpret it clearly and leaves us with two assumptions—first, that virtuous conduct was expected from the Brahmanas, and second, their virtuous conduct and customs adopted would set the trend for the rest to follow, thereby ordaining some kind of popular law or custom that could be imbibed by the people.

"Self-satisfaction" (*atmanastustih svasya priyam*) as the source of sacred law does not in any way seem explicable except that it puts a weight on one's own morality and conscientiousness to distinguish the right from the wrong, the wisdom to ascertain the lawfully accepted, and accept the truth from the false.[106] Medhatithi later on interprets it as self-satisfaction of only those who are learned in the Veda and good (*vedavidam sadhunam*). When these learned men felt satisfied by any action, it was to be taken as lawful, for such men could never be satisfied with wrong actions. However, this seems to be highly subjective source enlisted along with the rest.

In case of conflict, Manusmrti upholds both the texts. It says when two sacred texts (Sruti) are conflicting, both are held to be law for both are pronounced by the wise to be valid law.

The Yajnavalkyasmrti expounded the sources of law beyond those stated by Manu (book 1) although in a later verse Manu's fourfold Dharma-mulam is adopted.

"The Vedas with the Puranas, Nyaya, Mimamsa, the codes of law (*dharmashastra*) and the (six) Vedangas are the fourteen repositories (*sthananani*) of the sciences and of law (*dharmasya*)."[107]

The Vedas (*shruti*), traditional law (*smrti*), the practices of good men (*sadachara*), and one's own inclination are called the root of law.[108] The Yajnavalkysmrti too tells that in case of any conflict between shruti and smrti, the former shall prevail. On this analogy, the later *smrti* writers declared that statements of Smrti were to be preferred to those of *Arthashastra*. The influence of Arthashastra on the Smrti has yet to be ascertained.

However in the Arthashastra, sources of law have been spelt in clear terms. It says any matter in dispute shall be judged according to four bases of justice. These in order of increasing importance are Dharma, which is based on truth. Evidence, which is based on witness, Custom, that is tradition accepted by people and royal edicts, that is law promulgated by the state.[109]

Further, in case of disagreement between custom and the Dharmashastra or between the evidence and the shastra, the matter should be decided according to dharma. Evidently, Dharma was held above the customary law. And whenever there would be a conflict between the Shastra and the written law based on Dharma, then the written law shall prevail, for the reasoning explaining the derivation of a (particular) Shastra from Dharma is no longer available to us.[110] The Arthashastra also explicitly states that in case of conflict of sacred law (shastra) with rational law (*dharmanyaya*—that, is king's law), reason shall be authoritative.[111] In other words, in Arthashastra, the state and state-enacted laws under a conscientious king or head could not be overlooked even in the presence of smrti laws, which find a logical presence in the text, as indeed the work talks about assigning primacy to the authority of the ruler and the state. In fact, the text goes further to tell that the king who administers justice in accordance with Dharma, evidence, custom, and written law will be able to conquer the whole world.[112]

Although there is no suggestion that a king could create laws actually, the Arthashastra underlines the importance of a king in upholding justice in the state. He does not appear as a fountain of law from whom laws independent of Dharma enunciations could emanate but is seen as protector of Dharma and as a fountain of justice. This is made clear in this verse: 'Because the king is the guardian of the right conduct of this world with its four varnas and four agamas, he (alone) can enact and promulgate laws (to uphold them) when all traditional codes of conduct perish (through disuse or disobedience).'[113]

All systems of law, hence, have their origin in two sources: written and unwritten. The written sources enumerated in the textual sources under consideration more or less name Shruti and Smrti as their origin. Puranas works accessory to Shruti and Srnrti; and some miscellaneous sources like Tantras, Agamas, etc., constitute the other sources. The entire Veda has been declared to the treat of dharma (*Vedo dharmamulam*, 3.116).[114]

Narada states that Dharma, Vyavahara, Charitra (usage), and royal edict are the four feet (padas) of Vyavahara.[115] Katyayana, who represents the high watermark in the Indian legal tradition, speaks on sources at length.[116] Katyayana says, "Whatever a person practices, whether it be according to dharma (the letter of the sacred law) or not, because it is the invariable usage in a country, is declared to be *caritra* (usage)." His verses appear to be an elaboration of Brhaspati's teachings. Katyayana dwells on the definition of *Vyavahara*. In this verse, he defines *Vyavahara* in practical sense: "When the ramifications of right conduct that together are called Dharma and that can be established only with effect, have been violated, the dispute (in a law court between plaintiff and defendant) which springs from what is desired to be proved (such a debt) is said to be *Vyavahara*."[117] In the very next verse, Katyayana explains *Vyavahara* etymologically: "'*Vi*' is employed in the sense of various, '*ava*' in the sense of doubt, '*hara*' means removing. '*Vyavahara*' is so-called because of its removing various doubts."[118]

Katyayana sees the authority of a king to issue an edict but puts limits on its being legitimate. "What a king establishes as Dharma which is not in conflict with the *smrti* rules on justice and with the usages of the country as a righteous royal edict."[119]

Further, where a cause is tried by (an appeal to) reasoning and ordeals are eschewed, there (decision by) Dharma is overruled by Vyavahara and not in other cases. These sources, apart from the Vedas and Smrtis themselves, regard the customs and ways of learned men (*sadachara shistagama*) as the third source of law. Jolly, in his magnificent work Hindu Law and Custom, says, "In connection with law proper, particular customs and manners of particular countries, castes and families are often emphasised as standard of course only so far as they are not opposed to the sacred law."[120] According to Jolly, Katyayana is most emphatic on this issue. He says that the customary law shall be recorded in books and as much care should be paid to it as the Veda.[121] This implies that over a course of time—that is, by the time of Katyayana—customary law could not be ignored and assumed if not more as much significance probably as the Dharma.

NOTES AND REFERENCES

1.   K.K. Shah, *The Problem of Identity, Women in Early Indian Inscriptions*, Preface, p.viii.

2.   D.C. Sircar, *Glimpses of Achara and Vyavahara in Early Indian Literary and Epigraphic Records* in Richard W. Lariviere (ed.) Studies in Dharmashastra, p.3.

3.   D.C. Sircar, *Indian Epigraphy*, p.23.

4.   Ibid.p. 20

5.   Plates of the time cf. Sasankaraja, Gupta Samvat 300, (619–20 AD) cited in Epigraphia Indica, Vol.VI. p143, mention in line twenty-four customary verses found in Buguda Plates, too as quotations from the Laws of Manu.

6.   D.C. Sircar, *Select Inscriptions*, p. 112, in Nasik cave Inscription of Gautamiputra Satkami(C 106–30 AD).

7.   Ibid., Sanchi Stone Inscription of Chandragupta-Gupta Year 93 (412 AD)

8.   J. Jolly, *Hindu Law and Custom*, p 1

9.   Ibid., p. 33.

10.   Major Dharmasastras that Jolly speaks of are Apastamba, Hiranayakesin, Baudhayana, Gautama, Vasistha, Vishnusmrti, the Dharmashastra of Harita, Vaikhanasasutra, the spurious Buddhasrnrti smrtis of Kasyapa, Atri, Satapa, spurious Brhaspati smrti of Sankha, and Manavadharmasutra.

11.   M. M. Patkar, *Topics of Law and Litigation in the Dharmasutras*, Poona Orientalist, Vol. 26, pp. 65–104

12.   P.V. Kane, *History of Dharmashastra* (HD), 1.213.

13. Radhabinod Pal, *The History of Hindu Law* (HHL), p. 161.

14. Buhler, Laws of Manu, *Sacred Books of the East* (SBE), Vol.XXV, p.xi.

15. Ibid., p.xiii.

16. P.V. Kane, *History of Dharmashastra*, Vol. I, p. 148.

17. R.M. Das, *Manu and his Seven Commentators*, p .148.

18. Narhar Kurundkar, *Manusmrti; Contemporary Thoughts*, Tr. From Marathi by Madhukar Deshpande p.7. Manusmrti as it exists today is a book in 12 chapters and 2,684 verses. Some editions of the book have 2,695 verses. The 1877 edition of MS by Mrtunjai and 1927 edition by Bapat Shastri and Nimaya Sagar press edition with Kulluka and Bhatt's commentary all contain 2,684 verses.

19. Buhler, *Laws of Manu*, pp. 327–345.

20. K.V. Rangaswami Aiyangar, *Some Aspects of the Hindu View of Life according to Dharmashastra*, 1950, p. 5. In footnote he mentions the Burmese are governed by *Dhammatat*, based on Manusmrti. See Forschammer, Sources and Development of Burmese Laws by 1885.

21. Ibid., footnote. Manusmrti is still cited as an authority in the island of Bali.

22. P.S.Sivaswamy Aiyar, *Evolution of Hindu Moral Ideals*, p.xii.

23. Henry Maine, *Ancient Law*, 7th edition, p. 15.

24. R.M. Das, op.cit, p.5. Seven commentaries published by V.N. Mandalik are (1) Manubhashya of Medhatithi, (2) Manutika of Govindraja (3) Manvarthavivrti of Sarvajnananarayana, (4) Manavarthamuktavali of Kullukabhatta, (5) Manvarthachandrika of Raghavanda, (6) Manuvyakhyana of Nandana, and (7) Manu Bhavarthachandrika of Rarnachandra. He has also mentioned other commentators like Madhavacharya, Sridharaswami, Rudhidatta, Viswarupa, and Bharuchi.

25. Ibid., p.2.

26. K.V. Rangaswami Aiyangar, p.4 quoted from D.S. Sharma, *What is Hinduism?* (1939), p. 12.

27. Kurundkar, op. cit, p. vvi.

28. *Yajnavalkya Smrti* with the commentary of Vijnanesvara called the Mitakshara, Book I, The Achaya Adhyaya translated by the Late Rai Bahadur Srisa Chandra Vidyarnava, Allahabad 1918, preface.

29. J. R. Gharpure, *Yajnavalkyasmrti*, Part II, Vyavahara Adhyaya, Introduction.

30. Monier Williams, *Indian Wisdom*, p. 21 3. (Quoted in Yajnavalkyasmrti translated by Acharya Vidarnava).

31. *Yajnavalkyasmrti*, Introduction, p.xvii

32. Ibid., p.xviii. Vidarnava writes, "It should be remembered that it is not an authoritative Smrti for any Yuga. Manu was for Satya, Gautama for Treta, Sankha for Dwapara and Parasara for Kaliyuga. But Yajnavalkya is not mentioned tor any age."(Satyuga, Treta, Dwapara, Kali are concept of yugas or eras according to Indian mythology)

33. Buhler has compared this in his translation of *Laws of Manu*, SBE, Vol. XXV.

34. Jolly (in SBE Vols. VII and XXX III)

35. *Yajnavalkyasmrti*, Introduction, op.cit p.xviii.

36. Quoted from Buhler, note on the age of the author of Mitaksara read at a meeting at a Bombay branch of the Royal Asiatic Society, 1868.

37. *Naradasmrti*, SBE, XXXIII, Introduction, p.xvi.

38. P.V. Kane, HD, 1.205.

39. cf. *itimanavadharmashastre naradaproktaya sanhitam*

40. *Naradasmrti*, SBE, XXXIII, p.4. According to him, the original code of Manu consisted of 100,000 slokas or 1,080 chapters. This was reduced to 12,000, 8,000, and 4,000 slokas in subsequent versions.

41. cf, *Naradasmrti*, SBE, p.21.

42. Kane, *History of Dharmashastra* (HD) 1.202. Yajnavalkya recognises the right of widow to succeed to her deceased husband. Narada does not.

43. *Naradasmrti*, S.B.E. XXXII, Introduction p.xxi.

44. Mulla, *Principles of Hindu Law*, p.2.

45. Madhukar M. Patkar, *Narada, Brhaspati and Katyayana, A. Comparative Study in Judicial Procedure*, p. 17.

46. Kane, *HD*. 1.210.

47. Mulla, ibid., p.30.

48. Patkar, op. cit, p18. The distribution of slokas under different topics in the printed edition is as under.

Vyavahara verses	1,271	asauca verses	76
Samskara verses	557	apaddharma	51
Acara verses	101	prayaschitta	89
Sraddha verses	155	Total	2,300

49. Brhaspatismrti, p .233, v.13

50. Kane, HD 1.207
51. Brhaspatismrti, v .9, p.2.
52. P.V. Kane, *Katyayanasmrti on Vyavahara*, Introduction. In the present work, over 900 quotations from Katyayana have been collected.
53. Ibid., Introduction.
54. *Katyayanasmrti*, op. cit, Introduction, p.x.
55. Kane, *HD*, 1.213
56. Ibid. (distinction mentioned in Chapter on Procedural Law)
57. Patkar, op.cit, p.23
58. P V.Kane, *HD*, 1.344
59. Ratnamayi Dikshit, *Women in Sanskrit Dramas*, p.140. Merchand Lakshman Das, Delhi, 1964.
60. *Yajnavalkyasmrti*, op.cit, Introduction, p.xiv.
61. L.N. Rangarajan, *Kautilya: The Arthashastra*, p.16
62. Ibid., *On the Text, Commentaries and Translations*.
63. Ibid. The actual number of verses in Kangle's edition is 5,348.
64. Ibid., p 14
65. Ibid., p 13
66. Ibid., p. 14
67. Ibid., 4, 9, 18–0.
68. K.A. Nilkanta Sastri, *Age of the Nandas and the Mauryas*, p. 173. He maintained that the supremacy of royal decree (rajasasana) is exceptional among Indian writers and "marks an attempt to evolve a new norm in civil law in the establishment of which the royal authority would be actively exerted".
69. K.P. Jayaswal, *Manu and Yajnavalkya*, p.17.
70. Buhler, *Laws of Manu*, VIII, V-114-116.
71. Sri Henry Maine, *Early History of Institutions*, pp.382–83 said, "The influence of the Brahmanical treatises on mixed law and religion in sapping the old customary law of the country has always been very great and in some particulars it has become greater under English rule."
72. *Yajnavalkyasmrti*, Vidarnava, Introduction.
73. A. L Basham, *The Wonder That was India*, p.38 tells about the recent excavation of the ancient city of Hastinapura, the lowest level of which has been reasonably fixed at between 1000 and 700 BC by B. 3 Lal (Illustrated London News. 4.10. 1952, pp 551 ff)
74. Ibid., p.38.

75.	Ibid., p.39.

76.	*Mahabharata*, 1.1.204; *itihasa – puranabhyani vedani samupabrnhayet.*

77.	A.L Basham, op cit, p.80.

78.	E.W. Hopkins, *Origin and Historical Value of the Epic*, in Journal of Ancient Indian History, Vol.1 Parts 1–2, 1967–68, Calcutta, p. 331.

79.	Ibid., p. 332.

80.	Ibid., p.333.

81.	*Ramayana, Yuddha Kanda*, 113–41, 42, 43.

82.	Ibid., *Kiskindha Kanda*, 17–32, 33.

83.	G. S. Ghurye, *The Legacy of Ramayana*, p.6.

84.	Ibid., p.7.

85.	Benjamin Khan, *The Concept of Dharma in Valmiki Ramayana*, p.169.

86.	Ibid., p. 137, *Ayodhya Kanda*, 78–21.

87.	Ibid., p.137.

88.	Ibid., Ramayana, *Yuddha Kanda*, 81–23.

89.	Ibid., p.138, 139.

90.	Vishvamitra enunciated a good and sound law that if a woman is a confirmed enemy to social order, her sex ought to be no protection to her. This way, the killing of Tattaka is not a blot on Rama's character.

91.	T. R, Venkatrama Sastri, Foreword in *Lectures on the Ramayana* by V.S. Srinivasa Sastri, p. xiv.

92.	Ibid., p.xix.

93.	V. S. Srinivasa Sastri, *Lectures on the Ramayana*, First Lecture, p. 12.

94.	A.L. Basham, *The Wonder That was India*, p.253.

95.	Shakuntala Rao Shastri, *The Bhagvada Gita*, p.51.

96.	Shastri, op.cit, p.52.

97.	Ibid., 52. "Whenever, O Bharata, there is decline of righteousness and rise of unrighteousness, I create myself. For the liberation of the righteous and the destruction of the wicked, I am born age after age."

98.	Ibid., p.61.

99.	Mayne, *Hindu Law*, preface.

100.	Buhler. *Laws of Manu*, SBE, vol. XXV. p.25.

101.	Buhler, *LOM*, p.26.

102.	Ibid., p.27, v.108. "The rule of conduct is transcendant law, whether it be taught in the revealed texts or in the sacred tradition, hence a twice born man who possesses regard for himself, should be always careful to (follow) it."

103. Buhler, *LOM*, Ch. II, p.29.
104. Ibid., v.7. "Whatever law has been ordained for any (person) by Manu, that has been fully declared in the Veda; for that (sage was) omniscient," p.30.
105. Ibid., v.10, p.31.
106. Buhler, Ch. II, v.18. The custom handed down in regular succession (since time immemorial).
107. Buhler, op.cit, v.14. pp. 31–32.
108. *Yajnavalkya Smrti*, Book I, the Acharya Adhyaya translated by late Rai Bahadur Srisa Chandra Vidarnava, Introduction. I. 3.
109. Ibid., 1.7.
110. L.N. Rangarajan, *Kautilya, The Arthashastra*, Ch. VIII, p. 380–81 (V.3.1. 39, 40)
111. Ibid. (3.1.44–45)
112. Ibid.
113. Ibid. (3.1.43).
114. Ibid., v. (3.1.38) p. 377.
115. J.R. Gharpure, *Yajnavalkyasmrti*, Part II.
    Vedoakhilam dharmamulamsmrtishile cha taddvhidham
    Acharaschchev sadhunamatmanatushtirev cha
    Manusmrti (Ch. II, v.6)
    Yajnavalkya (Ch. I, v.6)
116. Jolly, *SBE, Naradasmrti*, p.7, and vv. 10–11.
117. Kane, *Katyayana on Vyavahara*, p. 122, v.25, 26.
118. Ibid., v.26/in.31. The (Vyavahara) is said to have four, i.e., viz. the plaint, the defence (or reply), the deliberation (as the burden of proof) and adducing of proof, p.122 and p.128.
119. Ibid., v.38, p.125.
120. J. Jolly, *Hindu Law and Custom*, p.3.
121. Ibid., from the footnote.
    yasya deshasya yo dharmah pravriti sarvakalikah
    Shruti smrtivirodhena deshdrishti sa uchyate

CHAPTER III

Procedural Law and the Concept of Justice

Understanding the Role of King, Origin of Procedural Law, and the Administration of Justice

Procedural law emphasises on the technical aspects of processing of law or set forms of trials that address the grievances in any set up in contrast to Substantive law which defines offences or crimes and sets the gamut of rights and obligations. The need for procedural law, according to Dharmashastra texts arose when the practice of Dharma declined. These Dharmashastra texts lay down somewhat an elaborate law of procedure with reference to the eighteen titles under substantive law Although the parts and proceedings of procedural law and a judicial system in early India is a core discussion in this section, it remains a point of debate whether they served only as norms or were actually administered in any court of law as they have been described in the Shastra texts. However, the detailed code of regulations, a set of people to administer these laws, and also guidelines for providing efficient justice as also substantiated by some inscriptions and secular literature indicate that legal procedure may not have been just an idea but could have existed in reality. It is possible that in practice there may have been some deviations under different rulers or in separate circumstances.

Maine commented that early India had not passed beyond a stage at which a rule of law had become a rule as distinguished from a rule of religion. In Manu and Yajnavalkya, law of procedure can hardly be traced on judicial lines. However, by the time of Narada, Brhaspati, and Katyayana, a definite effort and presence to lay down procedural law is noticed. Some of these

52

texts stand out in the advanced and meticulous thinking that is exhibited in jurisprudential concepts. The earlier as well as later Smrtis entail special role of king in the administration of justice, kind of courts and finer nuances of imparting justice. The Sanskrit term for Procedural law was *Vyavahara* which was defined by Katyayana as the process of removing doubts.

Narada's was the first purely judicial text to which is traceable to the nature and characteristics of judicial procedure while Brhaspati takes it ahead on several other aspects such as division of lawsuits into civil and criminal, functions of representatives of court, and different titles of law. In the work of Katyayana, it reaches a high watermark especially in the description of the constitution of *dharmadhikarana* (Court of Justice).

In the Rigvedic conception of law, there is no reference to positive law. Its conception of *rta*, the eternal law as firm and immutable *(rtasya drdha dharunani santi)*, is an inflexible bending force associated with rituals. Its transgression was not only violative of human laws but was supposed to be punishable even by supernatural forces.[1] Law in this sense was not only transcendental but presupposed its relation to religion as eternal and beyond the purview of any kind of litigation. As it remained pivoted on *rta*, from which was born the ideal of truth, it was natural divine law that formed the basis of law. Like the Rigveda, the Atharva Veda too looked upon *rta* and *satya* as the twin basis of law, declaring truth was equal to declaring the law.[2]

Dharma, as part of the *rta*, referred to a kind of moral function. It was the notion of dharma and its opposite adharma that gave rise to the idea of rewarding good and punishing the evil of mortals in society. In this Vedic conception of law, the king or sovereign was considered secondary to the cosmic law, and hence, law existed without and above the sovereign or political sovereign.

It is only in the Dharmasutra that the king appears to be invested with the special charge to administer justice, also at the same time when the divine theory of kingship seems to be favoured by the law writers. The Dharmasutra has covered a wide range of topics dealing with law, which were probably adopted by Manu, Yajnavalkya, and others. The topics were like (1) Legal procedure, (2) the Parishad or legal assembly, (3) Evidence, (4) Witnesses, (5) Marriage, (6) Niyoga, (7) Possessions and ownership, (8) Stridhana, (9)

Partition, (10) the Law of debt, (11) Relations between Masters and servant, (12) Trade laws, (13) Theft, (14) Gambling, (15) Sexual offences, and so on.[3]

However, these discussions pertain more to the ceremonial and religious conduct than pure law. Legal topics were referred to incidentally and not as a matter of deliberation. R.B. Pal has rightly analysed that "although purely legal matters are scanty in these books, they speak of law, in the course of their discussions, as much as it was necessary for the regulation of the society as a whole, with the king as the head of the administration of justice and the Brahmana as the head of the religion and society set up."[4] Nonetheless, law, civil and criminal, enforceable by the king and the court of law makes a rudimentary appearance in the Dharmashastras.

The codes of Manu and Yajnavalkya represent a vertical development in the concept of law. In them, the king is seen to assume wide powers and emerging as the fountainhead of justice. Attending to law and justice appears as among the primary duties of the king. The principal obligations of the king according to these lawgivers were deemed to be to protect the subjects, to maintain the status given with respect to varnas and ashramas, to punish the wicked, and to do justice to the persons wronged.[5] The king's role with respect to law emerged out of his duty of providing protection. Since it was the ultimate responsibility of the king to protect his subjects from any wrongs, he becomes the apex of the system of law and justice. He was not there to provide law as much as to ensure abidance by the law in society and state.

Manu and Yajnavalkya, in spite of being descriptive about *Achara* and *Vyavahara*, the approach in these texts is less juristic and more focused on sacerdotal issues or rules of conduct.[6] It is in the works of Narada, Brhaspati and Katyayana that the legal acumen in exponentiating juristic laws becomes more highlighted.

Kane aptly remarked them as the triumvirate in the realm of the ancient Indian law and composition of the Hindu Legal literature.[7] "So also in Patkar's study, the law codes of these authors belong to the latest production of the smrti epoch of Hindu law and their legal character as also their judicial content are decidedly more advanced than those of either Manu or Yajnavalkya smrti."[8]

Naradasmrti, available in the recensions, points out Patkar toeing the line of Kane, deals exclusively with the *Vyavahara* (procedural) aspects of law. Unlike the texts of Manu and Yajnavalkya dealing with Dharma and the *Vyavahara* portion containing mixed matter of law and religion, the *acharadharma, prayaschitta*, etc,. Narada covers the whole gamut of secular law, civil and criminal and so does Brhaspati and Katyayana.[9]

In the introduction, Narada professes himself as a compiler of traditional law from the source *Manavadharrnashastra*.[10] He states his work to be an abridged version of the larger Manusmrti. The extant Naradasmrti probably constituted the ninth chapter of the original code headed as 'judicial procedure'. This part is designated as *Matrka or Vyavaharamatrka*, containing a summary of proceedings at law or general rules of procedure.[11] The Naradasmrti can be bifurcated into two main divisions. The first part deals with the necessity of the administration of justice, the nature of plaint composition of court, evidence, witnesses, etc. The second handles the different topics of law and the eighteen titles of law, treated with remarkable clarity in approach. His famous aphorism with regard to judicial procedure is the one that regards it as having four feet, four bases, four means, it benefits four and produces four results.[12] Narada has laid down even the law of arrests.[13]

Brhaspati's work, which is available only in reconstructed form, has seven sections on Vyavahara, samskara, achara, shraddh, asauca, appaddharma, and prayaschitta, totaling a 2,300 shlokas.[14]

He has exponentiated on the principles of law and is the first lawgiver to make a clear distinction between civil and criminal suits. According to him, the lawsuits are of the two kinds: (1) *Arthasamudbhava* or civil and (2) *Himsasamudbhava* or criminal. The former originates in demands regarding wealth while the latter in injuries. Those originating in money are of fourteen kinds and those from injury of four kinds.[15] He has mentioned the different grades of court such as kula, sreni, and gana, ending with the king as the apex court of appeal,[16] as well as courts with different standing like those established (*pratisthita*), not established, those established by royal authority or those were king himself, participated in the administration of justice.

Katyayana's code, as available, deals primarily with Vyavahara, or civil law with only a small portion devoted to criminal law. Toeing the line of Narada and Brhaspati, Katyayana opines on the duties of king, the characteristics of judicial procedure, and the two branches of Vyavahara: the Dharmashastra or sacred law and the Arthashastra or science of politics and government. As Kane remarked, he closely follows both the writers in legal phraseology and in technique.[17] His treatment of *stridhana* (woman's personal possession) is exponential for which Kane remarked his treatment of topic as having 'attained classical rank'. He was probably the first to define carefully the several kinds of *stridhana* to lay down women's power of disposal over the several varieties of *stridhana* and the prescribe lines of devolution to *stridhana*.[18] Two terms indicating legal functionaries—'*Stobhaka*' and '*Suchaka*'—are used by Katyayana smrti for the first time. The first is a person appointed by king to apprise him of certain offences while the second acts as an informant of crime for the sake of remuneration. He has also described two types of documents: the *Pascatkara* and the *Jayapatra*.[19]

Besides these Dharrna texts, the Arthashastra has deliberated on various topics dealing with procedural law. In fact, the discussions in Arthashastra seem to be more logical and rational and has lesser scope for imposition of vested morality to prevail over letter of law. *Mrcchakatika*, *the Dashakumaracharita*, and the *Mudrarakshasa*, or the secular works help further in drawing a near-practical picture of law of procedure that might have existed in the period under study, although the references in nearly all of them are purely incidental. In Kalidasa, we came across references ranging from civil to criminal to court of law, role of king, law of punishment, and other aspects of judicial procedure. Among the inscriptions, the Chammak Copper Plate grant of Maharaja Pravarasena II has a term called '*dharmasthana*',[20] indicating probably a place connected with justice. Vishnusena's Charter has the mention of some legal functionaries in its clauses. The Nalanda Spurious Copper Plate Inscription mentions *Akshapatala* as the court of law or as the repository of legal documents. As much as can be pieced together from textual sources and epigraphic sources, it seems some elements from later smrtis can be in some ways compared to these inscription evidences though with a lot of caution.

Procedural law that might have existed in the period under study can be studied with respect to its various components such as (1) the administration of justice, the judicial procedure, and the structure and constitution of courts; (2) the law of evidence encompassing the documents, witnesses, possession, and ordeals; (3) the titles of law or categorisation into civil and criminal; and (4) the punishment, law of arrests and imprisonments, or the penal law.

ADMINISTRATION OF JUSTICE AND ROLE OF KING

> *Justice, being violated destroys,*
> *Justice being preserved preserves,*
> *therefore, justice must not be violated,*
> *lest violated justice destroy us.*[21]

The spirit of justice dreamt by Manu is worded in the above verse and also in verse 17 at the same place: the only friend who follows men even after death is justice, for everything else is lost at the same time when the body (perishes).[22]

To carry out this ideally efficient administration of justice, not only Manu but also all the smrti writers, as well as authors of Sanskrit dramas, stressed the cardinal importance of king in the setup of law. Presuming that protection and preservation are the twin roles of the state, the king was visualised by legal theorists and characterised by dramatists as an upholder of law as derived from Dharma, and he was supposed to be the fountainhead of justice. He was supposed to apply law as in Dharmashastra and as modified to some extent by usage. King is seen as the power to enforce laws by virtue of the institutional power. Law is deemed to be the king of kings, and there is nothing superior to law.

However, justice could not be neglected or be treated secondary by him. As Kautilya speaks, "a king who observes his duty of protecting his people justly and according to law will go to heaven, whereas one who does not protect them or inflicts unjust punishment will not."[23] The monarch is not only enjoined to protect the people, but he is also required to do so in accordance with the dharma and in a just manner. His spiritual remuneration for being just and not unjust is that he would be blessed with permission in heaven. The role as a protector of Dharma, hence, accrues from his role as a guardian of his subjects, and protection is not possible without punishing the wicked.[24] Emphasising this as a conscientious law for king, his role towards his subjects and pleaders of justice has been linked to the rewards in the notion of heaven.

Elaborating this role as a feature of law of procedure, the Smrti writes emphasised on the king (1) attending personally to the administration of justice, (2) acquiring knowledge for a first and equitable disposal of cases according to varna hierarchy and other distinctions, (3) appointing a body of Brahmana councillors or judges for the sake of application of law to the cases under litigation. The first implied that the king had to have a thorough knowledge of the scriptures or treatises. He had to be learned and "reverent of the sacred law and had to administer law in consultation with his Brahmana advisors". As Manu puts it, "having fully considered thee time and place (of the offence): the strength and the knowledge (of the offender) let him justly inflict that (punishment) on men who act unjustly".[25] Similarly, the Yajnavalkya smrti enjoined "a king should attend personally to the administration of justice everyday, surrounded by councilors."[26] According to him, the protection of the subject is the highest duty of a king possessing the (necessary) qualification of anointment. When the king was unable to try cases, he would appoint a learned Brahmana (and, by interpretation, even the Kshatriya and Vaishya if need be) (Katyayana, 63–67, Manu, VIII, and Yajnavalkya II, 37).

Secondly, in technical interpretation or application of injunctions, caste was a big factor in writing of Manu as we see he emphasised on cases being taken up according to the castes.[27] The Varna basis is equally explicit in his assertion that let a Brahmana interpret law for the king but never a Shudra, which is understandable as the Dharmashastra was in Sanskrit and knowledge or skill to understand was expected to be better with one who was well read and proficient in language. The injunction implied that the Shudra were emphatically forbidden to act as bearers or interpreters of law while Kshatriya and Vaishya could be employed in cases of necessity.

Third, the king was to be assisted in the task of administering law by a body of advisors such as *amatya* (minister), *purohita* (family priest), and *sabhyas* (assessors) as well as experts in law by procedure of litigation such as *pradvivaka* (judge). Katyayana adds *vanij* (merchants) to this list of advisors as well (Katyayana, verses 56–59). This indicates that since law by usage was also taken into consideration, it is possible that for matters pertaining to cultivators or merchants, non-Brahmins may have been roped in, where specialised knowledge of Sacred literature may not have been necessary.

This discussion also needs to examine the status of the king vis-à-vis law. Unlike the West where the king, being a temporal and ecclesiastical head, was deemed to be a creator of law, India had a notion of a positive law inherent in its tradition. The king, since the Vedic times, was seen as a seer and upholder; his role has been linked to the upholding of law. Law, whether cosmic or divinely sacred, was independent and above the sovereign. Law as derived from dharmashastra and king existed as two separate entities. Only the king was expected to administer the laws, in a just spirit, being the protector of laws created for the well-being of people. As kingship progressed, laws enunciated by powerful rulers came to be implemented as *rajashasanas* or state order.

In the Arthashastra, a verse says, "Because the king is the guardian of the right conduct of this world, with its four varnas and four asramas, he (alone) can enact and promulgate laws (to uphold them) when all traditional codes of conduct perish (through disuse or disobedience)."[28] However, this should not be taken to imply that Kautilya permits the king to create laws as an alternative or parallel to Dharma or overlook the Dharmashastra injunctions. What is suggested is that the king, being the ultimate guardian for the upkeep of law and justice, could enact or issue such laws as stated in shastra that uphold laws and maintain peace and harmony if there is such a need in cases of disruption of order. In other words, he makes a plea for the superiority of written law for the reason that explaining the derivation of a particular law shastra from Dharma is no longer available.[29]

The prime law and obligation of the monarch, hence, was protection and the maintenance of *varnasramadharma*. Manu declared protection to be the highest Dharma of king.[30] Narada states the king's duty to be to protect his subjects, listen to the aged and wise, look into the disputes of the people, and be energetic in the royal functions.[31] There are similar references in Kalidasa, Vishnudharmottara Purana, Kamandaka Nitisara, and Markandeya Purana.[32]

As an upholder of *varnashrama* based system of Dharma, the kings who appear in epigraphical evidence seem to corroborate this ideal that the king was the protector of the order. Ashoka went a step further by declaring that all subjects were like his children and he deemed their welfare the foremost. He stands out because he came out with edicts, the unique inscriptional evidence of king's or state's role in maintaining justice and spelling out the concerns with regard to law and its application (dealt in detail later). An inscription of AD 529 addressed for king Samskobha of Parivrajaka family describes him as devoted to the establishment of *Varnashramadharma*.[33] The Mandasor Stone Inscription of AD 532 of Yasodharman mentions one of his predecessors Abhayadatta as acting to the advantage of those who belonged to the four castes.[34] The Asirgarh CP inscription of the Maukhari king Sarvavarman compares the king to Vishnu for he preserves the *varnashrama* system.[35] Harsha's father Prabhakarvardhana claims to have overseered the system of all castes at all stages.[36]

Bhagwat Saran Upadhyaya, writing on Kalidasa's views on law and justice, remarked that the king's schooling in the scriptures, as well as treatises on polity, gave him a thorough knowledge of law with the help of which he was expected to administer justice.[37] The punishment of the criminals in proportion to their crimes (*yathapradhadandanam*)[38] required the king to have a sharp grasp of the judicial laws,[39] which alone could give him an idea of the legal remedies in proportion to the crimes committed. Upadhyaya says, "He was not a fountain of law but only its administrator as we find no reference in the writings of Kalidasa to the king being in any way connected with the making of laws."[40]

Interestingly, the king's coronation oath from the Mahabharata, which gives body to the idea that law existed prior to the king, spells out the restrictions on state or the king. It says, "Whatever law there is here and whatever is dictated by ethics and whatever is not opposed to politics I will act according to unhesitatingly. And I will never be arbitrary."[41]

This shows that the king himself had to revere the Dharma laws. The element of arbitrariness was not a virtue anyway and more so in the field of law and justice. The epic Ramayana talks of the virtues of judicial administrators of which the king himself was to be a part. It reads that an administrator "should set his heart on protecting the people. An administrator who carefully protects all the inhabitants of his dominion like his own life and like his own son endureth forever and attains the region of Brahma".[42] Also, "the administrator that carrieth away his royal affairs agreeable to justice, hath not to repent afterwards".[43]

However, one section of law in which the role of the monarch could be seen as proactive was in the awarding of capital punishment. Kalidasa enjoins upon the king to take a middle course as regards to the award of such a punishment. His ideal regarding this is summed up in the phrase *Yathapradhadanda*.[44] However, here it may be quoted that when the court reported the guilt of Charudatta to the king, it reminded him that, according to Manu, the Brahmana could not be subjected to capital punishment (*Vadhadanda*) and could only be banished from the country. But the king actually overruled the decision of the court and imposed capital punishment.[45] This would imply that in application of theoretical law, if the king thought that justice was inadequate or punishment less than the crime, he could apply his intellect in deciding capital punishment. The same may not have been true in any ordinary case, but this discretion seems likely to have been kept for extraordinary circumstances. It is also possible to look at it if one would be open to interpretation that if this was not the norm, the novel was asserting that the king was so powerful that he could or rather should play such a role in order to prevent justice being violated.

Among the inscriptions of Ashokan edicts, we came to know that Emperor Ashoka not only deemed his duty as the fountainhead of justice but also had an eye for details and loopholes that might creep in the judicial system. His exhortation to his people to cultivate moral qualities and righteous conduct in both his ministers as well as people is well-known. He calls upon his sons and successors to teach people by their own example[46] and underlines the need to administer justice, impartially, conscientiously, and honestly.[47]

Amulyachandra Sen studies that the separate Kalinga Rock Edict I undoubtedly presupposes grave miscarriage of justice and high-handedness on the part of some provincial administrators. Pillar Edict IV also hints at irregularities in judicial administration when it recommends uniformity of procedure and uniformity of decisions.[48] It is apparent that Ashoka paid heed to the application of laws re-enunciated and reiterated by him in detail and was aware of his responsibility as a king as the fountainhead of justice.

However, his professing of *ahimsa* (non-violence) did not lead him to abolish the capital punishment for criminals. This is clear from the respite he gives: three days to the prisoners condemned to death.[49]That law per se and its continuance was important, although he was endeavouring to standardise certain norms in pursuit of a common welfare state.

In the separate Kalinga Rock Edict I, Dhauli version,[50] Ashoka opines on the need of integrity on the part of judicial officers. In the administration of the law, it reflects not only his urge to ensure an efficient judicial set up but also his deeper understanding of justice as a concept and his relation with his subjects and concern for righteousness. In other words, the need to ensure that temptations that could have existed should not come in the way of justice being imparted by officers was being underlined.

The Mahamatras concerned with judicial procedure are addressed thus: "Whatever I conceive, I wish that to bring into practice by action and carry that into effect by (proper) measures . . . In this matter I regard my instructions to you to be the chief means because you are set or employed over thousands of human beings (with the idea) that you may surely secure the affection of all men (or goodman). All men are my children just as I desire for my children that they may be associated with all kinds of welfare and happiness both in this world and in the next, so also I desire (the same) for all men. Again there may be some individual person who incurs imprisonment or torture and for this reason, in this (matter), the result may end in captivity without a (due) cause and on this account, many other people may become graved deeply or intensively. In this case, you should deserve that you should follow a middle (i.e., impartial) cause (of justice) . . . In fulfilling (my) instructions, you will gain heaven and also discharge your debt (to me)" (SKRE, 1 Dhauli version).[51]

These lines of no less than Emperor Ashoka reflect his eagerness to apply and ensure in practice his benevolent thoughts on the matter of justice. He considers his instruction supreme for his administrators, who he feels have been appointed for the purpose of securing welfare of people over thousands of other people. He exhorts their status as representatives of state as well as people and reminds them that just as he, the monarch, is the patriarch of all his subjects, the officers should pertain as agents to secure the happiness of the subjects within this world and the next. Citing an instance, he says a person may be falsely convicted and on these grounds may be tortured or imprisoned. The officers ought to take an impartial stance and a middle path in justice and see that no person is aggrieved wrongly and welfare is enforced generally. And after giving such detailed instruction, he says the rewards for following such instructions in imparting impartial justice would lead him to heaven (spiritual rewards promised while exhorting), the ultimate bliss in the Indian conception, and also enable him to repay his debt to the king who gave them an opportunity to serve the people.

Ashoka exhibits the perfect specimen of a smrti-entailed monarch to quite an extent, in these lines as one who considers himself as the father of his subjects, one who attends to matters of justice personally or through his officers endeavours to ensure proper administration through his councillors, and one whose aim is welfare and happiness of men. In fulfilling the monarch's orders, the rewards of heaven would accrue, though he was under the influence of a new religion when he enunciated so. A word that creates ambiguity is *sumanushya*, which would imply that the officers (*mahamatras*) were appointed to secure the welfare of all good men. Sen explains that the officers must have been directed to win the affection of all people and not particularly of good persons alone.[52] Ashoka, however moves beyond the purview of Dharmashastra texts, by claiming equality of procedure and punishments and thereby setting a newer norm embedded in the idea of equality of all inspired by precepts of Buddhist religion.

In the Girnar Rock Inscription of Rudraman of the Saka year 72 (150 AD), the Kshatrapa king is discussed at length.[53] A.B. Diskalkar has pointed out the use of the word hastocheva. Some scholars suppose that epithet means that Rudraman made many religious gifts, but Dr. Kulkarni says that the expression "the raising of the hand of a person engaged in making any kind of gift, is that it is moistened by the water poured into the hand of the donee (cf Kadambari of *Anvartapravritidanardikrtkar* which implies occasionally a person making gift is described as taking or raising a pitcher from which the water is poured into the hands of the recipient)".[54] Diskalkar prescribes that in "the present case, the expression instead of meaning to convey the idea of donation should better be taken in the sense of dispensation of justice. For according to Manu (VIII.2),[55] a king, when investigating cases of law, should be seated or be standing 'raising his right hand'.

Rudraman must have earned the strong attachment of Dharma, i.e., justice thus by raising of his right hand, i.e., by the proper dispensation of justice.[56]

The Manusmrti describes how the king ought to maintain a dignified demeanour and examine 'daily (deciding) one after another question (all cases) which fall under the eighteen titles (of the law) according to principles drawn from local usages and from the Institutes of the Sacred law.'[57] And if he is unable to do so, then he may appoint Brahmanas to by them. Narada emphasises the personal role of a king thus: "After having seated himself on a judgment seat the king should be equitable towards all beings, discard selfish interests and act the part of Yama Vaivasvata being just in the reward or punishment according to good or bad actions of persons."[58]Smrti writers have prescribed a set of ideals and suggestions for the king to imbibe in the processing of dispensing justice. Manu says, "What may have been practiced by the virtuous, by such twice born men as are devoted to the law that he shall establish as law, if it be not opposed to the (customs of) countries, families and castes (jati)."[59] Further, this only suggests that certain general practices that stemmed from virtuous conduct of learned Brahmanas and that were in consonance with the customary laws could be legitimised. At another place, the Manusmrti opines: "(A king) who learns the sacred law must inquire into the laws of castes (jati), of districts, of guilds and of families, and (thus) settle the peculiar law of each."[60] This is a very important aspect as it allows law by usage or customary law to be taken into account along with Dharma clauses in imparting justice. It further envisages that the head of the state should be in the know of the local customs and peculiar laws of different groups or in various areas. An important observation here is the multiplicity of sources for emanation of laws in practice and the need to take into consideration as and when required as well as the necessity for king to be aware about these. One cannot rule out that deviations could have existed between Shastra law and laws in practice.

Upadhyaya's studies of Kalidasa verses on law and justice tells that king's schooling in the scriptures as well as treatises on polity gave him a thorough knowledge of law with the help of which he was expected to administer justice. The punishment of the criminals in proportion to their crimes (Hindi Raghuvamsa, 1.6) required of the king a sharp grasp of the judicial laws (Hindi. Raghuvamsa. 1.9), which alone could give him an idea of the legal remedies in proportion to crimes. The king was the protector (Gopta) of the people, and he applied law to the ends of justice.[61]

Manu enjoins that the king shall protect the inherited property of a minor until he returned from his teacher's house or until he passed his minority.[62] Likewise, he urges the monarch to take care of the barren women, of those who have no sons, of those whose family is extinct, of wives and widower faithful to their lords, and of women affected with diseases.[63] Thus, seen on humanitarian grounds and in special circumstances, the role of state was very crucial in ensuring that justice was not violated. Likewise, in the very next verse, Manu prescribes that "a righteous king must punish like thieves those relatives who appropriate the property of such females during their lifetime".[64] The very care taken in enunciating such a principle indicates that there must have been prevalent such cases of cheating, and in order to stop them or send a strong message as deterrent, the king was advised to not spare such malicious people. There cannot however be a generalisation asserting or crediting Manusmrti to be sensitive or in favour of women as the text appears to be contradictory when at other times it clearly tilts with verses entirely in favour of men and anti-women at several places. This is typically also indicative about a rescensionary text with heterogeneous authorship.

From Kalidasa's writings, we get to learn that the king sat in his court of justice along with his minister for law and justice and others as evident from the word *asmabhih*, used in plural. The court of justice was situated in the outskirts of the palace where the king sat at the proper time (Kale) marked out by the Shastra and looked into the lawsuits.[65] The seat of justice was variously described as *Vyvaharasana, Dharmasana*, and *Karyasana*.[66] The term *Vyavaharasana* analyses Upadhyaya, denotes the real capacity of the king as the dispenser of legal justice adjudicating on the points of law.[67]

The text Kadambari provides a description from which we come to know that the court was held in the morning time.. The *Dashakumaracharita* states that the king should look into the disputes of the people in the second part of the day divided into eight parts.[68] Katyayana srnrti prescribes the time for holding the court in the first part of the day which was divided into three parts, i.e., morning part being from 7 a.m. to noon. There were holidays on which the courts enjoyed holiday on eighth and fourteenth tithis (days), full noonday, and amavasya of every month.[69]

Katyayana exalts the role of a righteous king in the context of law, like other *smrti* writers. The king who looks (into causes) according to the sacred law along with the judge, the ministers, the Brahmanas, the family priest, and the assessors or jurors (sabhyas) attains heaven.[70] Elsewhere, he tells that where the king himself looks into all actions according to the dictates of Dharma, there the people behave well and reside in happiness.[71] And he (the king) should discard the teachings of politics and resort to the dictates of Dharmashastra (sacred law).[72] This seems to be similar to Yajnavalkya assertion, where the latter says, describing the rules of judicial procedure, that "the rule is that the science of law is stronger than the science of politics"[73]. Dharma, hence, was of primal importance over the realm of politics.

Manu prescribed that "having fully considered the time and place (of the offence, the strength and the knowledge of the offender), let him (firstly), inflict that (punishment) on men who act unjustly".[74] Likewise, Yajnavalkya spoke that the king divested of anger and avarice should administer justice, along with learned Brahmanas, in conformity with the principles of legal science.

Here, three instructions are combined: (1) that the king should maintain an unquestionable integrity and cool temperament, essential for maintaining balance, (2) that he should take the assistance of learned Brahmanas, and (3) that it should be in conformity with principles of legal science—or to say the rules of procedure.

Ancient jurists put a whole lot of emphasis on the mechanism for administration of justice. The king was pivotal in this execution of qualitative justice, and he was supposed to take opinion of the experts. The king had appellate jurisdiction or power to hear appeals from the lower courts, and there is a great sense of responsibility of the king that is spoken by the jurists. He was supposed to preside over the highest court in the capital and dispense justice with full responsibility. Katyayana, in fact, says where the king looks into the cases according to Dharma, people conduct themselves well and live in happiness.

Likewise, Vishnu enunciates that let the king dictate due punishment for other offences, also after having ascertained the class and the age (of the criminal) and the amount (of the damage done or sum claimed) and after having consulted the Brahmanas (his advisors).

In other words, in the works of Dharmashastra, the king has not just been ascribed role and responsibity for justice in society but has also been assigned a definitive role in procedural law as well as substantiated by the above-mentioned sacred and secular texts.

A question could be raised as to whether the king himself could take cognisance of any offence within his realm and initiate a legal suit *suo motto*. Manu's voice was that neither the king nor his servant should cause a lawsuit to be started.[75] This is opposed to the enunciation in Mahabharata, where Pitamaha permitted it.[76] Narada allows the king to recognise ten kinds of apradhas or offences of which the king should take note of without being approached by the parties.[77] It can also be read alternatively as in Katyayana's use of words "*Suchaka*" and "*Stobhaka*" and the role prescribed for them as informants of king, it appears that the king could have an independent stance in initiating suits in certain exceptional cases. Also, he explicitly tells that the king should not initiate any lawsuit under pressure from any litigants or for greed of wealth.[78]

Manu forbids the king from being a witness of law.[79] Also, the text declares that neither the king nor any servant of his shall themselves initiate a lawsuit or hush up a case brought by some other men.[80] Katyayana denunciated that "when a king directs (the judge or member of the court) to do injustice (to give a wrong decision in the case of) disputants, then a member of the court should beseech the king (that his order will lead to injustice) and should turn him away from wrong doing".[81] This appears to be thinking far ahead of its time. Katyayana is indeed a jurist with a special eye for progressive components in the law of procedure. The fact that the king could be beseeched appeared to be more a deterrent clause than a practical one. There are no such hard instances. Nonetheless, the principle of accountability of the head of the State as a fountain of justice is remarkable by its appearance.

In Vishnusena's Charter, we have an example of an order issued by a ruler endowed with subordinate titles like *Mahakarttakritika, Mahadandanayaka,*

Mahapratihara, Mahasamanta, and *Maharaja*. The designation might be indicating either a royal agent of a judge of a superior court or like the present-day Legal Remembrancer, inviting the attention of the king to what was done or left undone.[82] It seems to be a plea (*acharasthiti patra*) taken to Vishnusena by a community of merchants for incorporating elements of prevalent customary law that were either existent or were aspired to be brought into practice. This seems to be an extraordinary referential document as it speaks or rather presents a picture of judicial setup wherein there is not only a regard and attempt to include or merge the customary law but also a legal functionary who was in the nature of ombudsman in the issuance and implementation of laws. It even depicts the role of people in making Dharma or laws in Dharmashastras more effective and relevant by blending the customary laws, which would favour people themselves.

KING'S JUDICIAL AIDES

In the task of dispensing justice, the king was supposedly assisted by the learned Brahmanas and other court personages. Manusmrti says, "But if the king does not personally investigate the suits then let him appoint a learned Brahamana to try them."[83] This learned Brahmana along with three other Brahmanas versed in Vedas formed what Manu calls the 'court of (four faced) Brahman.' Further, he says that even a despicable Brahman who subsists merely by the name of race could interpret the law for king. Except the Shudras, the other two castes in the ladder along with Brahmins could play a role likewise.[84]Caste in other words was the primary bias in these texts, and status by birth was largely a determinant and debilitating factor in the field of law.

The Arthashastra prescribed that there shall be an established bench of three judges who shall hold court: frontier posts, subdistrict headquarters, and provincial headquarters (*samgrahanas, dronamukhas,* and *sthaniyas*).[85] The text suggests that impersonation might have been prevalent. In verse 3.20.17, the text says, "No one shall pretend to be a magistrate and examine a suspect under oath." Further, there is a verse that exhorts the judge to take an initiative in certain types of lawsuits. It says, "The judges themselves shall take charge of the affairs of Gods, Brahmins, ascetics, women, minors, old people, the sick, and those that are helpless (e.g. orphans) even when they do not approach the court. How and if at all this could have been practised seems difficult to visualise. The idea innate implies that judges ought to take care of those revered as well as those vulnerable across the society.

Vishnusrnrti too underlines the crucial role of the brahmanas in the legal matter as advisors.[86] Katyayana says in the absence of the king, a Brahmana who is well versed in the science of law should be appointed as Chief Judge to preside over the judicial proceedings.[87] Brihaspati declared the duty of the Chief Judge (*Pradvivaka*) was to put question to the applicant as well as to the respondent and to declare whether a prime facie case could be there. Because of this, he was called *Pradvivaka* [88] and as Katyayana has also defined, "it is settled that one who asks questions with reference to the matter in dispute is a '*prad*'(questioner), he who distinguishes in that (dispute as to what party is in the right), is hence called *pradvivaka* (a judge)".[89]

Narada considered *Pradvivaka* as one thoroughly conversant with the eighteen titles of law with their numerous subdivisions. He should be an expert in the science of politics. Being at the same time a devoted student of revelations and traditions, he should examine the law to the point under consideration and dispense judgement after careful deliberation.[90] Katyayana prescribes that a king should appoint such a judge who is not cruel, who is sweet tempered, kind, who is hereditary, clever, energetic, and not greedy.[91] He too, like Manu, forbids a Shudra (lowest in hierarchy of caste)in the role as judge but permits the Vanij (the merchant). He clearly states, "Where a Brahmana (evidenced with qualities enumerated) cannot be had, (the king) should appoint a Kshatriya or a Vaishya proficient in sacred law but he (the king) should carefully avoid shudra as a judge."

Pradavivaka, the judge was expected to be a learned man with adequate knowledge of substantive and procedural law as well as having the ability to interpret the sacred as well as customary law. A great amount of emphasis on the character and quality of judges being emphasised, it indicates that ancient jurists and seers probably objectified the goal of qualitatitive justice although all secular aspects could not be mooted as caste was a living reality and all Dharma was linked to the notion of caste. The fact that jurors were expected to be impartial and even bold indicates or underlines the important role they were supposed to perform. The situation of debarring of Shudras from becoming judges may have stemmed from the fact and the logic that they had restricted access to learning of these texts of judicial injunctions or Dharmashastras being in Sanskrit and not in vernacular languages. It was at the same time an effort to claim exclusivity for the ruling elite

Hence, the overall scenario was that a king was to administer law and justice personally by attending the *sabha* (the courthouse) and was to be assisted by advisors, the *pradvivaka* (judge), *amatya* (minister), *purohita* (family priest), and sabhyas (assessors), Katyayana adding *vanij* (merchants) to this list. If he is personally unable to carry out the task, he could appoint a learned Brahman as substitute (Katyayana- 63–67, Manu, VIII.9, Yajnavalkya, II, 37).

Interestingly, the judges are pressured by moral injunctions prescribing the rewards, guilt, and penances according to their performance. Manu says, "When an injustice is done, one-fourth of the sin attaches to the wrong doer, one-fourth to the witness, one-fourth to the judges and the remaining one-fourth to the king."[92] The Vishnusmrti enunciated that "that detestable judge who dismisses without punishment such as deserve it, and punishes such as deserve it not, shall incur twice as heavy a penalty as the criminal himself".[93] Likewise, Yajnavalkya says that if the members of the judicial assembly give any decision contrary to the law and custom through affection, temptation, and fear, each of them would be liable to double the punishment provided for the caste.[94]

Katyayanasmrti states that a judge, particularly assessors conversing privately with a party, is liable to punishment.[95] Further, it is the duty of the *Sabhya* not just to decide justly but also to prevent the king from being unjust.[96]

In two other verses, Katyayana describes the ultimate fall out of judges' misrule. In verse 72, he says where the sabhyas decide (a matter) in violation of the Sacred law, the Dharma (justice), being overcome by Adharma (injustice), does undoubtedly destroy (the king). And in verse 73, he declares where justice is slain by injustice while the *sabhyas* look on (with apathy), there the *sabhyas* (members of the court) are themselves destroyed.

These ideals prescribed for the king and his judicial aides not only were lofty and high sounding but raises curiosity as to how far these actually went to the court or mere professed by the jurists. These assertions, however, bring to table the point that in the early days, the judicial system was laden with high ideals, and a sense of juristic wisdom was coaxed upon the judges to imbibe and practise. Manu's assertion in the share of sins makes no sense unless we consider it to be an assertion towards declaring the shared responsibility of various agents of justice. Justice was never practicable by a single authority. It has always been a concept that needed to percolate down to the grassroots, with each level performing its said role.

The Ashokan edicts reflect upon the role prescribed for the judicial officers by the Emperor, the first clear reference to legal injunctions by a head of a first declared welfare state. The administrators or the judicial officers were designated as *Mahamatras*, and they were the highest class of officers. Those who looked after religious matters were called *Dharmamahamatras*. The *sutas* too belonged to the same class. Other officials of Ashokan records are the *Pradeshika, Rajiuka, and Rashtrika* who were styled as *yukta* who was like governor of the group of districts. Some of these may have been of the *Mahamatra* rank.

Ashoka emphasised on the need of integrity on the part of these officials in the administration of justice. In the separate Kalinga Rock Edict, he considers all men as his children, who he would like to associate with all kinds of welfare and happiness in this world; and further, he exhorts his judicial officers to understand this policy and adopt an 'impartial' course of justice. But it says, "Success may not be attained on accounting a certain (group) defects or mental inclinations viz, any, sudden loss (of mental balance), harshness, haste or impatience, want of application (or indiscrimination), laziness and awareness to you should desire that this class (of defects) may not be yours. The proof of the entire thing lies in the absence of sudden loss (of mental balance, or of perseverance) and also absence of haste in the application of the principles (of justice). The man who becomes languishing or weary cannot exert or get up to move properly. But (you are to) move, advance and proceed on (for reaching the goal)."[97]

One may argue that such assertions or exhortations, though they set the standards of state set morality, may not have been implemented fully, but what is worthwhile to note is that state had a role in defining duties or creating accountability. This assertion of Ashoka is important because this document is first of a kind in the early-recorded history where a head of the state exhibits immense concern for law and its administration and talks about a system that should ensure justice. It is a royal charter legitimately formalising the ideals of justice and well-being in order to serve as guidelines for judicial advisors and an instance where a king exhibits his own ideals by exhorting his officials to inculcate integrity of a high order. We should not assert that this is an example of textual law in practice, for matters of integrity can never be generalised or put as laws; secondly, these again talk about the ideals that needed to be put into practice. More than examples, they serve as aspirations representative of their times. There are, however, no windows providing the actual working of justice in the period. Whatever is possible to piece together is from the plays of the time, which are literary sources, and it becomes important to take note of who has written them.

P.E. 4 of Ashoka also throws light on his views on justice and sets the standards of state morality. We see an effort to goad people, particularly those employed by him, to apply dharma as far as possible in order to ensure justice in reality—the beloved of the good king.[98] Priyadarshi spoke thus: "This Dharma rescript has been called to be written by me (when) crowned twenty six years. y Rajjukas are occupied among the people, among many hundred thousands men (The hearing of) petitioners or (conduct of) by them has been made independent of me, in order that the Rajjukas may discharge (their) duties confidently (and) fearlessly, (and) may confer welfare and happiness on the rural people and benefit (them). They should bear in mind what causes happiness or pain (to the rural people) and learning (themselves) devoted to the Dharma, should exhort the rural people in order that they (the rural people) may attain (happiness) in this world and in the next world. They may discharge (their) duties unperturbed, fearlessly and confidently for this (reason) has (the hearing of) petitions or (the conduct of) trials by the Rajjukas been made independent of me. This indeed is desirable that there should be uniformity in judicial procedure as well as uniformity in sentences (passed). And even as far as this do I grant (viz) to imprisoned persons whose trials are over (and) who have been sentenced to death. a respite of three days is allowed by me."[99]

Three important facets emerge out of Ashokan judicial administration apart from the ideal of welfare of all people it sets up.

First, he makes the *Rajjukas (who were the officials responsible for welfare, deemed to be responsible for reward, punishment, justice and welfare apart from*

Mahamatras and Pradeshikas) independent of himself, the monarch thus emphasising the clause of impartiality of judicial authority, especially from the executive authority. This cannot be left unappreciated as to have a ruler with such clarity in operational issues of justice (under monarchy) is extraordinary.

Second, concepts like uniformity in judicial procedure and in punishments (*vyavaharasamata* and *dandasamata*) to be desired and practised by legal personages reflect the emperor's juristic instincts and conception of enlightened justice based on uniformity of procedure and judgements. Though the idea of equality of all humans may have been the impact of Buddhism which Ashoka adopted as his religion after Kalinga War (261 BCE), these ideas that he brought about in the legal arena preceded the later idea of 'Rule of law' became the guarantor of equality. They, infact were one of the earliest steps towards egalitarianism in law, a concept traced to much later period.

Third, his giving respite to prisoners sentenced to death brings to light three things—that capital punishment was not abolished by Ashoka, who believed in highest nonviolence, the principles of ahimsa. He was ready to give some respite (in this case, three days) to such prisoners convicted to death during which the thief's relatives could present an appeal to the *Rajjukas* (it probably could be a money fine), and if there be no relatives of such a convict, he may undertake some penance such as giving gifts or observing fasts. The principle of retrial or reinvoking the judgement already declared is also remarkable as he attaches a moral clause that those who do so would or make any attempt to correct the wrongs shall be blessed with permission in heaven.

This seems to be a departure from what the textual sources speak on it. Manusmriti words it that "whenever a suit has been decided or a fine declared, a wise man should consider it as (finally) decided, and must not annul it".[100] In case of punishment other than capital punishment, Narada, however, allows no reappeal. The 'retrial' is addressed as *punar-nyaya* in the texts and was allowed strictly where one of the litigants mostly originated from the lower courts to the higher and finally to the king.

Kautilyan Arthashastra uses the term '*Dharmastha*' in plural and less of *Sabhya* or *sabhasad*. The *Dharmastha* may have been experts in law while *Sabhasad* may not have been so as the references point out to. The *Dharmastha* were required to bring into the *Vyavaharika arthas*, cases arising out of mutual transaction.

Kalidasa refers to a Minister holding charge of twin portfolios of Revenue and Law and Justice. It seems that the Minister Pisuna in *Abhijnanashakuntalam*, as rightly studied by Upadhyaya, must have taken to his charge of the portfolios of Revenue, Law, and Justice apart from Finance. This Minister is referred as sitting in a court and disposing cases.[101] The Minister of Law and Justice sat with the king when the latter heard cases in his seat of justice (*Vyavaharasana*) and prepared a report of the cases thus disposed of.[102]

When the king was indisposed to sit in the open court, the Minister of Justice personally received petitions from citizens, examined them, and then sent them to the king in his seraglio. Upadhyaya writes, this has been graphically described by Kalidasa as an incident of common practice as can be inferred from the King's following utterances: "Speak to Minister Pisuna with my words thus, owing to having kept awake for long, it was not possible for us to occupy the judgment seat today. Whatever business of the citizens may have been looked into by his honor should be handed over, after being put on record."[103]

In Kalidasa, there is a reference to *Nagarika* as the Chief Police Officers of the town. Upadhyaya says the *Nagarika* of the *Abhijnanashakuntalam* was perhaps like the *Koshtapala* of the later times, the head of the establishment of the guards of the city. In the play, this official leads a criminal to the Court of justice with the help of guards *(raksinah)*. In other words, guards and police had a role to start with in addressing any breach of law but also that they had to play a proactive role by bringing them to Courts.

In the Vikramorvashi too, he is connected with the city administration. The king entrusted him with the task of hunting a winged offender when, at evening, it goes to its resting place.[104] The reference by the king to *Nagarika* of the Vikrarmorvashi suggests an officer of higher grade than the one referred in the Shakuntala. Upadhyaya studies that the latter was a petty offirer, placed immediately over the guards.

The court proceedings were probably started by the *Shodhanaka*, the Court persons entering to arrange the seating in the court, when the seats were arranged neatly. The Judge, accompanied by the *Sresthin, Kayastha*, and others was conducted to the courtroom by the *Shodhanaka*.[105] Next, the Judge ordered the *Shodhanaka* to go out of the hall and to call the plaintiff.[106] The judge used to be greeted on entering the court. Then the judge allowed the plaintiff to put up his case and ordered the *Kayastha* (scribe) to write from the statement, which was first recorded in the floor to make it easy for correction.

The *sabha* or some sort of judicial assembly has been described by nearly all the major smrtis as consisting of the king, the Chief Judge, and the assessors. It needs to be distinguished from the Vedic connotation of *Sabha*, which used to be an association of learned men, attended by the king frequently.[107] In the Vedic times, this *Sabha* used to be a part of selected men working under the larger assembly, the *Samiti*, as explained by K.P. Jayaswal.[108] The word *Sabha*, used in the legal context by the Smrti writers, was a body instituted to attend to the administration of law and justice. Its members were called *Sabhya*, and they participated in the judicial proceedings, according to the Smrti writers.

The king was supposed to attend to the administration of justice along with these Sabhyas, as comes out from Yajnavalkya's enunciation.[109] The *Sabhas* originally consisted of the Brahmanas alone while Katyayana distinguished between the Brahrnana *Sabhyas* and other *Sabhyas* who in his days consisted of merchant class of good birth and conduct, aged, wealthy, and free from greed.

From the inscriptions, we came across a number of officials and staff associated with law and the administration of justice. The *Chammak Copper Plate grant* of Maharaja Pravarasena II refers to the *dharmasthana* or the court.[110] From the grants addressed to various officers, we came across references about officers relating to the administering of law and justice. The excavations carved out at Basarh (ancient Vaisali) by Bloch brought to light numerous clay seals, which were issued by Prince Govinda Gupta. It mentions various officials of his administration including the *Mahadandanayaka* or the Chief Justice, and Vinayasthitisthapaka, the Minister for Law and order.[111]

The two Guhila grants, one of Bhavihita (Harsha, year 48) and another of Babhata (Harsha year 83), throw an interesting light on the judicial and police officials. The order of Bhavihita is addressed to several officials, including the *Chauroddharanika* (Police Officer to deal with cases of theft) and *Dandapasika* (Head of a group of policemen).[112]

There are many seals of the Gupta period referring to *dandapalakas*. The revised Corpus Inscriptionum Indicarum, Volume III, has analysed the use of three administrative terms together: (1) *Mahadandanayaka- Agniguptasya*, (2) *Dandapas- adhikaransya*, and (3) *Yuvaraja Bhattarakapadiya- baladhikaransya*.

Bloch interpreted it as judge while R.D. Banerjee took it in the sense of Principal Judge though later on he renders it to be general.[113] This term is mentioned thrice in the Allahabad pillar Inscription. In this inscription, the officer who got the prashasti executed, Tilakbhatta, the officer who composed it, the celebrated Harisena, is mentioned and even his father, Dhruvabhuti are called *Mahadandanayaka*. Similarly, in South Indian records, there is a reference of a Brahmana and his father, karana, as *Dandanayaka*. The usage of the term indicated that probably, more than just being a connotation for an officer connected with law and judiciary, it was a sort of hereditary title of nobility. There is a Kananda inscription (outside the period of study, dated Saka era 1030), which speaks of Malliyakka as *Dandanayakiti* on account of not her husband but rather her father, Ishvaramayya, who was a *Dandadhinatha* or *Dandadhipa*. This is similar to the titles of *Maharathi-Maharathivi*, *Mahabhoja-Mahabhoji*, and *Mahasenapati* and *Mahasenapatini*.[114]

In the earlier Corpus Inscriptions (Vol III, 1886), J.F. Fleet remarked the *Mahdandanayaka* to be a great leader of the forces, indicating it to be a military title. Moreover, as Danda means *fine* or *rod* (of chastisement) as well as army of forces, the titles that have this as a suffix or a prefix are explained as judicial or military. Bloch rendered it as judge while Sir John Marshall called him the Chief Police.[115] Vogel explained him as high judicial official[116] and Police officer.

Bhandarkar sees it in a slightly modified way. According to him, in the Gupta epoch, Dandanayaka is to be taken as an equivalent of Mansabdar. He has based his conclusions from Rajatarangini and a Bhita seal, which says *Mahasvapati Mahadandanayaka, Vishnurakshitapad anugrihita kumaramaty-adhikaranasya*. Here, a *Mahadandanayaka vishnurakshit* is mentioned as *Mahasvapati* or supreme commander of cavalry. Further, the grade of *Dandanayaka* surmised as it was ultimately merged with the mansabdari system of the Mughal period.[117]

On the other hand, it did not connote a general in several other sources. In number of inscriptions, like the Nagarjunakonda inscription, the Charter of Vakataka king Pravarasena II and another plate of a Pala King, the *Senapati*, are mentioned distinct from *Mahadandanayaka*. Another officer with the prefix of *Danda* is *Dandapasika* mentioned in the legend *dandapasikadhikaranasya* on the Basadh seal. Dandapasika is distinguished from the Chauroddharanika in the Valabhi and Chamba plates as well as Pala and Sena charters.[118] The Deo-Baranark inscription of Jivitagupta II also mentions Dandika, which is not a same as Dandapasika.R.G. Bhandarkar finally concludes that to him Dandika or *Dandashakti* implies a Kotwal or City Police Magistrate, *Dandapasika* to the Daroga or District Superintendent of Police, and *Chauroddharanika* to the head of the Detective Bureau, whose duty was to apprehend a thief.[119] The Mallasarul Copper Plate inscription of Vijayasena mentions them as Police Officers.[120] In Western India, the Palitana plate of Dharasena II and Valabhi grant of the same king refer to *Dandapasika* as officer in charge of punishment and criminal justice.[121]

As mentioned earlier, the Charter of Samvat 649 (Vishnusena Charter), which records an order issued from the Vasaka (residence) at Lohata by a ruler named Vishnusena (called Vishnubhata in the endorsement) who is endured with the subordinate titles like *Mahakarthakritika, Mahadandanayaka, Mahapratihara, Mahasamanta,* and *Maharaja.* The actual meaning of *Karttakritika* is unknown, but it may have indicated a royal agent or a judge of a superior court or an officer, like the present-day legal Remembrancer.[122]

The order of Maharaja Mahasamanta was addressed to subordinate officers such as *Rajan Rajputa, Rajsthaniya, Ayuktaka Vinyutaka, Chauroddharanika Vailabdhika, Drangika, Chata Bhata,* and other officers. Of these, the *Chauroddharanika* appears to be a prefect of the police while *Vailabdhika* may have been the custodian of recovered stolen property as the '*yukta*' of the Manusmrti (VIII, 34).[123]

The achara 15 in Vishnusena's Charter says *varikasya haste nyasako na sthapaniyah,* meaning the offers meant for the King were not to be deposited with the *Varika*. Monier Williams recognises the word *nagavarika* in his Sanskrit Dictionary and explains it as an elephant drummer or keeper and the Chief person in a Court or assembly. This seems like an attempt to avoid influencing court employees through gifts.

The Charter in achara 28 names '*uttarkulika*' who seems to be another class of *varika* or official, associated with the law court. The next achara 29 says *uttarkulika- varikanam =eva karana — sannidhari Chhatrena trir= aghushitanam riirupasthanad = vinaya rupaka _ dvayam sa — padam saha dharmikena*. Here, *karana* apparently implies short of *adhlkarna*, a law—court and *chhatra* seems to indicate a peon or constable. It implies that there was no excuse for the absence of the *varikas* of the *uttarakulika* class when summoned to court by a court peon. The fine for such offence was two and one-fourth silver coins if there was any good reason for absence.

The Charter also mentions the clerks who wrote down the statement of cases in the law court (*Vyavahara—abhilekhitaka*) and tells that if they were absent from the court after midday: they were liable to a fine of six and one-fourth silver coins.[124]

In the times of Harsha, the Banaskhera Copper plate and Madhubana Copper Plate refer to an officer *Pramatar* while Madhubana Copper Plate mentions the *dutaka* as *Maha pramatar*, Mahasamanta Skandagupta. The etymological meaning, however, points to a person who must have been either a judge or an assessor of revenue.[125] TheValabhi grant of Dhruvasena Ill (AD 654) mentions the messenger for this charter was the pramatr Sri Naga.[126]

The Sanchi Stone inscription of Chandragupta II (462 AD) mentions *Panchmandalya* (modern Panchayat) as the village jury of five or more persons. Sircar explains the word *rajakula*, which figures in inscription as meaning a person of royal family as well as it could mean the King's Court of justice.

In the inscriptions, another officer that we came across in the area of law and order is *Gaulmika*. He is mentioned in the Bihar Stone Pillar Inscription of Skandagupta. In the Hirahadagalli Copper Plate Inscription of Sivaskandavarman, AD 438, in South India, the word *Gaumika* is held by Buhler to stand for *Gaulmika*.[127] *Gaulmika* is explained as an officer in charge of a military squadron called *gulma*.[128] He appears to be a military officer performing police duties.

Among the associated functionaries, there is an officer mentioned called Araksadhikrta, who has been interpreted to be either a magistrate looking after the villagers or towns, or an officer responsible for protection of the king's person (D.C. Sircar, Indian Epigraphy, p. 357). The Bhamodra-Mohota Plate (582 AD) of the Maitraka Chief Dronasimha of Kathiawar offers a small list mentioning anorig other officers, Drangika. The term Drangika is derived from *dranga* similar to *udranga* and may have implied the officer of a watch station.[129]

Eran Stone pillar inscription of Samudragupta (335–76 AD) mentions *Dyuta*. Sircar says he may have been the head of the Department of superintending the gambling house.

Pradvivaka or the judge is mentioned in the Smrtis of Manu,[130] Brhaspati, [131] and Katyayana.[132] Brhaspati explained that the judge examines the plaint in the question and answer, and since he speaks gently at first (*pragvadati*) and so is called *pradvivaka*, Katyayana makes a *sandhi vigraha* and divides the word into *prad* and *vivaka*. With regards to "*pradvivaka*", Katyayana implies that when the judge would ask the plaintiff and dependents to explain the case, based on this hearing when the judge finds out what is right. Hence, two terms have independent significance. One implies listening to all aspects as told by both parties and latter means sifting through it to come to the right one. One implication of this would also be the careful selection of such men who should be learned and capable.

In the plays of ancient India, we come across different types of judges with different mental constitution. In the *Dashakumaracharita*, words from the mouth of the cynical jester, *Viharabhadra* to the king are that the judges decide matters just as they please after taking bribes and the king incurs infamy and the sin of doing injustice.[133] Sometimes the judges showed partiality towards the relatives of the king. In the text Mrchhakatika, the judge probably was unaware that the accused was the brother-in-law of the king and so postponed the case for the next day. But when Sakara, brother-in-law of the king, threatened to replace the judge by the king, the judge had to change his decision and had to hear the case on that very day.[134] Such instances would create doubt as to what extent dharma would have been practised in law. But as we know, in the practical world of justice and juridical setup, these challenges have existed in any society, and so it was in ancient India.

It means the judge could decide upon which case to hear and which one to postpone. People who were influential might have had at least same say to the judge in matters of hearing. From the *Mattavilasa Prahasana*, we came to know that riches were required to go to a court, indicating a degree of corruption in the courts of South India.

The Court proceedings were supposedly started by the *Shodhanaka*, the court people entering to arrange the seats in order. When the seats were ready, the judge accompanied by the *sresthin*, *Kayastha*, and others was conducted to the courtroom by the *Shodhanaka* (Mrcchakatika, IX, p. 457).[135]

Once they were seated, the judge ordered the *Shodhanaka* to summon the plaintiff. The judge used to be greeted on entering the Court. The judge then permitted the plaintiff to take down or record the statement, which was first recorded on the floor so as to make it easy for correction.

There are a number of enunciations that assert the responsibility of the Judge and the assessors. Yajnavalkya says if the members of the judicial assembly gave any decision contrary to the law and custom through affection, temptation, and fear, each of them would be liable to double the punishment provided for the case.[136] The Katyayana Smrti too states that a judge, especially an assessor conversing privately with a party, is liable to punishment. Similarly, an assessor who awards decision without proper consideration shall pay twice the amount involved in the suit.[137] It was the duties of the *Sabhya* to not only decide justly but also to prevent the king from acting unjustly.[138] Brhaspati prescribed banishment and forfeiture of all property of such '*Sabhyas*'.

Katyayana says that when a king directs the judge or court to do injustice, he could be secluded by a member of the court and be turned away from wrongdoing.[139] This could indicate there was a system to check the arbitrariness of the king if ever tried. He says when a *sabhya* decides wrongly through affection, ignorance, greed, or infatuation, he should be punished, for then he is not *sabhya* (becomes unworthy of being a member of court).[140] Where an error has been made by the assessors, Katyayana tells he has to make good the loss occasioned by his decision.[141]

The Chief Judge was expected to be well versed in eighteen titles of law with proficiency in logic and interpretation and one who would have capacity to extract the truth. He was supposed to be having full knowledge of Vedas and Smrtis.

These clauses are important as they not only reflect the ideal of integrity of judge but also at the same time bring the judges themselves within the fold of punishment and accountability. There was definitely a strong sense of responsible behavior being encouraged, and transgressions were accountable and had to be compensated, pointing to high standards that may have existed in the field of law and justice. A judge was not expected to be meek or fearful but rather had to exhibit impartiality, sharpness and independence.

THE COURTS

The king, being the fountainhead of justice, had the prime duty to ensure efficient administration of justice. If, for some reason, the king was unable to attend to the administration of justice, the *pradvivaka* of the Chief Judge supervised and controlled the proceedings of the court. The court presided over by king would have been the highest court. The king and the judge were assisted in their task by the *Sabhyas*, who were the assessors. In Manu and Yajnavalkya's time, it used to be a Brahmana court; but by the time of Katyayana, even merchants who belonged to a guild were of good purity, character, and fulfilled other eligibilities, which could be appointed. Katyayana mentioned five types of courts-*kula* (family councils), *sreni* (corporation), *gana* (Assembly), *adhikrita* (court that was appointed by king) and *nripa* (the king himself). *Sreni* had the right to review the decision of *kula*, and *gana* was supposedly having the power to review a decision by sreni. King was the highest court of appeal. Sasita was a court located at capital and presided over by the king.

The Arthashastra tells that there were two classes of law courts: the *Dharmasthiya* courts and the *Kantakshodhan* courts (literally, the courts for the removal of thorns or disturbances), as mentioned earlier as well.[142] As for the '*vyavaharashthapana*' or composition of the court, the *Dharmasthiya* court constituted of three persons proficient in *Shastra* or three ministers who together heard the cases. Similarly, in the *Kantakshodhan* court, three *dharmatyas* or assessors (pradesthirs) decided the cases.

A *Dharmasthiya* court had within its jurisdiction such cases that arose from personal grievances of one or few individuals against another or few individuals, and secondly, here the punishments were in fine, not very heavy. It seems that the *Dharmasthiya* court had no jurisdiction to penalise heavily or to pass judgements such as death. A *Kantakshodhan* court, on the other hand, looked into matters affecting the king, the government, and the public at large or even heinous offences like murder.

Fines for grave offences could be high, and the Court, it seems, had the power to inflict capital punishment with or without torture according to the gravity of offence.[143]

A *dharmasthiya* court was authorised to try the cases bearing on all of these matters.

i)   Validity of contracts
ii)   Violation of contracts of service
iii)   Relation between master and servant, employer and labourer.
iv)   Slavery
v)   Recovery of debts.
vi)   Deposits.
vii)   Rescission of Sale.
viii) Resumption of Gifts
ix)   Robbery and violence
x)   Assault
xi)   Defamation
xii)   Gambling
xiii) Sale of Property other than the owner
xiv)   Rights of ownership
xv)   Boundary disputes
xvi)   Construction of buildings

xvii) Sale of house property
xviii) Damage to agriculture, pasture
xix)   Miscellaneous hindrances
xx)   Duties of man and wife
xxi)   Partnerships
xxii) Inheritance and succession
xxiii) Miscellaneous offences
xxiv) Rules of procedure[144]

The *Kantakshodhan* court, on the other hand, had within its jurisdiction protection of artisans and merchants, measures against national calamities, detection of criminals by ascetic spies, arrest of robbers on suspicion or caught on the act, discipline in government departments, capital punishment with or without torture, improper social intercourse, etc.

Besides, these headmen and elders of the village supposedly played an important role in settling disputes. The headman could even 'deport' out of the village under his charge a thief or an adulterer if such a step became necessary.[145] The king with his learned Brahmana formed the highest court of appeal. The text of Manusmrti says 'where three Brahmanas versed in the Vedas and the learned (judge) appointed by the king sit down, they call the court of (four faced) Brahmana'.[146] Yajnavalkya mentioned three types of local courts: *puga*, *sreni*, and *kula*. Brhaspati too gave the same sequence of courts and ordained that an appeal shall be to the *sreni* from the decision of the *kula* court and the *puga* court from the decision of the *sreni* court.[147] The Puga court, as specified by Yajnavalkya had members from different castes.

In Narada's law text, king is expected to protect the practices and usages of different sections of the society. According to Narada, gatherings, corporations, associations, etc., are the other tribunals invested with the power of justice, in addition to the court established by the king and the king himself, of these each succeeding one is, superior to the one in the preceding order.[148] These courts were like the panchayats; and they were not, however, private or arbitrary courts but people's tribunals, which were a part of the regular administration of justice, and their authority was fully recognised.[149]

Brhaspati explains that 'when a cause has not been investigated by a *kula* tribunal it should be decided after due deliberation by companies (of artisans)'. When it has not been examined by companies, it should be decided by assemblies and then by the appointed judges and finally the king.[150] Further, the tribunals, other than the king and the one presided over by Chief Judge, had no jurisdiction in violent crimes or disputes involving violence (*Sahasa*).[151] The king alone had the right to impose fines or corporal punishment.

Brhaspati has entailed the functions of the guild courts(*sreni*). The right of making laws for the corporation and for settling disputes is given to farmers, craftsmen, cowherds, moneylenders, robbers, actors, and artisans. When a dispute lies between chiefs and the subordinates, the king shall interfere. Further, he even suggests that for the forest dwellers, the court shall be held in the forest for warriors in the camp and for merchants in the caravan.[152]

Sir Henry Maine considered these popular courts as stemming out due to the absence of regular royal court at village level owing to the prevailing anarchy in the country. But this seems to be inconvincing as popular courts were always encouraged as a part of established policy of the government. Guild courts were welcomed and encouraged for these settled matters at local level and lessened the burden of central administration, thereby contributing in imparting justice.

In fact, the guild courts (*sreni*) exerted some kind of local pressure in the sense that members of the guilds used to be in possession of relative faces of any dispute. The presence of such compeers', in fact, acted as deterrent to telling lies blatantly in the court.

The Chammak Copper-plate grant of Maharaja Pravarasena II refers to the *dharmasthana*.[153] Naradasmrti mentions '*Dharmasava*' as the king's court of justice.[154] S.K. Aiyangar considers '*Dharmasava*' as a permanently appointed hall of justice where the committee of village *Sabha* could assemble and carry on their work. The committee was in continuous session and more regular than any other committee.[155] But from the nature of work it did, C. Minakshi has opined that it seemed to be a court of the Central Government.[156] The *Mrcchakatika* mentions the court building as *adhikaranamandapa* while

Katyayanasmrti mentions *dharmadhikarana* where truth in cases were decided according to Dharmashastra.

Katyayana described the gradation among these who decide cases: family, council, corporation, assemblies, one appointed (as a judge), and the king. These have the responsibility in (deciding) disputes. Each is superior to the preceding one.

The Nalanda Spurious Copper Plate Inscription of Samudragupta mentions *Akshapataladhikrta*, or the keeper of records. Sircar explained *Aksapatala* as the court of law, a depository of legal documents.[157]

The king, hence, was the apex court of appeal with the tribunals under his jurisdiction. The right of imposing fine or corporal punishment was the sole prerogative of king.

Katyayana describes *Vyavahara as –*

When the ramification of right conduct, that together are called Dharma and can be established only with effort have been violated, the dispute (in a law court between plaintiff and defendant) which springs from what is desired to be framed (such as a debt) is said to be *Vyavahara.*[158] '*Vi'* is employed in the sense of various. *Áva'* in the sense of ðoubt' '*hara'* means 'removing', *Vyavahara* is so called because of its removing various doubts.[159]

Procedure is defined by Katyayana further as what the plaintiff complains of (before the court) is the root of the litigation, the two springs (of *Vyavahara*).

JUDICIAL PROCEDURE

'*Vyavahara*' is the Sanskrit term used both in theory and practice for judicial procedure. Narada has described judicial procedure at length, dividing into two types: one with a wager *(sapana)* and the other without a wager. Brhaspati mentions a few peculiarities and entails a review of the trials, summons, restraints, surely, retrial and the jury system, plaint and reply witnesses and documents, etc., are said to be nonrendition of what is due and urgency.

Vyavahara is envisioned to have four feet, i.e., stages, viz. the plaint, the defence (or reply), the deliberation (as to binder of proof) and the adducing of proof.[160]

The judicial trial in the Smrti period seems to have been attended by the King personally. In his absence, it was conducted under the supervision of the *pradvivaka*, or the Chief Judge. Manu prescribed that the king, desirous of investigating law cases, must enter the court of justice, preserving a dignified demeanour, together with Brahmanas and experienced councillors.[161] There, either seated or standing, raising his right arm, without ostentation in his dress and ornaments, he examined the business of suitors.

Here, D.B. Diskalkar has pointed out a similarity in raising hand (as mentioned earlier in the chapter), indicating a strong attachment to Dharma in the Girnar rock Inscription of Rudraman (Saka year 72–150 AD), which mentions the good deeds undertaken by Rudraman (which also speaks of the great Maurya Emperors Chandragupta and Ashoka and their interest in irrigation works in such a distant country from the capitals as Kathiawad and how Rudraman strengthened it further).

The sanctity of the court and judicial trial is emphasised by Manu in these words. The court must not be entered, or the truth must be spoken. A man who either says nothing or speaks falsely becomes sinful.[162] At another place, Manu says, as a hunter traces the kin of a (wounded) deer by drops of blood, even so the king shall discover on which side the right lies by inferences (from the facts). The king, in other words, was required to exercise his intellect with a great eye to sift the truth from available evidences and logic surrounding the case.

The trial began only when the plaintiff narrated his grievance caused by the defendant, who is then summoned; and if the king is satisfied that there is sufficient ground of investigation, the trial of case began before him. Both the parties had to furnish surety before the commencement of the trial, the failure of which would mean he was kept under the charge of a court officer called *Sadhyapala*. After the filing of the complaint and reply of the defendant, the assessors passed judgement after adducing to the proofs. The Chief Judge decided which side would begin the case. However, Narada and Katyayana tell that this right belonged to the one who suffered greater injury. Brhaspati advocated taking the castes of the concerned parties under consideration.

The Charter of Vishnusena (Samvat 649), which enlists seventy two acharas, says, in achara eight:

Arthi – pratyarthina vina vyavaharo na grahyah, i.e., a law suit could be taken up for disposal only when the complainant and the defendant were both present and never in the absence of both parties.[163]

Further, in the next achara, it recommends that

Apane asanasthasya chhalo na grahyah which implied (1) the pretext of being engaged in work at the shop should not justify the absence of a party to a lawsuit from the court or that no careless statement of accusation was acceptable from a person who had been at the time of occurrence of case been busy in selling things in shop or market.

Only a proper complaint was acceptable to the court. Achara 17 of the Vishnusena Charter tells

Avedanakena vina utkrishti na grahya

Avedanaka indicates a formal complaint in the court while *utkrushti*, derived from Pali *ukkutthi* and Sanskrit *utkrushti*, may imply wailing. Hence, a proper complaint and not mere wailing was acceptable to the court.[164]

The Smrtis have described the topic of summons. In the earliest times, there was no means at court's behest to summon the accused except that the plaintiff could produce the defendant. However, Narada, Brhaspati, and Katyayana have spelled rules for summons. The king could summon either through a letter under seal or through an attendant or defendant. There were rules for who should not be summoned. These provisions may be supplemented with the provisions communicated in Vishnusena's charter. Achara 21 in this Charter says:

Paren - arth – abhiyuktanam vada – pratisamasane
Yajna – sattra – vivah – adishu ahvanam na karayet.[165]

This implied that persons engaged in such works as sacrifice or a marriage ceremony should not be summoned to court to refute the charges against him. *Artha* may refer to 'originating' in wealth *(artha mula)* or civil and not *himsa mula* or criminal case. Or there may be reference to two different sets of persons who should not be summoned viz (1) one engaged in *yajna*, etc. (like Brhaspati includes such people in the list of the *nasedhyah* or who could not be summoned), and (2) one involved in other cases (as Yajnavalkya says at a place *abhiyuktam chananyena*).[166]

In the achara preceding this, the Charter says

Grih – apana sthitanam mudra - patraka dutakaih sahasa- varjjam – ah vanam na karaniyam.[167]

Persons engaged in the work at home or at their shops should not be summoned to court by means of a seal ring or letter of by a messenger unless they were involved in a criminal case.

Achara 29 of the same charter tells about a situation of the absence of *varika* class.[168] It seems there was no excuse for the absence of the *varika* (officials) of the *uttarakulika* class when thrice summoned to the court by a court peon. The fine for the offence was two and one-fourth silver coins even if there could have been a good reason of absence.

In this context, the next clause seems quite interesting that if the clerks who wrote down the statements of cases in the law court were absent from the court after midday, they were liable to a fine of six and one-fourth silver coins.[169] No pretext tells the achara 31, of the absence of *uttarakulika – varika*, absent from the court (a – *madhyahnad -urdhavam)* after mid-day was to be accepted.

Katyayana advocated that a king should not summon a young woman whose family is dilapidated, a lady of good family, a woman who is recently delivered a maiden who is of higher caste than the claimant (since). These are declared to be under the tutelage of their kinsmen.

Summoning is declared with cases of these women on whom family depends—women who are unchaste courtesans, women without family, and degraded women.[170]

Fines were there for disregarding orders of summons.

Restraint, i.e., *asedha* was probably some sort of imposition upon the movement of the defendant either by plaintiff or by the court pending the arrest of the defendant, if there was an apprehension that the latter could abscond. However, in times of Narada, a royal order or court order was necessary to arrest the defendant. Katyayana made concessions with respect to arrest for husbandmen or soldiers or one who has already promised. Law of surety was present too in early procedural law. This surely was for the appearance of the litigant parties as distinguished from the surety for monetary transactions. However, reservations seem to have existed with those who could act as sureties. Katyayana tells if any of the parties failed to provide a surety, as required by law, he would be kept in charge of a person called *Sadhyapala*, who was like a modern bailiff.

Katyayana vividly put forward the method of questioning. The plaintiff (the king or Judge) should question the litigant (who approaches) at the proper time (of the Court) who bows (to the King or Judge) and who stands before him: 'What is your grievance? What is the injury done to you? Don't be afraid. Speak out, man!' The (Judge), presiding in the court, should ask by whom, where, at what time and why (the grievance or injury caused). When this was asked, whatever he replied should be considered (by the judge) with the assessors and the Brahmana; and if the cause he judicially entertain able, then he (the Judge) should deliver the (Court) seal to the plaintiff for calling (the defendant) or he should order the (Court's) officer (to call the defendant).[171]

Katyayana has same interesting provisions regarding the nature of plaint. The plaint that is opposed to the interests or usages of the country, that is prohibited by the king, and that contains a mixture of several titles of law does not succeed (i.e., must be rejected as bad).[172] Further, that plaint is regarded as unacceptable which lacks (the mention of the time and place (of the cause of action), that awaits the (statement of the) material (*dravya*) claimed or the amount and that is wanting in the dimensions of the thing claimed. It (the plaint) should be concise in words, abounding in meaning (contexts), unambiguous, not self-contradicting, free from arguments that would defeat it and capable of refuting opposite statements.[173]

Elsewhere, Katyayana tells He (the scribe) who writes down the words of the plaintiff or the defendant be punished as to thief, by the king who desired to enforce Dharma.[174]

Katyayana, who represents the high watermark in the judicial procedure, takes about the duration for reply and the kinds of reply too. He says time should be granted (to the defendant to file his reply), viz a day, a month of a fortnight or a season (two months) or even a year or even beyond that according to the requirement of the importance or otherwise of the cause.[175] He makes a reference to regard to tradition and prevalence when he says the king should able (the defendant) to give a reply according to the requirement of justice after paying regard to whatever rules of practice have been handed down traditionally in matters (of dispute).

Katyayana enunciates that a reply could be of four kinds: admission of the truth (of the plaint), denial, a special plea, and the rule of former judgement (or *res judicata*).[176] He tells that there can never be a (proper) reply that is ambiguous, irrelevant, incomplete, too wide, covering only a part of the plaint.[177] Dwelling on the matters that cause failure in litigation, which does at length, he declares that "one who changes his pleading should be fined five *panas*, one shunning judicial investigate (kriyadvesi *or one who hates kriya*, i.e., members of the court and their intentions) should be fined ten *panas*, one failing to appear twelve *panas*, one who remains silent sixteen and one who absconds after receiving summons, twenty *panas*. Katyayana calls a person cast out in their pending suit as *hinavadi*. According to Narada, there were five classes of *hinavadisanyavadi*, *kriyadvesi*, *nopasthata*, *niruttara*, and *ahutaprapalayi*. [178] *Anyavadi* implies a person who after lodging a complaint abandons or puts forward a different one. *Kriyadvesi* means one shunning judicial investigation. *Nopasthata* implies a litigant who does not present himself before the court after being summoned. *Niruttara* means a litigant who on questioning remains silent.

The stage of adducing proof comes next, which implies the law of evidence (*kriyapada*), which is dealt separately.

Katyayana also describes *sadhya* (the claim to be established), which the plaintiff himself proposed to clearly establish, and *adhara* (means of proof), by which the entire claim (of the litigant) is established.[179]

The decision rendering or the judgement is the final stage of the judicial procedure known as *'nirnayapada'*. This aspect has received an elaborate treatment at the hands of the smrti writers. The final decision is declared by the king and arrived at after king's consultations with the learned members of the court, after the establishment of evidence in support of the case according to the laws as laid down. A party is declared successful when it establishes its point of view by means of evidence to the satisfaction of the court. The copy of the judgement in his favour is designated as *'jayapatra'* or the document of victory corresponding to the modern day decree of the court. One who fails to establish his case or exhibit a case contrary to one in question or is found guilty of a vitiated case is termed as the defeated party.

The advanced Smrti writers—Narada, Brhaspati, and Katyayana—spell out the fourfold character of a judicial decision, as depending on moral law or Dharma, the issue of the case, custom, and an edict of the king.[180] Law— without adducing to proof, oral or documentary—is a decision by Dharma. In Kautilyan times, it was law as administered by *Dharmasasthas*. When a decision is according to *Vyavahara*, the decision is taken by applying principles of Dharmashastra in judicial procedure, resting on the testimony of witness or documentary evidence. When any decision is according to the local custom or in conformity with prevalent tradition, it is termed a decision based on custom or *achara*. Finally, a decision based on the royal command is in the form of edict. This could be at variance with local custom. Katyayana, however, had cautions and urges that decisions based on royal order should not be in conflict with the rules laid by Smrti.

The content of the deed of judgement is described briefly by Narada and Brhaspati and has been dealt in detail by Katyayana. The latter lists that the decree ought to carry the following:

(1) The statement of the plaintiff and defendant
(2) The reply claimed by plaintiff
(3) Documentary evidence or testimony of witness

(4) The decision for the dispute

(5) The manner in which the matter is considered by the king or the *pradvivaka* (Chief Judge)

Katyayana tells of two kinds of judgement: one that was awarded after the success of the party with much contest (*pascatkara*) and the other given to a party on success in a suit without full or complete trial of an action (*jayapatra*).

Some provisions have been spelled out for ex-parte decree. According to Katyayana, in the adduce of the defendant at the time of trial, an ex-parte decree could be passed in the form of plaintiff (except when the defendant has been prevented to be present for reasons beyond control).

Rules regarding adjournments are visible, although ancient India did not allow any permission to plaintiff to ask for time to prepare his claim. It was Katyayana who allowed the plaintiff a time period of three to seven days to collect his wits and for the ground that defendant gets time to file his reply too. It was allowed in both civil and criminal cases. Where however time value was important, no additional time was permitted. Brhaspati does not favour adjournments and allows it when *God* or king prevented an accused concerned from making his defence. All the Smrti writers unanimously oppose a cause of adjournment in criminal cases such as abuse, assault, adultery, or theft. Kane has observed that rules for adjournments were more rigid in times of Kautilya than Katyayana.

There are scanty references to pleaders or recognised agents who appeared in courts on behalf of the contenders. Pleaders were permissible only where one was timorous, idiotic, mad, sick, kinsman, slave, pupil, and so on. Narada permitted recognised agents *(prativadin)* and even brother, son, or father of the litigant to appear in court.

As regards to retrial, or *punar-nyaya*, there seems to be few rules in the Smrtis. From times of Manu, it was deemed that once a legal transaction was over, the decree executed, no retrial was allowed.[181] Retrial was allowed if the decision was contrary to justice. Recalling Manu, Brhaspati declared that the king should punish the judges' party to the trial along with victorious party therein. Where the successful party has been instrumental, he along with assessors was liable to fine. In such cases, the king should try the suits himself and punish the ministers and judges for miscarriage or non-deliverance of justice. In cases where a party is not satisfied with the decision of a lower court or false evidence of the witness has led to urgent decision, the case is reopened for trial. We hear about punar nyaya in Ashokan edicts as well which has been mentioned earlier.

Mm Kane observes that same sort of jury system was resorted to for settling disputes, although references to it were not very conclusive.

LAW OF EVIDENCE (or *Kriyapada)*

Evidence, which forms the third stage in the judicial procedure in early India, has been dwelled at great length by the Smrti writers Narada and Brhaspati ordained that after. The case been filled, the plaint should present the evidence and establish the truth. Hindu jurists declared that evidence could be from these sources: (1) documents, (2) witnesses, and (3) ordeals. The broader category is, however, human comprising the first two and divine consisting of the third. Ancient legal jurists also looked upon possession as an additional means of human proof. Brhaspati used the expression inference (*anumana*) for possessions.

The human proofs were given more preference by the smrti writers than the divine ones. In the presence of human proof, divine proof was not resorted to, even though they will be covering a small part of allegation of the plaint. Divine proofs were resisted

(1) if human proofs were unavailable;
(2) in cases of assault or heinous crimes, as enunciated by Katyayana (v. 229);
(3) where there was doubt with regard to validity of documents or witnesses; and
(4) where the witnesses are equally balance or disputes about loss of life.

Moreover, documentary evidence was declared to be more suitable or to be accepted with regard to transactions such as sale, mortgage, partition, etc., of immovable property, similar to the practices prevalent in our times. Katyayana prefers documents, if available to witnesses or ordeal (V.223).

Katyayana even asserts somewhat a rule of closure in modern judicial system, which he tells that it was the duty of the litigant to resort to more weighting means of proof and once he took recourse to weaker means, he was not allowed to take recourse of the stronger one and thus could lose the case.[182]

DOCUMENTS

Documents are and were considered the supreme with respect to their evidential value. In monetary transactions, documents served as an important means of apprehending frauds. Compared to witnesses where the possibility of deliberate error was always existent, the worth of documents was greater. However, the earliest Hindu legal procedure relied more on the testimony of witnesses and ordeals. Documents were deemed valid, however, if they were in proper formation, free from ambiguity, and perfect in all respects.[183]

Documents could be declared valid or invalid. In order to be valid, it was not to be adverse to the usages in the country and Smrti laws.[184] The Smrtis talk of causes that could invalidate a document. Narada tells (V.137) a bond written by an intoxicated person or a person charged with a crime, a woman, a child, or a document caused to be written by force is considered invalid.

The royal documents or *rajasasanas* needed to have the royal seal compulsorily to be valid while public documents (*laukika*) were expected to conform to a particular format.

The *laukika* document, the Smrti writers tell that should have mentioned that name of the royal family in order, the year, the month and day of the transaction. The name of the creditor and debtor preceded by father's name, the nature of property, and rate of interest were to be vividly enlisted. And lastly, the document should also bear signatures of the witnesses. Any script could be used for the sake of writing of the document.

Narada and Katyayana permit the validity of secondary evidence as well. When a document is split or stolen burnt or if writing of the original document is obliterated, a fresh document could be executed by the parties to the suit.[185] However, this could be allowed only be if the court was satisfied to the reasons for the loss of the original document.

Narada deals with documents briefly. Brhaspati is more elaborate, and he warns us against clever forgeries. In Katyayana, the provisions for documents, types, nature, and validity are even more comprehensive. He devoted seventy-four verses to the topic of documents. He is more elaborate about the needs of testing the documents.

Interestingly, in the inscriptions, there is an allusion to a forged *shasana*, which shows that ancient forgeries existed too. The Madhuban Copper Plate of Harsha (632 AD),[186] which furnishes great information on great Harsha as an eminent king of India, tells about the transfer of the village of Somakundika situated in the *vishaya* (District) of kundadhani and in the *bhukti* (Province) of Sravasti to two learned Brahmanas: the Samavedi Bhatti Vatasvamin of the Savarna gotra and the Rigvedi Bhatta Sivadevaswamin of the Vishnuvriddha gotra. This village, it is told, had formerly been enjoyed on the strength of a forged *shasana* (kutashasana) by one Vamarathya, from whom it was then taken after destroying the old plate. Buhler tells this incidence shows that the rules of the Smrtis, which settle the punishment for forgers of royal edicts, were not unnecessary and that ancient forgeries did exist.

Documents could be of different kind. Brhaspati names three types: those written by (the order of) the king, those written in a particular place, and those written by a person in his own hand. Royal writings were called "*rajkiya*" documents known as *shasanas* or grants. These could be made under the king's seal and were executed or copper plate or piece of cloth. The second type was a *jayapatra* or a deed of victory to the successful party in a lawsuit (this could have been like a modern day court decree). Katyayana uses *pascatkara*, another deed for judgement given in a case after thorough contest. A fourth type of document was *prasada—patra* or a deed of favour. This was issued by a king to a person for his faithful services and laudable virtues in the form of landed or other property.[187]

(a) Narada mentions two categories of documents: one, in the hand writing of the party and (b) other, in the handwriting of another person. Vishnu declared documents to be of three types attested by the king or by (other) witnesses or unattested.[188]

A document, he tells, is said to be attested by the king when it has been executed (in a Court of judicature), on the king ordering it, by a scribe, his servant, and has been signed by his Chief Judge, with his own hand. It is unaltered when it has been written (by the) party himself) with his own hand. Vishnu especially tells that should the debtor or creditor or witness or scribe be dead, the authenticity of the documents has to be ascertained by (comparing with it other) specimens of their handwriting.[189]

Brhaspati and Katyayana have described various kinds of *janapada* (of the people) documents. Brhaspati talks of *vibhaga pattrka* or *vibhaga lekhya*, *simapattra*, *danalekhya*, *krayalekha*, *adhilekhya*, *samvit patra*, *dasa patra*, *malekhya*, while both Brhaspati and Katyayana talk of *Sthiti-patra*, *visuddhi patra*, and *sandhi pattrka*.

A *vibhaga–pattraka* describes Brhaspati (V.11) as a deed of partition effected by brothers being divided in interest. *Simapattra* is a deed defining the boundary line, made by villages of two adjoining villages (Br. V.3, Kat, v.257). *Danelekhya* was a deed of gift made when any property was given as a gift (Br. V.12)

Krayalekhya was a deed of purchase (of immovable property) while *adhilekhya* was mortgage deed. *Samvit patra* was a deed of agreement (Brhaspati, V.15) not opposed to the king or the sacred law. *Dasa patra* was a deed of bondage or contract for labor (Br. V.16). Rnalekhya used to be a deed of debt. Katyayana describes *sthitipatra* (deed of conventions) as made for the validity of (for preserving intact) the usages of men versed in the four Vedas: of a city, of corporations, of groups and of citizens.[190] *Visuddhi, patra* (deed of purification), was given to persons with attestations of witnesses when they performed penance and became free from sins. *Sandhi patra* (deed of peace) is used to write what happened when a person has been accused in the presence of the best of the people.[191]

WITNESSES

In the determination of truth, the deposition of the witness or the testimony of the person or persons who witnessed the event is very important. Documentary evidence was admitted much later in the ancient judicial procedure. It was witness, which constituted the primary evidence. The evidence should be direct and not hearsay. In the Smrti period, we came across detailed provisions with regard to the witnesses; and these mention their number, qualifications, manner of deposition, etc. Similarly, from the Vishnusena's Charter, we came to know about the witnesses, who could be and could not be, in various civil and criminal cases.

Manu describes the kind of men who could be witnesses and the manner in which those must give true evidence. According to him, householders, men with male issue, and indigenous (inhabitants of the country, be they Kshatriyas, Vaisyas, or Shudras) are competent when called by a suitor to give evidence, not any persons whatever their condition be except in cases of urgency.[192] This implied that, probably, the bachelors were not considered trustworthy to depose, or it could be that householders were imagined to be more responsible to depose. Either way, it is strange that such qualifications as these or having a male issue should have determined the eligibility to be a witness.

Manu, in the next two verses, emphasises that in all the four castes, men could depose, provided they were trustworthy, knew their duty, and were free from covetousness. However, what could have been the yardstick for determining such subjective elements in a witness is difficult to imagine. He further tells that those who have interest in suit, are familiar friends or enemies of parties, or convicted of perjury or suffering witness or tainted by some mortal sin should be excused from the ring of permissible witnesses. He declares, "The king cannot be made a witness, nor mechanics and actors, nor a Srotriya, nor a student of the Veda, nor (an ascetic) who has given up (all connection) with the world. Nor one wholly dependent, nor one of bad fame nor a *dasyu*, nor one who follows forbidden occupations, nor an aged (man) nor an infants, nor one (man) alone, nor a man of the lowest castes, nor one deficient in organs of sense. Nor one extremely grieved, nor one intoxicated, nor a madman, nor one tormented by hunger or thirst, nor one oppressed by fatigue, nor one tormented by desire, nor a wrathful man, nor a thief."[193] Manu's emphasis seems to allow men who would have some sort of balanced judgement, who would be neither sick nor in want of something that could make them fallible, or who would be capable of understanding and deposing to be a witness.

In another gender- and caste tainted clause, Manu tells that "women should give evidence for women, and for twice born men twice born men (of the same kind) virtuous Shudras for Shudras, and men of the lowest castes for the lowest".[194] However, he permits that "on failure of qualified witnesses, evidence may be given (in such cases) by a women, by an infant, by an aged man, by a pupil by a relative, by a slave or by a hired servant." But the judge shall consider their testimony as untrustworthy.[195] In Manu's thoughts, there is clearly evidenced a reserve towards women being trusted as witness except where women was in question, indicating for rest her evidence was considered non serious. He brings the caste biases in declaring the qualified evidence sources, thereby restricting justice in many ways. Manu is, however, firm in asserting that in all cases of theft and adultery or defamation and assault (where it is difficult to find witnesses, hence above qualified one, the competence of witnesses), the competence of witnesses should not be examined too strictly.[196]

The ideas of Manu against women seem to reflect in his verse 77 of the same chapter, which tells, "One man who is free from covetousness may be (accepted as) witness, but not even many pure women, because the understanding of female is apt to waiver, nor even many other men, who are tainted with sin." At the same time, he does not waver from showing concern for women if witnesses spoke false. He says, "Whatever places (of torment) are assigned (by the sages) to the slayer of a brahmana, to the murderer of women and children, to him who betrays a friend, and to an ungrateful man, those shall be thy (portion), if thou speakest falsely."[197] Here, it seems to take a tough line on men with respect to false deposition. The inconsistencies of clauses of Manusmrti, however, cannot be ruled out given the heterogeneous or rescenscionary character of the text.

Kautilya, on law of evidence, tells that in any case before the judges, admission (by the defendant of the claim against him) is the best. If the claim is not admitted, then the judgement shall be leased on the evidence of trustworthy witnesses, who would be persons known for their honesty or those approved by the court.[198] Kautilya also debarred the following from the purview of qualified witnesses: the brother of the wife of the claimant, his (business) partner, a dependent, a creditor or debtor, an enemy of his, a cripple, or anyone with an earlier correction (3.11.28). The following were allowed to be called as witnesses in cases concerning their own groups: the king, Brahmanas, learned in Vedas, village officials, lepers, people with open wounds or sores, an outcast, anyone having a despicable profession, blind, deaf or dumb persons, women, government officials, and those who volunteer to be a witness.[199]

Kautilya's thought with respect to witness seems to be a step above Manu. The Arthashastra does not impose insensible qualifications for witnesses as much as Manu does. Although Kautilya too emphasises the element of trustworthiness in witnesses, he differs from Manu in that he allows the king to be a witness in certain cases as well as a *Chandala* (untouchable). By asserting that men who volunteer as witness should not be accepted, it may be seen as an apprehension that these men could be a secret witness or a spy too.

Similarly, Yajnavalkya, too distinguished between competent and incompetent witnesses – Seen men who were devoted to religious austerities, men liberally disposed, men sprung firm high families, fulfill men, men devoted to religious observances, straightforward men, men blessed with loss and men possessed of wealth (were deemed) competent witnesses, (provided they are) not less than three and devoted to the performance of *Srauta* and *Smrta* rites, each respectfully according to their caste or class or all for all (castes and classes).[200]

A women, a minor, an old man, a rogue, an intoxicated person, one infatuated against whom an accusation has been brought, a stage drama, a heretic, a forger, one deformed, one degraded, a relative, one having an interest in the subject matter, an ally, an enemy, a thief, a desperado, one who has been found guilty, an outcast, and others are incompetent witnesses (V. 70–71). Yajnavalkya presents a quick proposition in verse 83 (1) that where man of the four orders are (likely) to suffer capital punishment, there a witness may speak the untruth, and by this prohibition against true evidence, Gharpure explains, a permission for refusing to give evidence or for giving false evidence is given for witnesses of whom it has been prohibited before.[201] In 82(2), Yajnavalkya suggests a purification from that (sin). The special oblation of rice known as the *Sarawata* should be presented by the twice born.

Narada (Ch. I.139) distinguishes eleven types of witnesses in law by the learned. Five of them are known as appointed (*Krta*) and the other six as unappointed *(akrta)*. A subscribing witness, one who has been reminded, a casual witness, a secret witness, an indirect witness—these, Narada says, are the five sorts of appointed witnesses.[202] The unappointed witnesses are the king, the judge, the people of a village who are acquainted with affairs of the two parties, one deputed by a claimant, and a family witness who represents in family quarrels.

Brhaspati has described these twelve witnesses in detail—subscribing witness *(Likhita)* who enters in the deed, the name of caste, his father's name, place stay, etc., a witness distinctly mentioned in a deed *(Lekhita)*, a secret witness *(gudhasaksin)* who stays cancelled at the time of occurrence when a person is invited to attend to a transaction of money *(smarta)*, in events of family partition, sale, gift, etc., the persons who are invited for in a good terms with both sides, called family witness as *(Kulyas)*, a witnesses by chance or spontaneous witness who happens to offer his witness *(Yadracchika)*, a messenger witness *(dutaka)* deputed by the parties, an indirect witness who tells what somebody has told before going abroad or about to die, a common witness *(Karyamadhyagata)* to whom both parties communicate, a king, who could be summoned under special circumstances, the judge, together with the assessors in a fresh trial and villages who could act as witnesses in case of boundary disputes.

Narada enjoins that all men of all castes, free from blemish, could depose either in disputes pertaining to respective castes or in all cases in general. Katyayana is, however, more explicit in enunciating that, normally, a litigant of lower caste should not engage witnesses of higher castes but only men of lowest castes alone. When disputes are between different groups such as guilds, corporations, etc., heads of such groups should be considered appropriate witnesses.[203] An exception is when, in the same group, same person harbors ill will against persons of the same group. And in cases of disputes among women, same group should preferably be women.

Narada explains the reasons for excluding a child, a woman, a single witness, a relative, and an enemy from being witnesses. Regarding child not being taken as witness, he says a child would make false statement through ignorance, from affection, and an enemy from a desire of revenge.[204]

Katyayana maintains in a similar manner that women should be a witness for women (when women are litigants), for (litigant of) the first three castes (witnesses should be of) the same caste as themselves, well-balanced Shudras for Shudra (litigants), and men of the lowest castes, such as chandalas should be witnesses for lowest castes.[205]

Brhaspati entails that in boundary disputes relating to house and field, peasants, artisans, hired labourers, headmen, hunters, gleaners, root diggers, and fishermen are to act as witnesses. In relation to boundary disputes, Narada's list of false witnesses encompasses jugglers, public dancers, sellers of spirituous liquor, oil pressers, elephant drivers, leather workers, Chandalas, Shudras, peasants, son of Shudra women, and outcastes. Narada moderated the earlier provision regarding Varna witnesses and provided that members of all varnas could depose as witnesses in case of all varnas.[206]

When the witnesses differ, the Smrti writers emphasise that the statement of majority has to be accepted; but if there was no clear majority, the statement of those who were purer was to be accepted. If the meritorious were divided equally, then those who were best were to be accepted as true.[207] Indicative of the exercise of subjective intellect, these clauses envision sharp legal mind and functionaries in early India.

As for the number of witnesses, Manu and Narada declared that at least three witnesses were required in a cause.[208] Brhaspati tells they could be nine, seven, five, four or three witnesses or only two if they were learned Brahmana.[209] He tells that a single witness would never be sufficient in deciding the matter. However, if he is a *dutaka*, Manu and Brhaspati allow him to be a single witness.[210] Brhaspati tells that a single witness could furnish valid proof if he was a messenger, an accountant, a King, or a Chief Judge.

The Charter of Vishnusena in the nature of *achara sthiti patra* throws some light on the witnesses' aspect of judicial procedure as it may have prevailed in actuality. Achara 16 in this document reads,

Para-vishayat – karan – abhyagato vanijakah
Para – reshe na grahyah –

This could have meant that a merchant belonging to another district or kingdom should not be accepted as a witness in a criminal case involving persons of a locality where he happened to be present on account of some reason or other.[211]

Further, achara 18 tells,

Vakparushya – dandaparushyayoh, sakshitive, sari na grahya –

This implies the *sarika* bird could not be allowed to be a witness in cases of defamation and assault. The *sarika* bird refers to a singing bird (myna), which could capture conversation. This bird, coincidentally, has been mentioned in the Sanskrit drama Ratnavali, written by Harsha, where Sagarika confesses her love for Udayana to her bosom friend and the bird overhears sagarika's confession of love and reproduces at another place.

The concept of witness has been studied by Dr. Kane very exhaustively. His concept of witness is based on the Vishnu Dharmashastra. VIII 13 and Medhatithi on Manusmrti, VIII. 74 S.G. Moghe has examined the concept of witness in, the Mahabharata and Dharmashastra literature in an article in the compilation "A peep at Indology".

In the Dharmashastra literature, the concept of witnesses was connected with a merit or demerit.[212] In the Mahabharata, this concept was dissociated from heaven and earth. According to Moghe, the concept of witness in the epic is associated with *punya* and *paapa* (good deed and sin). There lies the benefit for telling the truth in the form of heaven and hell for telling lies. In the Mahabharata, 11.61.76, [213]it is pointed that he is called a witness when he has directly heard (the conversation or) speech between the concerned persons, kept in mind, and spoken the truth. It is further said that such a witness is never dissociated from *Dharma* and *Artha*, the two important goals of human life. What is interesting is that it tells whenever any sin takes place and is not censured, the person who is the seniormost and who is particularly present on the spot incurs half the sin. One who is the direct performer of a sin incurs one-fourth of the sin. One-fourth of the sin is, however, incurred by the members of the assembly who did not censure the censurable deed.[214]

This implied that the performer of the sin was given equal blame as those seniormost person and members who did not forbid the considerable deed. Further, the Mahabharata (11.61.71) tells that the seniormost person becomes free from sin once they blame or condemn such wrong deeds. In such a situation, the performer of the sin is held responsible.

The text metes out a different treatment to the witnesses speaking untruth. The text (in 11.61.74) tells that those who speak untruth destroy the effect of Istapurta of seven generations on both the sides (of father and mother) and they further experience the sorrows of other ladies. [215]

It is here that the text of Mahabharata stands out with respect to treatment of false witnesses. It talks of the dire consequences of speaking untruth in their life in present birth rather than advancing the concept of going into a hell.

Moghe has pointed out another novel view from Mahabharata as to who should not be accepted as witnesses. The Mahabharata (V.35.37) points out that a palmist, a merchant who was formerly a thief, a medical practitioner who was formerly a painter, an enemy, a friend, and an actor should be treated as unacceptable witnesses in the court matters.[216] This view point of the Mahabharata has no parallel in the entire Dharmashastra literature. This view seems to be based on the point of view of witnesses' professions. The Dharmashastra bases the concept of witness on the fruits of heaven and hell while Mahabharata bases it on the direct consequences (in respect of istapurta).

POSSESSION

Possession was regarded by ancient Indian jurists as one of the modes of evidence especially in disputes of immovable property. Possession was recognised to be of two types: one with title *(Sagama-bhukti)* and, two, possession without title *(anagamabhukti)*.[217] And Katyayana tells documents, witnesses, and possessions are regarded as three *pramanas* (means of proof). Among human pramanas, possession is regarded as equal to a faulter's (valid) document.[218] In the earlier verse, Katyayana took possession, which continues for three generations is independent (means of proof of ownership without for three generations), then it (is proof of ownership) if accompanied with title.

Title, along with possession, gave rise to ownership of property. However, it is debatable whether title alone without possession could create ownership.[219] Narada explicitly prohibits ownership if there is no possession and only title. On the other hand, he declares possession without title as theft. Similarly, Katyayana states that mere possession cannot prove ownership in certain cases such as female slaves, property of a temple, state property, property of minors and of men learned in Vedas, as also what was inherited from father and mother.[220]

However, long possession led to ownership provided it was uninterrupted and continuous. Narada, Brhaspati, and Katyayana laid down that possession for three generations or beyond human memory created ownership without title. Rules were also provided for an adverse possession that matured into possession, although the time period for such cases was different according to various Smrti writers.

ORDEALS

Ordeals were the divine means of proof that supposedly showed themselves from very early times. The most common instance of ordeal was the fire ordeal head of undertaken by Sita at the behest of Rama to prove her purity and innocence. Ordeals were supposed to be resorted only in the absence of human proofs. However, Katyayana laid down that in a dispute, if one party resorted to human proofs and other to divine ordeals, the human proofs alone are to be taken into account.

Narada tells that ordeals are to be resorted when a transaction takes place in a forest or with regard to an act of violence or in lonely place, at night, inside a house, or when a bailee denies a deposit. Similarly, Brhaspati advises that a forger of gems, pearls, or coral, one withholding a deposit, a ruffian, or a person accused of adultery should be tested through ordeals. In charges of grave offences or misappropriation, transactions that took place in remote past, truth was suggested to be established by means of ordeals.

Manu described two kinds of ordeals: fire and water.[221] Yajnavalkya and Narada prescribed five ordeals—consecrated water, scale, poison, fire, and water—to be administered only on serious charges. Brhaspati enunciated nine ordeals: fire, water, scale, poison, ploughshare, sacred litigation, grain of rice, hot gold, price, and lottery. Katyayana described seven ordeals.

The *Kadambari* of Bana mentions four ordeals: fire, water, poison, and balance. Account of the Chinese traveler Hiuen Tsang refers to four ordeals: water, fire, weighing, and prison.

Ordeals of balance were prescribed for offences like treason, sedition, etc., or for persons involved in scandals or involved with people of suspicious character. *Kosa* ordeal was administered on charges of suspicious at the time of family partition. Brhaspati tells an ordeal of person was to be resorted to when the property in dispute was of the value of 1,000 panas. When this value was 300 panas, six ordeals or ordeal by *kosa* (sacred liberation) was used. Theft of one hundred panas was to be settled by ordeal of Dharma while theft of cows was to be subjected to ordeal of plough-share *(phata divya)*.

Titles of Law

The Smrti writers recognise the division of law into eighteen topics of law (litigation). They differ only in their order and nomenclature. These eighteen topics of litigation are popularly called *vyavaharapadani*. There seems to be no clear-cut division of civil and criminal laws, but Narada and Brhaspati seem to be aware of this distinction. Brhaspati distinguishes between two types of suits, *arthasamudbhava* and *himsasammubhava*—that is, those suits originating in wealth and those in violence. However, there are no references to two kinds of courts looking into the two aspects: civil and criminal separately. It is more probable that the same courts tried both kinds of cases. There are references to some miscellaneous suits *(prakirnaka)* in which the king and his officers could take initiative instead of the plaintiff.

Madhukar M. Patkar has analysed that these eighteen topics of law could be arranged under five broad categories: (1) Monetary Laws, (2) Service laws, (3) Group Laws, (4) Land disputes, and (5) Criminal Laws.[222]

Monetary laws deal with topics such as debt and deposits. The law of debt lays down rules for interest, sureties, repayment, and liability, and so on. Service laws imply laws that would explain the relation between master and servant, teacher and apprentice, or employer and employees. Group laws tell of partnership, joint undertakings, safe and purchase, etc. Land disputes referred to laws regarding boundary disputes. Criminal laws could be classified under six heads:

(1) Offence by words *(vakparusya)*
(2) Assault *(dandaparusya)*
(3) Theft *(asteya)*
(4) Violence resulting in injury *(sahasa)*
(5) Adultery *(strisamgrahana)*
(6) Miscellaneous offences *(prakirnakas)* in which the King and his officials could initiate litigation

Rules for trying the two types of cases were the same. As Mm. P.V. Kane observed, "It appears that the set of rules and procedure in both were the same (except as to the time allowed for reply, as to the qualifications of witnesses and as to the proxies) the same courts tried both kinds of disputes and not as in modern times when civil disputes are tried in one class of courts and criminal complaints in another and when the procedure also in both differs a great deal.[223]

Further, these eighteen titles did not exhaust the entire realm of law. Several disputes such as relating to collection of taxes, treasure trove, etc., were there that could not be brought within the fold of litigation. Narada declared these 18 titles as having 132 subdivisions.

These eighteen titles of law have been described in varied sequence by the respective smrti writers.

Manu declared the cases fall under eighteen titles of law according to the principles drawn from local usage and from the institutes of the Sacred law.[224]

Of these title, the first is the nonpayment of debts (then follows), (2) deposit and pledges, (3) sale without ownerships, (4) concerns among partners and (5) resumptions of gifts,[225] (6) nonpayment of wages, (7) nonperformance of agreements, (8) rescission of sale and purchase, (9) disputes between the owner (of cattle) and his servants (10), disputes regarding boundaries, (11) assault and (12) defamation, (13) theft, (14) robbery and violence, (15) adultery, (16) duties of man and wife, (17) partition (of inheritance), and (18) gambling and betting. These give to rise to lawsuits in this world.

Narada has included theft (steya) and adultery (strisamgrahana) under one category, viz *sahasa* (violence), while Brhaspati, in line with Manu mentions them as two different topics. Also, Narada and Brhaspati divide *parusya* into *vakparusya* (abuse) and *danda parusya* (violence) while Manu has only one title under sahasa.

The procedural law, hence as described in the Dharmashastra texts or inscriptions or as gleaned from secular literature indicate the embedded consciousness that early India exhibited with regards to various components of procedural law and quality of justice being delivered. From clearly stating the occasions for rise of litigation and endeavour to prevent any discrimination in procedural justice, the effort seems to be to maintain Dharma or order. Law, in other words seems to be embedded in the larger circle of intentions to sustain Dharma based order. Paradoxically, the cross currents that stemmed from vested interests marred the theoretical law but in procedure, there seems to be greater application of reason and precision based on perceptiveness of the age to which it refers. Some of these constitute finer threads of early jurisprudence in India.

NOTES AND REFERENCES

1. N.C. Sengupta, *Evolution of Ancient India Law*, p.3
2. Cf.*Brhadaranyakupunisad*, 1.4.14
3. M.M. Patkar, *Topics of Law and Listigation in the Dharmasutras*, Poona Orientalist, *vol.26* pp.65–104.
4. R.B. Pal, *History of Hindu Law*, p.55.
5. P.V. Kane, *History of Dharmashastra*, 3.57.
6. For instance, 420 verses in Manu are devoted to civil and ceremonial law, 336 verses on duties of husband and wife.
7. Ibid., *HD*, 1.213
8. M.M. Patkar, *Narada, Brhaspati and Katyayana; A Comparative Study in Judicial Procedure*, p.9.

9.   Ibid., p.14

10.   Cf.

11.   *Naradasmrti*, Eng Tr. SBE, XXXIII, p.21.

12.   Ibid., p.6, v.8

13.   J.R. Gharpure, *Yajnavalkyasmrti, Book II, p.8, v.1, 47-54.*

14.   M.M. Patkar, op.cit, introduction, p.18.

15.   Ibid., p.18
      Cf *Brhaspati smrti*, p.2, v.9

16.   Aiyangar, *Brhaspati smrti*, p.1

17.   P.V. Kane, *HD.* 1.213

18.   Ibid.

19.   Discussed later under documents.

20.   *Corpus Inscriptionum Indicarum*, Vol. XXV, Chapter VIII, v.15, p.255.

21.   Buhler, *Laws of Manu*, SBE, Vol.XXV, Chapter VIII, v.15, p.255.

22.   Ibid.

23.   L.S. Rangarajan, Kautilya, *The Arthashastra*, Part VIII, p.377.
      Similarly, *Brhadaranyaka Upanishad* says-
      Law is the king
      Nothing is superior to law
      The law aided by the power of king
      Enables the weak to prevail over the strong
      (quoted in *Legal and Constitutional History of India, Ancient Legal, Judicial and Constitiutional System* by Justice M Rama Jois, p-10)

24.   J.R. Gharpure, *Yajnavalkyasmrti*, Part II, Ch.1, v.360.
      The protection of the subjects is the highest duty of a king possessing the necessary qualification of anointment. That (i.e., the protection), however, is not possible without (restraining the wicked) punishing the guilty.

25.   Buhler, *Laws of Manu*, Ch.VII, v.16, p.218.

26.   J.R. Gharpure, op.cit, Part II, Ch.1, v.360, p.1.

27.   Buhler, *Laws of Manu*, Ch.VIII, v.24, p.256 "Knowing, what is expedient or inexpedient, what is pure justice or injustice, let him examine the causes of suitors to be order of the castes (varnas)."

28.   L.N.Rangarajan, Kautilya, *the Arthashastra*, (3. 1. 38), p.377

29.   Ibid., (3.1, 45), p.380

30.   Buhler, *LOM*, ch.VII, III.

31.   Jolly, *Naradasmrti*, *SBE*, Vol.XVIII, 33.

32. Kalidasa, *Raghuvamsa*, 14.67, VK, PP, III.323, 35–26, Kamandaka. *Nitisara*, 1.12, *Markandeya Purana*, 130,33–34.
33. D.C. Sircar, *Select Inscriptions*, p.375.
34. *CII*, III, No.35, ii.15017, p.157.
35. Ibid., No.47, p.220.
36. Ibid., No.52, p.232.
37. B.S. Upadhyaya, *India in Kalidasa*, p.143.
38. Kalidasa, *Raghuvamsa*, 1.6.
39. *Raghuvamsa*, 1.9 quoted by Upadhyaya, p.144.
40. *Upadhyaya, op.cit, p.144.*
41. Mahabharata, *Shanti-parva IIX, 107; Kumbakonam, LVIII, 116, quoted from Upadhyaya, op.cit, p.144.*
42. Benjamin Khan, *The Concept of Dharma in Valmiki Ramayana*, Quoted from Ayodhyakanda, 46–23, 30, 3707,8)
43. *Ramayana*, *Yuddha Kanda*, 12–30.
44. B.S. Upadhyaya, *India in Kalidasa*, p.146.
45. Proceedings of the Indian History Congress, 1959, p.130.
46. A.C. Sen, *Ashokan Inscription*, referring, to RE.406.13 SKRE 1, PE.7, p.35.
47. Ibid., referring to SKRE 1, PE.4.
48. A.C. Sen, op. cit, p.37.
49. Ibid., referring, P.E.4.
50. Regnal Year B.C. 256 B.C.
51. A.C. Sen, op. cit, English Translation, p.119.
52. Ibid., word-notes, p.121.
53. The inscription actually speaks about the great Maurya Emperors, Chandragupta and Ashoka's interest in irrigation works in so far a country from the capital, as Kathiawad.
54. D.B. Diskalkar, *Select Sanskrit Inscriptions*, p.14.
55. Buhler, *Laws of Manu*, SBE, Vol.XXV, Ch.VIII, v.2, p.253, describes that after the king enters the court, "there, either seated or standing, raising his right arm, without ostentation in his dress and ornaments, let him examine the business of suitors".
56. Diskalkar, op.cit., p.14.
57. Buhler, *Laws of Manu*, SBE, Vol.XXV, Ch.VIII, v.3, p.253.
58. J. Jolly, *Naradasmrti*, SBE, v.34, p.15.
59. Buhler, *LOM*, Ch.VIII, v.46, p.262.
60. Ibid., v.41, p.260.

61. B.S. Upadhyaya, *India in Kalidasa*, p.143.

62. Buhler, *LOM*, Ch I viii, v.27, p.257.

63. Ibid., v.28, p.257. However, this appears inconsistent with its verse that tells the years in which the brave women, the sonless women, and women bearing daughters should be abandoned.

64. Buhler, *Laws of Manu*, Ch.VIII, v.29, p.258.

65. B.S. Upadhyaya, op. cit, p.145
     Raghuvamsa, XIV.24.

66. Kalidasa, *Raghuvamsa*, XVI.39/VIII.18

67. Upadhyaya, ibid.

68. G.P. Sinha, *Post- Gupta Polity* (AD 500–750), p.175.

69. P.V. Kane, *Katyayanasmrti*, v.61–62, p.129.

70. Kane, *Katyayanasmrti*, v.56.

71. Ibid. v.14

72. Ibid. v.20

73. Ibid. v.21(2)

74. Buhler *LOM,* Ch.VII. v.16, p.218.

75. Buhler *LOM,*VIII v.43

76. Cf *Smrtichandrika*

77. Cf Naradasmrti, quoted in *Smrtichandrika*, II, p.27.

78. P.V. Kane, *Katyayana on Vyavahara*, v.27.

79. Buhler, LOM, Ch.VIII, v.65, p.265.

80. Ibid., Ch.VIII, v.43, p.260–261.
     Katyayana states that the king either because of the person from litigant parties or through greed for wealth should never cause to be started a case among men who have not dispute.
     Kane, *Katyayanasmrti*, v.27, p.3.

81. P.V. Kane, *Katyayanasmrti*, v.78, p.131.

82. EI. Vol.XXX, p.170.

83. Buhler, *Laws of Manu*, Ch.VIII, v.9.
     v.1o Says that (man) shall enter that most excellent court accompanied by three assessors and fully consider (all) cases before the (king) either sitting down or standing.

84. Ibid., Ch.VIII, v.20.

85. L.N. Rangarajan, Kautilya, The *Arthashastra*, (3.1.1.)

86. Vishnusmrti, Ch.V, v.194, p.42.

87. P.V. Kane, *Katyayanasmrti, v.63, p.11*

88. Aiyangar, *Brhaspatismrti*, v.69, p.11.
89. Ibid., *Katyayanasmrti*, v.69, p.130.
90. *Smrtichandrika,* on Narada II, p.14.
91. *P.V. Kane, Katyayanasmrti*, v.56, 129.
92. Buhler, *Laws of Manu*, Ch.VIII, v.18, p.255.
93. *Vishnusmrti*, ch.V, v.195, p.42.
94. *Yajnavalkyasmrti*, Ch.II, v.4.
95. *Katyayana smrti*, v.70.
96. *Ibid., v.72-78.*
97. *A.C. Sen*, Ashokan Inscriptions, Separate Kalinga Rock Edict (SKRE)-1, 256-B.C., p.108.115.
98. R.G. Basak, p.150–153.
99. R.G. Basak, p.150-152.
100. Buhler, *Laws of Manu.*
101. *Malavikagnimitra*, p.219, ibid., p.198.
102 Ibid
103. *Malavikagnimitra*, p.178.
104. *Vikramorvashi*, p.124
     Likewise in *Shakuntala*, V
105. *Mrcchakatika*, IX, p.454.
106. Ibid., p.459.
107. P.V.Kane, *History of Dharmashastra*, 3.92.
108 K.P. Jayaswal, *Hindu Polity*, pt.1, p.11.
109. Cf. *Yajnavalkya* 2.2
110. CII, III, pp.248.49
111. Radhakumud Mukherjee, *The Gupta Empire*, p.48.
112 E.I. Vol.XXXIV, ed by D.C. Sircar, pp.170–71.
113. CII. Vol.III, p.95.
114. Ibid.
115. A.R. ASI, 1911–12, p.54.
116. *Epigraphia Indica*, Vol.XX, p.32.
117 *Indian Historical Quarterly*, vol.XII, pp.225
118. CII, Vol.III (Revised), p.98.
119. E.I. XI, No.5, p.83.
120. Ibid., p.99.
121. I.A. XV, p.187.
122. E.I. Vol.XXX, p.169.

123. Ibid.
124. Ibid., P.174.
125. Monier Williams, *Sanskrit English Dictionary*, p.686.
126. *Dashakumaracarita*, VIII, p.131.
127. *E.I. I, No.13 pp.88–92.*
128. G.P. Sinha, *Post Gupta, Polity* (AD 500–750), p.192.
129. R.C. Majumdar, H.B.1, pp.285–86
130. Buhler, *Laws of Manu*, IX.234.
131. Brhaspati, 1.12
132. P.V. Kane, *Katyayanasmrti, 69.*
133. D.C. Sircar, *Indian Epigraphy*, p.361.
134. G.P. Sinha, *Post Gupta Polity*, p.173 quoted from proceedings of I.H.C, 1959, p.130.
135. Ibid., p.174.
136. Yajnavalkya 11.7
137. Katyayana, 40, 79.
138. Ibid., 72–78
139. Ibid., v.78
140. Ibid., v.79
141. Ibid., v.81
142. N.V. Law, *Studies in Ancient Hindu Polity*, Vol 1, p.117–18.
143. Ibid., p.119
144. Ibid.
145. Ibid., p.120.
146. Buhler, *Laws of Manu*, Ch.VIII, v.11.
147. Aiyangar, *Brhaspati*, 1, 28.30.
148. Cf, Naradasmrti, p.6, v.7
149. Mayne, *Hindu law and Usage*, 11th edition, p.13.
150. *Brhaspati*, p.16, vv.93–94.
151. cf, Br,p.15, v.92
152. *Brhaspati*, I.25–28
153 *C11*, III, pp.248–49
154. *Narada, 1–34*
155. *S.K. Aiyangar, Hindu Administrative Institution in South India*, p.203.
156. *C. Munakshi, Administration & Social Life under Pallavas, p.59.*
157. D.C. Sircar, *Select Inscriptions*
158. P.V. Kane, *Katyayanasmrti*, v.25, p.122.

159. Ibid., v.26, p.122
160. Kane, *Katyayanasmrti*, v.31, p.123
161. Buhler, *Laws of Manu*, Ch.VIII, v.1.
162 Ibid., v.13, p.254.
163 *Epigrphia Indica*, Vol.XXX, No.30 Charter of Vishnusena p.171.
164. EI. Vol.XXX, p.172.
165. Ibid., achara, 22.
166. EI.Vol.XXX, p.172.
167. Ibid
168 Ibid., p.174.
169. EI.Vol.XXX, p.174.
170 *Katyayana*, v.97, 98.
171. *Kane*, Katyayana, *v.86–88, p.132.33.*
172. Ibid., v.136–138, p.142, 143.
173. Ibid., v.142, p.145.
174. *Katyayana*, v.132, p.141.
175. Ibid. v.148, p.145.
176. Ibid. v.165, p.147.
177. Ibid. v.188, p.152.
178. *Naradasmrti*, v.33, p.31.
179. *Katyayanasmrti*, v.213, p.158
180. *Brhaspati*, vi18, p.4
181. Buhler, *Laws of Manu*, IX, v.233
182. *Katyayana*, v.221, p.31.
183. *Katyayana*, v.253, p.34.
184. *Naradasmrti*, v.136, p.86.
185. *Naradasmrti*, v.146, p.90.
186. *Epigraphia Indica*, Vol.I, p.67.
187. M.M. Patkar, *Narada, Brhaspati and Katyayana*, p.77.
188. Vishnu VII, v.1, 2.
189. Ibid., VII, v.13.
190. Katyayana, v.254, p.166.
191 Ibid., v.256, p.166.
192. Buhler, *Laws of Manu*, v.62.
193. Buhler, *Laws of Manu*, Ch.VIII, v.65–67.
194. Ibid., v.68.
195. *Manu*, Ibid., v.70, 71.

196. Ibid., v.72.
197. Ibid., v.89.
198. Rangarajan, *Kautilya Arthashastra*, VIII, p.386.
199. Ibid., (3.11.29.33), p.93.
200. Gharpure, *Yajnavalkyasmrti*, v.68–69, p.103.
201. Ibid., p.121.
202. Gharpure, *Narada* in Ch.I, 150, p.103.
203. *Naradasmrti*, v.155, p.93.
204. Ibid., v.191, p.101.
205. Kane, *Katyayana smrti*, V.351, p.184.
206. *Narada*.1, 154.
207. *Manu*, VIII, v.73, *Brhaspati*, VII, 35, *Katyayana*, 408.
208. *Manu*, VIII, v.60, *Narada*, I.153.
209. Brhaspati, VII.
210. *Manu*, VIII, 77, *Brhaspati*, VII, 18.
211. E.I. Vol.XXX, p.172.
212. S.G. Moghe, *A Peep at Indology – He tells in the Tantara Dharmasastra*, B 7–8.
213. P.V. Kane, *History of Dharmashastra*, Vol.III, p.330.
214. S.G. Moghe, *A Peep at Indology*, p.20.
215. Ibid
216. Ibid., p.21
217. Katyayana, v.317, p.176
218. Ibid., v.313.
219. Narada, v.77, p.66
220. Katyayana, v.330, p.180
221. Buhler, Laws of Manu, v.
222. M.M. Patkar, *Narada, Brhaspati and Katyayana, A Comparative Study in Judicial Procedure.*
223. P.V. Kane, *History of Dharmashastra*, 3.259.
224. Buhler, *Laws of Manu*, Ch.VIII, v.3, p.253.
225. Ibid., v.4–7, p.25.3.

Chapter IV

Civil Law and Society
A Comparative Perspective on Norms and Practice

Any sustainable society can be based on stable economic and legal relations. It is the body of civil and criminal laws that lays the foundation of the kind of society that is aspired for. The ideals of the smrti writers in India with respect to civil laws were lofty but not altogether divorced from the practicality of the times they represented. In the earliest past, it was thought that in the Golden Age, men were impersonations of righteousness (Dharma), and there hardly existed any disputes. However, this is belied by the fact that no matter how far we go back in our history, personal liberty and duties have coexisted, and the clash between individual rights and social obligations always existed. They not only gave rise to disputes but thereby also necessitated such enunciations, which could govern the men in their social, economic, and legal relations in a civilised society.

Ancient Hindu jurisprudence, in earliest Dharmashastra as Manu's did not recognise a clear-cut demarcation between the civil and the criminal laws. There were no technical terms to describe or distinguish them as such. However, Narada and Brhaspati seem to be aware of this distinction. Brhaspati further distinguished two types of lawsuits: those originating in wealth and those in violence. Nonetheless, the body of Hindu laws, as deduced from the Smrtis, is fairly complete on contracts, debts, deposits, pledges, sale, mortgages, immovable property, etc. These constituted the mass of civil laws that supposedly were adopted and administered at various levels of providing justice. Of the 18 titles under substantive law treated by Dharmashastra authors, 14 fall within the category of civil laws.

The 14 topics arising out of disputes are listed as moneylending, deposits, invalid gifts, concerns of partnership, non payment of wages, disobedience of contracts, boundary disputes, sale without ownership, revocation of sale and purchase, breach of agreements, law between husband and wife, theft, inheritance and dice gambling.

The legal history presupposes this body of laws to be evolutionary and organic having grown over a long period of time and not without adjusting itself to different milieus. The law of usage *(charitra)* was incorporated to the extent that it was not contradicting Dharma laws. In this context, one may remind oneself of the understanding of Valmiki about human nature and social wants as reflected in the Ramayana. He advocated that Karma, Artha, and Dharma are not eternal, absolute, and immutable values but relative to time and place.[1] Rama, the incarnate of Dharma, had to undergo several trialsome moral situations, and every situation required a unique and special adaptation.

Among the inscriptions, there are some scattered references about debts or inheritance. But it is surprising that we have not come across any charters or private document telling about the civil laws as such. In such a situation, it may be inferred that the Smrtis themselves served as the code of regulations for governing and administering civil law in the courts. Nonetheless, there are some references in the plays of Kalidasa that help us in understanding the application of these civil laws in reality.

Debts

Law of debt is the first topic, which has been treated by the smrtis as part of the judicial procedure. In early times, it seems that the creditor could recover debt without even taking recourse to law. It was more of a moral responsibility rather than a legal liability. Manu has treated debt more as a plea to moral obligation than as a matter of law. The later Smrti writers, however, are more elaborate on the matters pertaining to debt. They cover aspects like who could be or could not be made responsible for the debts contracted, how they could be recovered or those debts which debts were irrecoverable.

According to Manu, when a creditor sues (before the King) for the recovery of money from a debtor, let him make the debtor pay the sum, which the creditor proves (to be due).[2] This shows that lawsuits pertaining to debts could be brought to the King's notice though not necessarily. It was necessary for the creditor to prove the sum in order to sue the debtor. Manu recognises five modes of recovery of debt: "By moral suasion, by suit of law, by artful management or by the customary proceeding, a creditor may recover property lent; and fifthly by force."[3] This implied that besides litigation, persuasion, fraudulent means, and customary proceedings, even force could be resorted to recover property. The sanction to use force shows that in order to recover debts, private means could be resorted to rather than relying only on litigation. Manu permits force even in possession. In V.168, he says, "What is given by force, what is enjoyed by force, what has been caused to be written by force and all other transactions done by force, Manu has declared void."

However, about the validity of contracts, he says "that agreement which has been made contrary to the law or to the settled usages (of the virtuous), can have no legal force, though it be established by for."[4] Hence, it appears that, in order to be valid, a contract was needed to be in consonance with the settled usages—that is, practice adopted by the wise. It did not matter if it was contracted by force.

Kautilya, earlier to Manu, has spelled the law of debts more explicitly. He says debts mutually contracted between the following are not recoverable in law:

- A husband and a wife
- A father and a son
- Brothers in a joint family[5]

A wife shall not be sued for a debt incurred by her husband if she had not agreed to the borrowing (this rule does not apply to the herdsmen families or farmers leasing land jointly). However, a husband shall be responsible for the debts incurred by his wife if he has gone away without providing for her.

The Arthashastra further tells in case a debtor dies, the responsibility for repayment with accrued interest shall devolve upon sons, heirs inheriting the property of the deceased, cosignatories, and sureties (3.11, 14, 17 and 18).[6]

The topic of recovery of debts, according to Yajnavalkya, has these points: the kind of debt that should be paid, by what person should be paid, at what particular time to be paid, and in what way to be paid – in all, four points for the debtor, and for the creditor, concern such as, viz – the mode of advancing a loan as also the mode of recovering it.[7] Similarly, Narada has made clear about which debt must be paid and which may not be paid, and the rules of advancing and recovering of (loans) are said to make up the (title) of recovery of debts.

In Yajnavalkya's enunciation, we get a glimpse first of the varna based distinction when (in v.43) he says, 'An insolvent debtor of a lower class should be made to work for his debt, a Brahmana insolvent, however, should be made to pay by installments according to his ability" – second, we get the principle of shared responsibility of the joint family and of the wife, where the contract was done by her consent (verse 49). Yajnavalkya tells, "A debt agreed to by her, or which was contracted by her jointly with the husband or by herself (alone) should be paid by a woman. A woman is not bound to pay any other debt." This implied that in any contract that took place without her consent, a woman was not to be held responsible to pay the debt. Here, Vishnu enuniciates that a woman (shall)

1) Not (be compelled to pay) the debt of her husband or son (V.31)
2) Nor the husband or son (to pay) the debt of a woman (who is his wife or mother) (V.32)
3) Nor a father to pay the debt of the son (V.33)
4) A debt contracted by parceners shall be paid by any one of them who is present (V.34)
5) And so shall the debt of the father (be paid) by any one of them who is present (V.35)
6) After partition, they shall severally pay according to their shares of the inheritance (V.36)
7) Where husband is supported by wife, Vishnu tells a debt contracted by the wife of a herdsman, distiller of spirits, public dancer, washer, or a hunter shall be discharged by her husband (for she supports him) (V.37)
8) A debt of which payment has been (previously) promised must be paid by the householder

Hence, Vishnu tells that neither woman is responsible (compulsorily) for a debt by husband nor a husband or son for a debt by wife or mother. Even the father is not responsible for a debt byson. Only he who is present, is responsible for his father's debt. What is interesting is where woman is an independent earner or supporting the husband, the husband is liable for a debt incurred by her.

Yajnavalkya states (V.117(1)) the sons should divide equally both the assets and the debts of the parents after them (in equal shares only).

He provides that if the father has gone abroad, is dead, or immersed in difficulties, his debt should be paid by sons and grandsons, when established by witness in case of dispute.[8] For the same situation when father is dead, Narada (Ch. 1, 2) propounds that the sons should pay the debt each according to his share, when they are divided or if undivided by one who holds the lead (in the family).[9]

Brhaspati, however, is explicit in transferring the responsibility of father's debt on the sons. He says, "The debt of the father which has been proved, should be paid by the sons as if it were their own (debt), the grandfather's debt should be paid in an even amount, his (i.e., grandsons) son, however is not liable to pay any debt." Brhaspati, hence, relieves the fourth generation from incurring any liability to pay debts of his ancestors.[10] Katyayana endorses that in the absence or death of the son, grandson should pay the debt but he too relieves the fourth generation from this duty.

Brhaspati states a practical maxim that a creditor should not give loan without securing a pledge of adequate value or trustworthy surety. Likewise, unless the debtor executes a bond duly attested by subscribing witness, loan should not be advanced.[11]

Katyayana states that "one should prove a debt by means of these in order, viz, urging the debtor (to pay) on each occasion, putting forward some argument and third being oaths.[12] If the debtor being repeatedly urged does not refute, it amounts to the acceptance of creditor's plea, and then he must pay the debt. If the creditor tries to remind the debtor of the details—time, place, amount, and so on—and the latter denies, Katyayana permits the application of ordeals such as fire, water, righteousness, etc., commensurate with the amount of debt and capacity of the defendant.

Brhaspati is most juristical in stating the rules of procedure regarding debt. He states that when time fixed for repayment lapses, the amount of debt becomes due. In such a case, the creditor has two options: either to recover the loan or execute a fresh bond for the debt as well as interest. If the debtor denies the liability, lawsuit could be filed with the support of documents and witnesses.

INTEREST

The Smrtis provide detailed rules on the rate of interest, kind of interest, cessation of interest, exemption from interest, and so on. There is a distinction between lawful interest and one that is not lawfully permissible.

According to Manu, 'a money lender may stipulate as an increase of his capital, for the interest allowed by Vasistha, and take monthly the eightieth part of a hundred'.[13] Remembering the duty of goodman, he may take two in a hundred (by the month), for he who takes two in the hundred becomes not a sinner for gain.[14] But if a beneficial pledge (i.e., one from which profit accrues has been given), he shall not receive interest on the loan or keep such a pledge for a long time, give, or sell it.[15] Also, "in money transaction, interest paid at one time (not in installment) shall never exceed the double (of the principal) on grain, fruit, wool, or hair (and) beasts of burden. It must not be more than five times (the original amount)."[16]

Yajnavalkya allowed the rate of interest to vary to two, three, four, or five per hundred according to the order of the caste of the debtor.[17]

It was generally acceptable among the Smrti writers that interest should not exceed the principal at any time. Narada allows the rules to vary according to the usage of the country (v.105, p.76). Brhaspati is more specific and lays down that on gold, the interest may be double its value, triple on clothes and base metals, and fourfold on grain and edible plants, beasts of burden and wool, on potherb, it can be quintuple, on salt, oil and intoxicating drinks, octuple, so also on honey is the loan long standing.[18] Katyayana too more or less takes the line of Brhaspati.

The Smrti writers have dealt with the topic of interest in details. About the kinds of interest, they generally stipulate four types of interests:

(a) *Kalika* or periodical interest
(b) Karita *or stipulated interest*
(c) *Cakravrddhi* or compound interest
(d) *Kayika* or bodily interestin the form of manual labour[19]

Katyayana and Brhaspati added two more types to the list: *Shikhavrddhi*, or hair interest, and bhogavrddhi, or interest as enjoyment. The first type of interest is so-called because it is recovered from time *(kal)* to time (kal); hence, it is periodical *(Kalika)*. When the interest has been agreed or stipulated to be paid at a certain rate, it is called stipulated interest *(Karita)*. *Kaika* interest, which implies bodily labour, includes in its fold the labour of cattle and the products pledged from it. Where interest is recovered upon interest monthly, it implies compound interest. *Shikhavrddhi* is so named as it is an interest that grows like hair and would cease only on chopping the head, i.e., on repayment of debt. *Bhogavrddhi* is interest in the form of enjoyment gained on the pledged property of the debtor.

These interests, especially hair, bodily, or enjoyment interest, could be accepted by the creditor so long as the principal was unpaid. Brhaspati especially enunciates that the use of pledge post the realisation of double the principal amount, compound interest, and the recovery of the principal and the interest as principal amounts to usury is condemned.[20]

The Smrti writers have demarcated certain cases when interest on debt should be let gone and not be recovered. Narada provides that "the price of a commodity, wages, a deposit, a fine that was fixed, a gift without consideration and a stake at dice do not bear any interest.[21] Likewise, Katyayana would exempt interest on hides, crops, distilled liquor, gambling, debts, price of commodities, and on a woman's *sulka*". Also, any debt under surety or liability is exempted from the range of interest. Katyayana provides for articles borrowed and not returned within a certain period. An interesting verse of Katyayana tells that "on a loan taken from a friend, interest, should not be recovered as long as it is not demanded, but when demanded and not paid, the interest rate would be five percent."[22]

The Charter of Vishnusena, in achara 23, talks of debts (*rnadana*). It says,

Rin - adan – abhilekhita – vyavahare–– kashtha –
Loha – baddhena krita – pratibhuvena (bhuva) guptir – upasya

It implies that in case of written complaint about the realisation of borrowed money, the debtor, when he was not under wooden or metal handcuffs, because of security having been furnished for him by somebody, should enjoy the protection of the court. It would infer probably that, in the case of a debtor for whom security had been furnished, neither handcuffs nor guards at court were necessary.[23] When no *pratibhu* (surety) was furnished, the court had to arrange for the person's security and the cost was to be borne by the parties. A similar provision has been stated by Katyayana (quoted in Yajnavalkyasmrti, p. 126, N. Sagar Press Edition) which means the same. –implies a similar cause.

atha chet pratibhur = n = astikarya = yogyas = tu vadinah
/ sa rakshito dinasya = ante dadyad = bhritgaya vetanam.[24]

PLEDGE (*Niksepa or Upanidhi*)

Manu and nearly all the Smrti writers have talked about pledge. It is called *adhi* by Narada and *bandhaka* by Brhaspati and is distinguished from deposits that form a separate title of law. Manu declared that neither a pledge nor a deposit can be lost by lapse of time. They are both recoverable, though they have remained long (with the bailee).[25] According to Narada, a pledge is something that is mortgaged to the creditor as a security against loan received whereas a deposit means a man's entertaining of his property with another person in confidence and without suspicion.[26] The differentiations between these aspects in civil law are indicative that there was a consciousness and sensitiveness to various kinds of sureties and pledges. It additionally highlights that individual property could not just be appropriated or confiscated without a procedure. There is an effort to see that he creditor too was not at unknown risk.

A pledge brings in its fold a title for the creditor over the thing pledged, but in a deposit, there is no legal title that accompanies. Pledge has been treated as a subtopic by the Smrti writers, treating debt a topic.

Narada has divided pledges into two main types: (a) one that is to be redeemed within a period and (b) another that is to be retained till the debt is cleared. These two are further divided into *gopya* (to be kept) and *bhogya* (to be enjoyed) categories (V.124–125). Brhaspati, who names pledge as bandhaka, distinguishes its four types: (a) movable or immovable (b) to be kept or used, (c) to be released at any time or limited as to time, (d) stated in writing or orally in the presence of witnesses.[27] Katyayana tells of pledge effected by documents and through witnesses and consider those in writing as superior to those effected in the presence of witnesses.[28]

Manu talks about the creditor's liability and says a fool who uses a pledge without the permission of the owner shall remit half of his interest as a compensation for (such) use.[29] Likewise, he opines, a pledge (to be kept only) must not be used by force (the creditor), so using it shall give up his (whole) interest, or (if has been spoilt by use) he shall satisfy the (owner) by (paying its) original price; else, he commits a theft of the pledge. Narada too talks of these safeguards against misuse by the creditors. He tells that in case of loss of the pledge by the creditor, the principal is forfeited unless the loss was due to an act of God or King.[30] Brhaspati opines that in case of lost pledge due to some calamity, the debtor should either provide another pledge or pay the debt (along with interest, adds Katyayana).[31]

On the other hand, it is also the duty of the debtor to ensure that the article pledged is in good condition and capable of being returned. If during the stipulated period the value of the pledge declines despite adequate care by creditor, the debtor should either replace it or pay the debts off.[32]

Simultaneous mortgages, in which is a person pledging the same property to two or more creditors was decried and punishable (as a theft).[33] The Smrti writers accepted that if two or more persons possess the mortgaged property for an equal period of time, it is to be held in common and to be shared proportionately. But Katyayana states that if one was effected by document and other in the presence of witness, one effected by means of document was superior.

Rules regarding the redemption of pledge have been dealt by the Hindu jurists. The general rule seems to be that on the payment of the debts, i.e., principal along with interest thereon the creditor should restore the pledge to the debtor or else invite punishment. Brhaspati states that in case of field or other immovable property, the debtor could redeem the pledge after the creditor had enjoyed it or received more than double the principal and conditions were expressly stated. A pledge would not be redeemed by the debtor by force or deceit (whereas Manu permits force for obtaining the debt).

When, however, on expiry of the period of pledge, the debtor is required to redeem it by satisfying the creditor's debt and he is unable to do so, the creditor can become the owner of the pledge. Brhaspati permits a period of ten days to the debtor to enable him to redeem the pledge.[34] Brhaspati also states that in case of gold, when interest on it doubles the principal and where a pledge is deposited for a certain fixed period, the creditor becomes the owner of the pledge after having waited for a fortnight if the debtor does not redeem the pledge within the period of grace.[35]

SURETY

The law of debt entails that when a person borrows money from another, he has to nominate someone who could assure the creditor that the amount advanced by him to the debtor would be safely returned in case the debtor fails to do so. The Smrti writers have dwelled on kinds of sureties—their liability and their competence.

Hindu lawgivers recognised two to five kinds of sureties. Manu has mentioned two kinds of sureties: (1) Surety for appearance (before the court) and (2) surety for payment of debt. Narada has added one for honesty.[36]

A surety of appearance used to be given by the plaintiff and the defendant, assuring the court that he would produce before the court the person concerned whenever required and that the court decree would be carried out. If none of the parties supply surety for appearance, the party unable to offer a surety is to be kept in the custody of a court official called *sadhyapala*. A surety for payment called the *danapratibhu* could get the repayment of debt in case the debtor failed to pay it. Likewise, a surety for honesty vouched for the reliability of the debtor. Vishnu spoke of the three kinds, as mentioned by Narada. Katyayana mentions surety for oaths and ordeals too, making it of five kinds.

Surety generally implies that if the debtor failed to repay the debt, it was to be paid by the surety. However, surety of appearance was responsible for the presence of the party at the appointed time and place. Certain time period was also granted (three fortnights) to produce the debtor, or the liability was of the surety. The Smrti writers allowed the surety to recover from the debtor whatever was paid by it to the creditor. He should not be harassed by the creditor, and if he is, then he could recover twice the amount paid by him from the creditor.

Narada prohibited the coparceners from acting as sureties. Katyayana entails a longer list of those who could not be accepted as sureties, such as a master, an enemy, one representing the master, one under restraints, a convict, one who is of suspicious character, an heir, a friend, a resident student, one on king's mission, an ascetic are incapable of paying debt or find to the king, one whose father is living and one whose attendants are not known (V.114–116).

DEPOSITS

To the Hindu jurists, a deposit (*Upanidhi*) was not just a legal responsibility but a moral obligation too. Brhaspati extols the religious merit of a person who preserves a deposit as equal to the merit of one who gives gold, base metals, or clothes and the sin of one who consumes or spoils the articles deposited as great as that of a *mahapatakin*.[37]

Manu talks about the sensibility of making deposits. His verse (179) tells a sensible man should make a deposit with a person of (good) family, of good conduct, well acquainted with the law, veracious, having many relatives, wealthy and honorable (arya). The deposit was to be returned in the same manner as it was received. Manu prescribes that "he who restores not his deposit to the depositor at his request may be tried by the judge in the depositor's absence".[38] He further details the rules regarding open or sealed deposits and goes on to enunciate the punishments for not restoring deposit.

Manusmrti says "(a deposit) which has been stolen by thieves or washed away by water or burned by fire, (the bailee) shall not make it good unless he took part of it (for himself)".[39] Those who appropriate a deposit or those who falsely ask for it without having made a deposit are liable to be brought to court and should be punished like thieves. For a man who possesses himself of another's property, Manusmrti prescribes punishment by various (modes of) corporal (or capital) chastisement, together with the accomplices.[40]

Yajnavalkya defines a deposit as an article enclosed in a box or like made with another without telling him of the contents of the box.[41] According to Narada, when a person entrusts a property of his own with another in confidence and without suspicion, it is called *Upanidhi* or deposit.[42] Brhaspati speaks of *mudrankita*, or sealed deposit, and *nyasa* deposit, the latter implying that when a thing deposited in the house of another person, through fear of the king, robberies, or other dangers or for the purpose of deceiving the heirs. A *niksepa*, according to Katyayana (V.592), implies a deposit entrusted to a man in his presence after counting before him coins.

Different kinds of deposits have been spoken about by the Smrti writers like an article that is sold a deposit made when one goes on a journey, a pledge, a bailment to one for delivery to another at an appropriate time (*anvahita*), a loan of ornaments or clothes, or a thing for sale.[43] Katyayana too says like Manu and others that a deposit should be preserved, and if it is lost due to his fault (not the fault of fate or king), then he should be made to pay the thing along with interest.[44] Also, he who, having taken the loan of an article, does not deliver it on demand should be restrained and forcibly be made to return and fined if he does not return.[45]

Katyayana has spoken of especially a deposit made with an artisan or craftsman (*silpinyasa*). He says if an article was retained by an artisan beyond the stipulated days in which it was agreed to be worked up, he should be made to pay the price even if lost by fate.[46] However, the artisan shall not be responsible for loss of an article due to defects in it. If the article is lost after working little on it, then the artisan loses wages on it; but when an artisan delivers a good after it is finished, the loss belongs to the owner.

SALE WITHOUT OWNERSHIP (*asvamivikraya*)

Sale without ownership was considered by the Hindu jurists a serious offence comparable to theft. Selling an article without being its owner gave rise to litigation between the owner of the article and the purchaser. The term has not been defined as such, but nearly all the Smrti writers have expounded on it. Manusmrti opines, "If anybody sells the property of another man, without being the owner and without the assent of the owner, the (judge) shall not admit him, who is a thief, though he may not consider himself a thief as a witness."[47] Manu forbids such a person from being a witness in any case. He says, "If the (offender) is a kinsman (of the owner), he shall be fined 600 panas, if he is not kinsman, nor has any excuse, he shall be guilty of theft."[48] Any such gift or sale is to be considered null and void. Title is considered a greater proof of ownership as Manu says, "Where possession is evident, but no title is perceived, there the title (shall be) a proof (of ownership), not possession, such is the settled case.[49]

Narada mentions that when a thing deposited or the property of a stranger lost and found by another person or stolen property is sold in secret, it is considered a sale by one who is not the owner.[50] Katyayana too candidly declared that a sale, gift, or pledge made without ownership should be rescinded.[51] He further states that the purchase should establish his purchase to be overt by (the testimony of) his own kinsmen who are respectable. In this case, no other means of proof, whether human or divine, were proper.[52] He too considers a man who fails to prove his ownership be punished like a thief. But once the party (the purchaser) proves his property as overt and legal, with the help of kinsman, he should not be blamed by the king.

Katyayana forbids being careless about preservation of one's good or purchasing from a man whose habitation was unknown. He considers both these reasons as the cause to loss of property.

PARTNERSHIP

Talking on laws concerning the partners, Manu gives two rules with regard to the contract of marriage. First "if, after one damsel has been shown, another be given to the bridegroom, he may marry them both for the same price that Manu ordained."[53] Secondly, he who gives (a damsel in marriage) having first openly declared her blemishes, whether, she be insane or afflicted with leprosy, or have lost her virginity, is not liable to punishment. The first case is one of cheating—hence, the permission to take two brides for a single bride price— while in the latter since the blemish is first confessed, no punishment was called for such a person. The next few verses in Manu talk about partnership applicable to performance of rites where several priests jointly officiate. The rule for shares in such partnership was enunciated by Manu—thus, the (four) chief priests among all (the sixteen) who are entitled to one-half, shall receive a moiety (of the fee) the next (four) one-half of that, the set entitled to a third share, one-third and those entitled to a fourth, a quarter. Hence, allotment of share was according to these rules.

Narada, however, defines partnership as the conduct of business by traders or others jointly. Katyayana expanded the term to include business of the artisans and of unseparated brothers. Kautilya's Arthashastra systematically treats reference to (a) contract between traders or cultivators and (b) the shares of priests officiating a sacrifice.

The Arthashastra tells that those who engage in work like traders and cultivators shall apportion among themselves the profits after the performance of work in hand and before entering a fresh one. The work, if performed by a substitute, does not abate the share of profit due to a partner. Any losses sustained in transmission had to be borne by the partners equally. It tells abandoning the partnership halfway shall be a punishable offence.[54] If he is in good health and abandons work, he shall be fined twelve panas. Further, a partner who was suspected of embezzlement shall be caught (made to confess) by promising him forgiveness and a continuing share in the partnership. If it is the first occasion, he should be pardoned; if it is the second occasion, he shall be thrown out of partnership. And if he commits a serious offence, he shall be treated as traitor and ostracised. As for the concelebrating priests, the text tells that a priest abandoning a ritual or its principal organiser halfway is punishable.[55]

Brhaspati and Katyayana have applied the laws of partnership to artisans when a pillaging party brings booty from an enemy king. At the command of the king, the artisans share profit in the proportion of one, two, three, or four shares according to their grades. Likewise, he spells the shares for a dancing party as well.

It was quite understood that the partners had shares in profit as well as loss according to their contribution. If a partner causes some loss due to negligence or without authorisation, he was individually responsible for the loss so caused.[56] But if any one partner was responsible for rescuing the property, he was entitled to a tenth part of the property rescued as reward.[57] That is to say that the liability in case of loss was high. On death, the partner's share went to his heirs; and in the absence of heirs, it reverted back to the surviving partners.

Rules on partnership, overall, are meagre in the Smrti texts. This may imply that business by mode of partnership was not much in vogue. It contains a few provisions regarding tolls. Tolls—that is, the duty that a trader was supposed to pay to the king—was not to be evaded. Taxes were imposed on goods and merchandise and not on articles of home use. If, however, the evasion occurred, the trader had to pay eight times the amount of toll due as punishment.

RESUMPTION OF GIFTS *(Dattapradanika)*

Gifts that are taken back after having been made come are covered this topic of law. The topic includes what may be given or not given, valid and invalid gifts, and so on. Manu discusses it as lawful subtraction of gifts. The text tells should money be given (or promised) for a pious purpose by one man to another who asks for it, the gift shall be void.[58] But in case the recipient, out of pride or greed, tries to enforce (the fulfillment of the promise), he shall be compelled by the king to pay one suvarna as an explanation for his theft.[59] Narada mentions these kinds of gifts as valid: price paid for merchandise, wages, something offered for amusement, a gift from gratitude, a nuptial price, and a gift for favour.[60] Brhaspati too mentions eight kinds of gifts, more or less on the lines of Narada. Katayana defines wages *(bhrti)* and a gift obtained through gratitude *(pratyupakara)*.

Narada forbids the following eight categories: *anvahita* deposit, a *yacitake*, a pledge, joint property, a deposit, a son or wife, the whole property of one who has offsprings, and what was promised to another person. These gifts are not alienable in times of distress.[61] Katayana differs from Narada to enunciate that in times of adversity, one may sell or gift one's wives and sons, but he should not do this otherwise.[62] Whatever belongs to oneself over and above what is required for maintaining one's family may be subject of gift except one's house or entire wealth.[63] Here too the varna distinction makes headway when Katyayana mentions that he who, having voluntarily promised a gift to a Brahmana, does not deliver it should be made to pay it as a debt and should be awarded lowest amercement. In fact, he adds a metaphysical punishment by telling that one who does not honor what is promised or takes back what is donated is born for hundreds of births in the form of lower animals.

Likewise, Brhaspati tells that property received in marriage and ancestral property cannot be given except with the consent of wife, co-heirs, kinsmen, and others. Likewise, he tells, a single co-parcener has no power of disposal by gift, sale, or mortgage over the whole of the property.

Sixteen invalid gifts have been declared by the Smrti writers. Katyayana mentions what is promised through lust or wrath or by those who are dependent (like servants or slaves), by those distressed, by those who are cowards (or are frightened), by lunatics and by those who are infatuated, or through misapprehension or joke may be taken back.

Katyayana has devoted six verses on the topic of gift offered as bribe. It has been ridiculed as the worst kind of offer. What is promised as a bribe to somebody for accomplishing a certain object need never be given, though that object is accomplished. But if the bribe was already paid, it should be returned, and a fine of eleven times as much the bribe should be levied.[64] He defines *'Utkoca'* or bribe as that which is obtained by giving information about a thief, about a fellow, about one who breaks rules of decent conduct, or about an adulterer by pointing out those who are of bad character or by spreading false reports about a person. In such cases, the person offering the bribe is not be punished or fined, but the intermediary deserves blame.[65] Likewise, Katyayana tells that if a man is appointed to do certain duties by the king and he obtains a bribe, he should be made to return the whole of the money (or bribe) and pay a fine, eleven times of it to the king. However, if a person who is unappointed receives a gratification in the nature of return for a deed, he incurs no blame.[66]

These two verses of Katyayana have been referred in Shri Sitaram versus Shri Harihar (I L.R., 35, 169, p.180) wherein it was held that if an adoption was induced by a bribe given to a widow, the bribe was an illegal payment and cannot support a sale or gift.[67]

Gifts that were prohibited hence fall into two types according to the Smrtis: (1) those that cannot be made (*adatta*) and (2) invalid gifts (*adeya*). Katyayana tells that avoidable gift could be a gift, which is promised in distress and could be revoked later.[68] Besides, if anybody had surplus wealth, he could make gifts for charitable and religious acts, and this was irrevocable. If donor died before honoring a promise of gift, his son was to fulfill the wishes." [69]

B.S. Upadhyaya has pointed to a reference in Kalidasa where there is allusion to bribe. The *Nagarika* of Shakuntala was supposedly a petty officer above the guards. These constables were stern in treating the fisherman, the supposed criminal, before the verdict of court had been passed against him. They were even threatening him with capital punishment. But they did not accept bribe to the detriment to the aims of justice. However, when the fisherman was acquitted of charges with rewards, he offered half the reward to them, which the *Nagarika* accepted. This money accepted from the fisherman could not be named as bribe as it was from the reward money, received only when the accused was acquitted. It was not accepted during the hearing of case for the sake of an end but after it. Hence, it was not really bribe but a sort of gratitude expressed out of the reward received by the accused.

NON-PAYMENT OF WAGES

According to Manusmrti, a servant or workman who, without being ill, out of pride fails to perform his work according to the agreement was to be fined eight *Krshnalas* and no wages ought to be paid to him. But if he was genuinely ill and after recovery performed the deed according to original agreement, he shall receive wages even after a long time. But if the work was not performed, whether sick or well, wages shall not be given, even if they are little incomplete. That is to say wages would be in proportion to the work.

Katyayana tells that when no wages are settled, the trader, the cowherd, and husbandman should get a tenth part of the profit of the milk and of the crops.[70] He strictly advocates imposing fine by the king on one who does not accomplish the said work. Likewise, he tells a palanquin bearer who obstructs the start of a work should be made to pay double the wages. But a servant should not be made to pay if a thing was plundered, burnt, or carried away by flood. Katyayana imposes a first amercement fine on a master who would abandon a servant tired or diseased on the road. When the goods were carried by road, the servant was to be given wages in proportion to the distance traversed.

TRANSGRESSION OF COMPACT *(Samayasyana pakarma)*

Compact means an agreement, and transgression implies a break or breach of the agreement. Compact in ancient India could imply a local caste usage, convention, or association or corporation formed by group of people for different purposes with certain rules and established usage among specified groups such as *naigamas*, guilds of merchants, or corporations. It was deemed the responsibility of the king to ensure the continuance of these usages among these groups and to honor them like customs if they were not at variance with the established custom or public interest.

Manu states the law of transgression in some of these verses, "If a man, belonging to a corporation inhabiting a village or a district, after swearing to an agreement breaks it through avarice (the king) shall banish him from the realm.[71] "Fines on such an offender was six *nishkas*, four *suvarnas* and one *satamana* of silver.[72] This was to be applied in villages and castes for all transgressors of any compact.

Yajnavalkya advises that there should be a committee of advisors on affairs of an association. Brhaspati prescribes two, three, or five such members. Narada stated that transgression of these rules formed a separate title of law.[73]

Brhaspati has dealt with these laws in detail. According to him, an association or compact could be formed with a valid purpose such as relief for poor or construction of houses, gardens, temples, and such other objects. An association should be formed in writing, and for their proper conduct, there should be heads and advisors. If any member fails to maintain the agreement, his property should be confiscated, and he should be either banished from the town or fined. Katyayana too imposes a fine on one who opposes what is reasonable.[74] The king should act as intermediary in between the heads of association and their members. Katyayana provides that he who is guilty of *sahasa* (heinous crime), who causes a split (in the group), or who destroys the wealth belonging to that group should be proclaimed to the king and destroyed (by the group).[75] Further, he tells that whatever is obtained by the advisors of the group or saved or whatever debts are incurred by them should be shared equally by them.[76]

He then names the different types of 'vargas' or groups:[77]

(a) *Naigama*—a group of several inhabitants of the same city.
(b) *Vrata*—a troupe of persons bearing various kinds of weapons.
(c) *Puga*—a group of merchants.
(d) *Pasandas*—heretics who have forsaken rules of ascetics.
(e) *Gana*—the corporation of Brahmanas.
(f) *Craftsman*—those who subsist by some craft.
(g) *Sangha*—followers of Jainism and Buddhism
(h) *Gulma*—the companies of *chandalas* (outcastes) and *svapas* (those who eat dog flesh).

Yajnavalkya (II 189–190) tells that when the principal men of group wait on the king, the latter should listen to them and send them away with honors and gifts, and whatever they obtain from king should be handed over as property of the group. This is (*rajaprasadalabha*), the benefit derived from meeting the king.

REPENTANCE AFTER SALE AND PURCHASE OR NON-DELIVERY AFTER SELLING
(Krayavikrayanusaya)

This rescission of purchase and sale has been regarded as a title of law by Narada.[78] Manu has treated it under a single topic while Narada has put it under two heads: (i) *kritanusaya*, i.e., repentance of purchase and (ii) *vikrayasampradana*, i.e., non-delivery of the thing sold.

In the contract of marriage, Manu entails that in case of one who gives a blemished damsel to a suitor without informing him (of the blemish), the king shall himself impose a fine of ninety-six panas. Also, if somebody, simply out of malice, calls that a maiden is not a maiden or accuses her of not being a virgin, he shall be fined one hundred (panas).[79] Also, Manu declares emphatically that with the seventh step (of bride around the sacred fire), the marriage ceremony was complete and nobody could resolve it after that.

Narada has dealt with the topic in detail on various aspects such as buyer's rights and liabilities, seller's rights and responsibilities, preemption, adequate or inadequate price, etc. Some of the interesting provisions may be studied. Narada tells that if a buyer purchases an article with full knowledge of its defects, he loses the right of returning it back.[80] The buyer should take the delivery immediately after it is sold to him.[81] If he fails to do so, the vendor may sell the article to another buyer. Katyayana provides that if any seller shows an article free of defects and delivers one full of defects, he should be made to pay double the price to the buyer and an equal fine as punishment (to the king).[82] And if an article having sold is undelivered due to being burnt or stolen, the loss falls on the seller only.

Katyayana also provides that if any article is purchased from a disqualified person such as a lunatic or for an inadequate price, the safe is lawful and the article belongs to the seller.[83] Brhaspati gives a list of persons disqualified as purchasers: sudras, degraded persons, chandalas, and desperate persons.[84]

Katyayana follows Manu (VIII.222) and states that if a seller repents after sale, he could rescind the sale but return the price of the article to the buyer.[85] If the buyer has already paid any earnest money and the lender fails to give effect to sale, then according to Yajnavalkya, he fails to pay double the amount of earnest money to the buyer.

With regard to sale of land, Katyayana states that there can be no lawful sale of purchase of land without securing the approval of the kinsmen (of the seller and buyer) who are neighbor, i.e., owners of the neighbouring lands and who are respectable men. Also, the sale could be vetoed by the kinsmen within a time period[86] in Yajnavalkya (*Mitakshara* on Yajnavalkya, II,114) implies the consent of the villagers, kinsmen, and co-heirs was taken simply for the purpose of giving notice to them of the intended sale and of neighbours for avoiding disputes about boundaries in future.

BOUNDARY DISPUTES

Manusmrti deems that it was the duty of the king to settle the disputes regarding boundaries. This should be ideally undertaken in the month of '*Gyaistha*', which (Medatithi explains) means May–June, when the grass has been dried up by heat, when the landmarks are mostly distinctly visible.[87]

The boundaries, the text tells, should be marked by trees such as vyagrodhas, asvatthas, cotton trees, palmyra, and trees with milky juice by clustering shrubs, bamboos of different kinds, samis, creepers, reeds, thickets, etc., and should not be forgotten. Tanks, wells cisterns, temples, and fountains should be built where the boundaries meet.[88] However, Manu also tells that if there be slightest doubt on inspection of marks, the dispute should be settled with the help of witnesses.[89] If the witnesses determine it unjustly, they shall be compelled to pay a fine of two hundred (panas). Further, the text lays down that if anybody takes possession by intimidation of a house, a tank, a garden, or a field, he shall be fined five hundred (panas). (If he trespassed) through ignorance, the fine (shall be) two hundred (panas). And finally, if the evidence available does not help in ascertaining the boundary, the righteous king can himself assign the land to each.

Narada talks of this title of law as 'disputes concerning land' *(Kasatrajavivada)* for which he devoted forty-three verses. Brhaspati has used the term *bhuvada* for this while Manu Yajnavalkya. Kautilya and Katyayana have all used the term *Simavivada* or disputes relating to boundaries. Narada's *Ksatrajavivada* is, however, more comprehensive as it includes not only boundary disputes but disputes pertaining to land, fields, embankments, wasteland, etc. Narada mentions that in disputes regarding landed properties or boundaries, the decision shall rest with the neighbours, the inhabitants of the same community, the elders of the village, and those living on the outskirts or by tillage of fields such as herdsmen, bird catchers, hunters, and other inhabitants of the woods.[90] Like Manu, Brhaspati too puts emphasis on visible and invisible signs as boundary marks. These boundary marks should be shown by one generation to another to avoid any confusion or dispute.

Narada has described five hinds of boundaries: (a) *Dhvajini* or that shown by trees like a flag; (b) *Matsyini* or a river flowing by the side of the village and containing fish, tortoise, etc.; (c) *Naidhini* implying boundary indicated by signs concealed in the ground such as treasure or other articles; (d) *Bhayavarjita*, implying free from danger, settled by agreement; and (e) *Rajasasananita*, i.e., fixed by royal command.[91]

INHERITANCE AND PARTITION

The Hindu Law of inheritance does not presume the property rights of sons or daughter till the parents are alive. Manu speaks that it is "after the death of the father and of the mother, the brothers, being assembled may divide among themselves in equal shares for the paternal (and the maternal) estate for they have no power (over it) while the parents live."[92] The text of Manusmrti advocates the law of primogeniture by which the eldest son succeeds to the property. The text puts it thus: "The eldest alone may take the whole paternal estate, the others shall live under him just as they (lived) under their father."[93] The eldest son should shoulder the responsibility and support the younger brothers, and the brothers should regard the eldest brother as sons behave towards father. They could either live together or separately. By living separately, the text tells their merit increases, and hence, 'separation is meritorious'. The additional shares (deducted) for the eldest shall be one-twentieth (of the estate) and the best of all chattels; for the middle, most half of that; but for the youngest, one-fourth.[94] The eldest is supposed to get the best articles, chattel, and best of ten (animals).

If additional shares are deducted, one must allot equal shares (one of the residue to each); but if no deduction is made, the allotment of shares among them shall be that the eldest son takes one share in excess, i.e., two shares, the brother born next to him one share and a half, and the younger ones one share each.[95]

The rule with respect to sisters as stated in the Manusmrti is that to the maiden (sisters), the brothers shall severally give (portions) out of their shares, each of out of his share one-fourth part. Those who refuse to give (it) will be outcastes. Yajnavalkya too propounds a similar rule (II, 124). According to the commentators, it may imply that if a man leaves children by wives of different castes, the brother should provide for the dowry of unmarried sisters of the same caste, i.e., a Brahmana's sons by a Brahmana wife for the daughters of the latter, the sons of a Kshatriya wife for the daughters of the latter. This duty, Kulluka adds, far from day for sisters devolved first on brothers of full blood and in default on half brothers.[96] These provisions reflect or assert two aspects-the rights being asserted for the maiden sisters and second, the principle that brothers were supposed to take care of the sister financially and undertake these responsibilities. The caste undertone still prevailed imposing a layer of segregation between brothers and sisters.

Another verse in Manusmrti tells that "if a younger brother begets a son on the wife of the elder, the division must be made equally, thus the law is settled.[97]

Also, if there is a doubt as to how the division shall ensue in case of a younger son born of the elder wife and the elder son of the younger wife that is, if the seniority be according to the mothers or according to actual birth, most often than not, seniority of the mother was regarded as important for the law of inheritance. In verse 125 too, however, Manu mentions that "between sons born of wives equal (in caste) and without (any other) distinction no seniority in right of the mother exists, seniority is declared (to be) according to birth.[98] In case of twins, the seniority is declared (to depend) on (actual) birth."[99] Medatithi, the commentator on Manusmrti, however, denied any legal force in these verses.

Manu tells that the rule of inheritance applies to ancestral property and not to self-acquired property. Manu says that if a father recovers lost ancestral property, he shall not divide it unless by his own will with his sons (for it is) self-acquired property.[100] Kautilya too, more or less, speaks a similar rule. The Arthashastra enjoins that partition of inherited property shall be made in accordance with the customs prevalent in the region, caste, guild, or village (of the family).[101] Sons whose fathers are alive cannot be (independent) masters of the (ancestral) property.[102] A father may, however, divide his ancestral property among his sons during his lifetime. In the case of such a partition, the father shall neither show a special favour to anyone nor exclude any rightful heir from the inheritance without good reason.[103] The Arthashastra clearly mentions that the laws of inheritance do not apply to self-acquired property *(swayamarjitham)* but only to ancestral property and that part of the property earned by using ancestral property.[104] If there had been no division of ancestral property in the lifetime of father, a partition could be made after the death of the father (3.5.2).

Yajnavalkya (V.118–119) tells that whatever is "acquired by a man himself without detriment to the paternal estate, as a present from a friend as also as a nuptial present, shall not belong to the co-heirs. He says there is no need to give to co-parceners, that which is recovered as hereditary property taken away or that gained by learning (119). Further, the wealth given by the parents to one belongs to him and of the heirs, dividing after (the death of) the father. Let the mother also take equal share. Yajnavalkya too advocates giving the sisters a fourth part of one (each brother's share).

In the case of one who has no son, the Manusmrti advocates that he may make his daughter an appointed daughter (putrika) by making her say that "the (male) child born of her, shall perform my funeral rites."[105] Manu tells about the legend of Daksha (in the Mahabharata and the Puranas) who himself, lord of created being made all his female offsprings, appointed daughters in order to multiply the race. Manu holds this appointed daughter as rightful heir in case of no sons. He tells, "A son is even (as) oneself (such) a daughter is equal to a son, how can another (heir) take the estate, while such (an appointed daughter who is even) oneself, lives?"[106] Three important enunciations follow this in the Manusmrti.

First "between a son's son and the son of a (appointed) daughter there is no difference, neither with respect to worldly mattes nor to sacred duties, for their father and mother both sprang from the body of the same (man)."[107] Second, if a daughter is appointed and a son is born (to her father), the division (of the inheritance) must in that (case) be equal, for there is no right of primogeniture for women.[108] "And third if the appointed daughter dies without (leaving) a son, the husband of the appointed daughter may, without hesitation take the estate."[109]

In the whole issue on inheritance, the son seems to be pivotal. Verse 138 says, "Because a son delivers (*trayate*) his father from the hell called put, he was therefore called *put-tra* (a deliverer from put or hell) by the self existent (*Svayambhu*) himself. Also, through a son, he conquers the worlds; through a son's son, he obtains immortality; but through his son's grandson, he gains the world of sun. These verses clearly seem to be the product of a patriarchal mind-set and a society that regarded women as second by gender, right from the birth. There seems to be no legal logic in it but merely indoctrination to the theory of salvation, which envisaged the son as the salvator. What is more interesting to note is that Manusmrti, in defiance to the proposed bias, regards the son of a son and son of a daughter as equal in this world and in getting salvation. Probably, the idea must have been to ensure that the estate did not pass on to outside heirs in the presence of female issues.

Kautilya has talked about the order of inheritance. The Arthashastra tells that in the first four types of marriages, the order is as follows:[110]

- Sons, if they are leaving sons
- Daughter, if there are no sons
- The father, if alive, of the deceased

- If father has died, then equally between brothers and nephews while in the second four types of marriages the order is
- Sons, if they are living sons.
- Brothers, or persons who had been living with deceased
- Daughters

For a son, born of *Niyoga*, the Arthashastra allows him to get his share of the property (3.5.33). As far as entitlement is concerned, the text explicitly tells that (among children from the same wife), daughters do not have a share in the father's property. They can only inherit bronze household utensils and their mother's jewellery.

Regarding wives of different castes, Manu speaks, "Let the son of the Brahmana (wife) take three shares of the (remainder) of the estate, the son of the Kshatriya two, the son of a Vaishya a share and a half and the son of a Shudra may take one share."[111] Caste hierarchy was applied explicitly to the issue of inheritance and thereby distinction made in priviliges and status of different stratas of society The text further specifies the list of legitimate and illegitimate heirs. Verse 159 specifies the legitimacy of rights of son begotten through wife, an adopted son, a son secretly born and even a son cast off. "The next verse specifies the kinsmen: "The son of an unmarried damsel, the son received with the wife, the son bought, the son begotten on a re-married woman, the son self-given and the son of a Shudra female, (are) the six (who are) not heirs but kinsmen." Legitimacy of heirs, hence, was based on begetting the son lawfully within the permitted rules. Those outside this ring were prohibited from being heirs. They were declared to be kinsmen alone and the legal heirs offer funeral oblations while the illegal sons do not inherit but offer libations and are regarded as remoted kinsmen.

The caste rules were harsh on the Shudra wives. The text (V.155) tells the son of a Brahmana, a Kshatriya, and a Vaishya by a Shudra (wife) received no share of the inheritance; whatever his father may give to kin, that shall be the property while inheritance was enjoyed equally by sons born of the wives of same caste. It says (V.156) all the sons of twice-born men, born of wives of the same castes, shall equally divide the estate after the others have given to the eldest an additional share. (The Arthashastra permits one-third of property to a son of a Brahmana born of a Shudra's wife.)

The Manusmrti talks of eleven categories of sons.[112] The legitimate son and the son of the wife share the father's estate while the other ten inherit according to their order. This order is thus:

1. *Aurasa* or the son begotten on his own wedded wife (V.166).
(2) *Kshetraja or a son begotten according to peculiar law of niyoga on the appointed wife of a dead man, of a eunuch, or of one diseased (V.167).*
(3) *Datrima* or the son received from one equal of caste, whom his father or mother affectionately give with (a libation) of water, in times of distress as adopted son (V.168).
(4) *Kritrima* or a son made owning to being equal in caste, acquainted with distinctions between right and wrong, and endowed with filial virtues (V.169).
(5) *Gudhotpanna* or a son born secretly, whose father be not known. He belongs to him of whose wife he was born (V.170).
(6) *Apaviddha* or a son cast off or deserted by one or both parents (V.171).
(7) *Kanina* or son of an unmarried damsel. The son would belong to him who weds her afterwards (V.172).
(8) *Sahodha* or the child born of an already-pregnant (bride) or a son received with the bride (V.173).
(9) *Kritika* or a son purchased, whether equal or unequal (in qualities) from his parents (V.174).
(10) Son of a *Punarbhava* or son born of a woman abandoned by her husband, or a widow, or one who contracts a second marriage. *Punarbhava* implies a remarried woman.

Further, the text talks of two additional categories, where a son gives himself having lost his parents or being abandoned is called *Svayamdatta* while a son begotten by a Brahmana through lust on a Shudra female called *parasava* (a living corpse).[113] However, the text permits the son begotten by a Shudra on a female slave to take a share in inheritance if the father permits. In a verse (V.184) which talks on merit of sons, the text tells that "on failure of each better (son) each next inferior (one) is worthy of the inheritance but if they are many (of) equal rank, they shall all share the estate." However, it is the sons and not the brothers who take the paternal estate as said in the text. Also, Manu tells that if a son leaves no male issue, the father and brothers take the inheritance. For the adopted son, the Manusmrti tells that (the *datrima*) possessing all good qualities shall take the inheritance (V.141). He never takes the family and estate of his natural father. Likewise, Narada too tells that "it has been declared that an adopted son receives a share like the chief son, when he is eminently virtuous".

On the share of women as wife, daughter, and mother, the Manusmrti devotes a good number of verses. In verse 131, it says, "Whatever may be the separate property of the mother that is the share of unmarried daughter alone, and the son of an (appointed) daughter shall take the whole estate of (his maternal grandfather) who leaves no son. Manu hence, recognises a separate property of women—that is the *stridhana*, and that was for the unmarried daughters alone. "If the widow of a man, says the text, who leaves no issue dies and a son is raised by her widow from a member of the family, she shall deliver the whole property to that son (of the deceased). But if two sons contend for the property (in the hands of) their mothers, each shall take to the exclusion of others what belonged to his father."[114] Moreover, when the mother died, all the uterine brothers and uterine sisters shall equally divide the mother's estate.[115] Even the grand daughters ought to receive something out of grandmother's estate.[116]

Manu has defined *stridhana* as what (was given) before the (nuptial) fire, what (was given) on the bridal procession, what was given in token of love, and what was received from her brother, mother, or father as the sixfold property of a woman (V.194). Such property and what was given affectionately by her husband shall go to her offspring if she died, in the lifetime of her husband.

The Manusmrti further tells that in the case of four approved forms of marriage—the *Brahma*, the *Daiva*, *Arsha*, the *Prajapatya* and including *Gandharva* (one of the unapproved forms)—her property would belong to her husband if she be issueless. Whereas in *Asura* or other blamable marriages, the property shall go to her mother and father in the absence of any issues.[117]

Manu, sounding like a patriarchal protagonist, asserts (V.199) that "women, should never make a hoard from (the property of) their families which is common to many nor from their own (husband's particular) property without permission". Firstly, the women are discouraged to hoard from the common property, and if she does so, she is expected to take permission, obviously from her male masters in the form of husband or father.

The ornaments, which women wear during her husband's lifetime, the Manusmrti (V.200) tells should not be divided by the heirs. Those who do so become outcastes. Some other assertions regarding inheritance in Manusmrti are as follows. V.201 tells that eunuchs and outcastes, persons born blind or deaf, the insane, idiots and the dumb, and those deficient in any organ receive no share. They are, however, entitled to maintenance. And if any of these marries, the offspring of such union is worthy of a share (V.203). Debts and assets are to be duly distributed equally (V.218) while a dress, a vehicle, ornaments, cooked food, male and female (slaves) property destined for prior use or sacrifices and a pasture ground are declared to be indivisible.

On partition, the Manusmrti tells that "if brother (once) divided and living (again) together as (coparceners) make a second partition, the division shall in that case be equal, in such a case there is no right of primogeniture."[118] If the eldest or youngest brother is deprived of his share or if either of them dies, his share is not lost (to his immediate heirs).[119] If the eldest brother tried to defraud, his additional share was done away with, and he was punishable by the king.[120] What a brother acquires by his labor without using the patrimony, he shall not share unless by his own will.

On the issue whether a property without heir could go to the king, the Manusmrti tells that the "property of a Brahmana must never be taken by a king that is settled rule, but (the property for men) of other castes the king may take on the failure of the (heirs)."[121] The Arthashastra too forbids the king to take the property of a Brahmana without heirs while it allows in the rest of the cases to go to the king except allowing a basic maintenance for the widow and the funeral rites (3.5.28.29).[122] The text also prescribes a fine of one hundred panas for misappropriating family wealth (3.20.16).[123]

While in te above verses, the caste bias is clearly visible, in the Charter of Vishnusena, the text of achara 1 tells,

Aputrakam na grahyam

Aputraka means the property belonging to a person who died without leaving a son. This seems to say that such property should not be confiscated by royal officials, disregarding the claim of any legal heir other than the son.[124]

The concern for illegitimacy of confiscation by government is being voiced in this particular achara irrespective of any caste reference.

Similarly, of the comparatively scanty reference to civil law in the writings of Kalidasa, there is one positive reference to such a property of a childless. In Shakuntala Act VI where the king orders his Minister for Justice to look into the case filed to him by the citizen and then to submit a report on it, the Minister reports thus a leading merchant name Dhanamitra, carrying on business by sea, died in a shipwreck. And childless, they say is the poor man, his store of wealth goes to the king".[125]

"However, after reading the documents, the king orders the Minister to enquire if any of his wives was pregnant; on enquiry it, came to light that one of Dhanamitra's wives had her *punmsavana* ceremony performed only recently. The king orders the Minister to restore the property of Dhanamitra to his family with the remark that 'surely the fetus deserves the paternal property."[126] The sensitiveness of the state and idea of transferring a property to the rightful owner throws light on the kind of commitment of king towards ensuring justice. This case incidentally also shows that a regular record of tried cases was kept.

Hence, it appears that, by law, the property of a deceased person in the absence of the male heir did lapse to the treasury of the crown. It appears that the widow probably had no right to inherit the property of her deceased husband. Additionally, the later jurists allow the widow some concessions with regards to inheritance based on her behavior and character possibly highlighting that virtues of wife needed to be cultivated consciously, if inheritance held any significance to her.

Brhaspati, one such law giver among later jurists, declared, "The wife is pronounced successor to the wealth of her husband, and in her default the daughter." Katyayana puts a rider that if the widow be chaste, she could take the wealth of her husband (an, in her default, the unmarried daughter).[127] But a wife who is full of evil deeds, is immodest, wastes her property or is given to adultery does not (deserve) to inherit the wealth of her husband.[128]

Katyayana, representing the advanced Hindu legal thought, has propounded rules on partition of heritage. He devotes ninety-four verses to this topic, including about twenty-three verses on stridhana alone.

Katyayana declares that a lawful division of property is where the fathers and brothers divide the whole property in equal shares (V.838). Both father and sons have equal ownership in the property of the grandfather while the son is not entitled to ownership over what is acquired by the father. This verse embodies the central conception of the *Mitakshara* School as to the equal ownership of father and son in the ancestral property.[129] The grandfather's property, the father's property, and whatever was acquired by joint efforts are divided when there is a partition among co-heirs (or coparceners) (V.840), and partition is ordained among those who attain an understanding of affairs at the age of 16 (V.844). The father should not deprive any son of his share if the partition takes place in his presence (V.843). The debts must be equally shared as tells Manu too. After paying of the debts only, the rest of the property should be divided (V.849–50). The father, says Katyayana gets two shares or half from the wealth acquired by the son. When the father is dead, the mother also gets a share equal to the son (V.851). A single coparcener has no right to make a partition. He can only enjoy it and not even make a gift mortgage or sale of it (V.853). If any brother dies, his son gets a share in inheritance (line Manu tells). Even the son's son gets this right, but beyond that, there is a cessation of inheritance.

Like Manu, Katyayana too ordains one-fourth share for the daughters unmarried (Manu IX.118 and Yajnavalkya 11.124 both prescribe a fourth share) (V.858). The Mitakshara explains that this one-fourth share is not of the whole estate but one-fourth of what the unmarried daughter would have got if she had been a son of the same class as herself. Kane tells that vide Bhagavati Shukul V Ram Jatan, I.L.R. 45, [130] where it was held that the quarter share in the Sanskrit texts means as much money as will suffice for marriage expenses, that the provisions of a dowry for a daughter was a legal necessity and that where the daughter was a cripple and blind and all the property was a meager sum of Rs.500 an alienation of the whole of it by the widowed mother for raising a dowry for the daughter was justifiable.

Katyayana has listed the property that does not come within the fold of permissible partition that wealth which was taken away by force and recovered by father, that gained by learning (*Vidyadhana*), what is acquired from pupil, by performing as priest, by exhibiting one's knowledge and deep learning, whatever is earned by an artisan over and above the price of an article, wealth due to value received as reward from the king, wealth of the wife (*Kanyagata*, coming with the maiden, vaivahika (nuptial wealth), whatever meant for the bridegroom, whatever wealth was set apart for religious purpose, pasture for religious purposes and *dhvajahate*, or that received from a battle are impartible (V 866–884)

Katyayana suggests fresh partition to conceal heritage. Joint fields and all could be partitioned even after long time. When, however, for ten years the brothers reside (separately) and have separate transactions, they should be regarded as separate as far as ancestral property is concerned.

Katyayana's treatment of *stridhana'* is, however, the most remarkable. Kane remarks that he attained a classical rank in the treatment of *stridhana*. He reiterates Manu's verse (IX-94) on what constitutes the *stridhana* (V.894). He too enumerates six kinds of *stridhana*. Here, it is worth mentioning Kane's reference to Taittreya Samhita VK.2.1.1, which reads the wife is master of the household gear. This is the germ of the law of *stridhana*.[131] Katyayana lists the following types of *stridhana*:

(1) *Adhyagni*—that which a woman receives at the (V.895) time of marriage before the (nuptial) fire.
(2) *Adhyavahanika*—that which she receives when (V.896) being taken (in a procession) from her father's house (at the time of *vidai* or *dviragmana*).
(3) *Pritidatta*—whatever is received by a woman (V.897) through affection from father-in-law or mother-in-law or by saluting the feet of elders.
(4) *sulka*—that which is obtained as the price of (V.898) household utensils, of beasts of burden, of milch cattle, ornaments, and slaves.
(5) *Anvadheya*—whatever is obtained by a woman (V.900) from the family of her husband and family of (father's kinsmen).
(6) *Saudayika* (V.901)—that which obtained by a married woman or by a maiden in her husband's or father's house from her technical word, used in a peculiar sense by Katyayana. Over *saudayika*, a woman has absolute power of disposal even during her husband's lifetime. It signifies the wealth received from her brother or parents and not from her husband or his relations.

Katyayana mentions that the father, mother, brother, and kinsmen should give stridhana to women according to their means up to 2000 panas except immovable poroperty.[132] The commentaries, however, clarify that the limit of 2,000 panas was fixed with reference to annual payment. If it was going to be once in a lifetime, they could give more than 2,000 panas. Kane has cited that the Smrtichandrika quotes a similar verse from Vyasa, Kautilya (111.2) that says that '*vritti*' and jewellery constitute *stridhana*. The limit of *vritti* was fixed up to 2,000 panas and there was no limit for jewellery.[133] Katyayana further tells that if a father, brother, or husband in fraud of his coparceners gives some family property to daughter or that cannot be termed *stridhana* (V.903). If any property was acquired by her labour, Katyayana recognises the wife's ownership of the property, but her right of alienation was restricted and made subject to husband's wishes.

About the gifts a woman may receive from her husband, Katyayana propounds that she could dispose of the affectionate gifts of her husband only with his consent (excluding the immovables). After his death, she could dispose of it as she pleases, except the immovable property (V.907).

If the husband has two wives and does not honor or reside with one of them, he should be forced to return (by the kind the *stridhana* of the ill-treated wife (V.908). Where basic maintenance is denied, she may extract her *stridhana* and also the share (that would have been her husband's on partition) from the coparceners. And when she receives (her wealth), she should reside in her husband's house (except when afflicted with deadly disease) (V.910). This again echoes the grand old Hindu sentiment that a wife must never abandon her husband's house even if the husband does not honor her.

None of the male members had any right by law over the women's *stridhana*. If anybody forcibly consumes *stridhana*, he should be forced to return it with interest and should be fined as well. Kane (has cited that the Smrti Chandrika III, p.6.56) points out that by marriage, a wife gets a sort of dominion over her husband's property, though she is subordinate to him, but the husband has not even that dominion over his wife's *stridhana*. Another verse (V.916) makes it binding for sons to pay the *stridhana* promise to a woman by her husband as seriously as a debt.

As to the heirs to the *stridhana*, Hindu jurists depict a great divergence of views. The Mitakshara on Yajavalkya II, 145 speaks of two lines of devolution— one for sulka and other for all kinds—while the later commentaries speak of five different lines of devolution. Katyayana's verses imply that unmarried daughters got preference over the married ones and sons in succeeding to *stridhana*. "In the absence of daughter, it goes to sons; and in the absence of (of even) sons, this wealth goes to such relatives (who gave this wealth) or in their absence to the husband."[134]

NOTES AND REFERENCES

1. *Ramayana*, Ayodhya Kanda, 100-62-63
    Dharmascarthasca Kamasca Kaleksama Samahitah
2. Buhler, *Laws of Manu*, ch.VIII, v.47.
3. Ibid., v.49
4. Ibid. v.164.
5. L.N. Rangarajan, *Kautilya, The Arthashastra*, (3.11.21–24). p.423.
6. Ibid., p.424.
7. J.R. Gharpure, *Yajnavalkyasmrti*, p.64.
8. Ibid., B-II, V.50, p.75.
9. Ibid., p.77
10. Ibid., p.77
11. cf.*Brhaspatismrti*, v.21, p.303.
12. Kane, *Katyayanasmrti*, v.234, v.162
13. Buhler, *Laws of Manu*, Ch.VIII, v.140, p.278.
14. Ibid., v.141, p.278.
15. Ibid., v.143, p.278.
16. Ibid., v.151, p.280.
17. Brhaspati, v.17, p.101.
18. cf *Yajnavalkyasmrti*, 2.37.
19. *Naradasmrti*, v.102, p.75
20. *Brhaspatismrti*, v.21, p.102
21. *Naradasmrti*, v.36, 0.36.
22. *Katyayanasmrti*, v.505, p.63.
23. *Epigraphia Indica*, Vol.XXX, p.172–173.
24. Ibid., footnote 1.

25. Buhler, *Laws of Manu, Ch.VIII, v.145, p.279.*
    Vishnu, VI.7–8, Yajnavalkya, II.58, have also spoken of pledge. Buhler explains Medatithi's version: The pledge spoken of here is a pledge for keeping, which is forcibly used, *Upanidhi*, a deposit means according to Medhatithi, Govindraja and Kulluka, anything lent to another out of friendship.
26. *Naradasmrti*, v.1, p.129.
27. *Brhaspatismrti*, vv.38–39, p.105.
28. *Katyayanasmrti*, v.518, p.218.
29. Buhler, *Laws of Manu*, VIII, v.150, p.280.
30. *Naradasmrti*, v.126, p.83
31. *Brhaspatismrti*, v.41, p.105.
32. *Naradasmrti*, v.130, p.84
33. *Katyayanasmrti*, v.517, p.219.
34. *Brhaspatismrti*, v.49, p.107.
35. Ibid., v.189, p.287.
36. *Naradasmrti*, v.118, p.80.
37. *Brhaspatismrti*, vv.7–8, p.121.
38. Buhler, *Laws of Manu*, VIII, v.181, p.286.
39. Ibid., v.189, p.287.
40. Ibid., VIII, v.193, p.288.
41. *Yanjavalkyasmrti*, 2.65.
42. *Naradasmrti*, v.1, p.129.
43. *Katyayanasmrti*, v.592, p.240.
44. Ibid., v.593–594, p.240.
45. *Katyayanasmrti*, v.610, p.243.
46. Ibid., v.603, 0.243
47. Buhler, *Laws of Manu*, VIII, v.197, p.289.
48. Ibid., v.198, p.289.
49. Ibid., v.200, p.290.
50. *Naradasmrti*, v.1, p.155.
51. *Katyayanasmrti*, v.612.
52. Ibid., v.616.
53. Buhler, *Laws of Manu*, VIII, v.209, p.291.
54. L.N. Rangarajan, *The Arthashastra, 3.24, p.456.*
55. Ibid., p.457.
56. *Naradasmrti*, v.5, p.133.

57. *Brhaspatismrti*, v.1, p.131.
58. Buhler, *Laws of Manu*, VIII, v.212, p.292.
59. Ibid., v.213.
60. *Naradasmrti*, v.8, p.138.
61. *Naradasmrti*, vv.4–5, p.137.
62. *Katyayanasmrti*, v.638–39, p.250.
63. Ibid., v.640, p.250.
64. *Katyayanasmrti*, v.646, p.251.
65. Ibid., v.60–651, p.252.
66. Ibid., v.652–653, p.252.
67. Ibid., Notes.
68. *Katyayanasmrti*, v.646, p.251.
69. Ibid., v.566, p.234.
70. *Katyayanasmrti*, v.565, p.253.
71. Buhler, *Laws of Manu*, VIII, v.219, p.293.
72. Ibid., v.220, pp.293–294.
73. *Naradasmrti*, v.1, p.163.
74. *Katyayanasmrti*, v.671, p.256.
75. Ibid., v.672, p.256.
76. Ibid., v.677, p.257.
77. Ibid., v.678–681, p.257–258.
78. *Naradasmrti*, v.1, p.160.
79. Buhler, *Laws of Manu*, Ch.V.
80. *Naradasmrti*, v.4, p.160.
81. *Ibid., v.4, p.159.*
82. *Katyayanasmrti*, v.689, p.260.
83. Ibid., v.692, p.260.
84. Brhaspati as quoted in *History of Dharmashastra*, 3.496.
85. *Katyayanasmrti*, *cf.*HD, 3.490.
86. *Svagramhantisamantadayadanamatena ch.....*
87. Buhler, *Laws of Manu*, VIII, v.245, p.298.
88. Ibid., v.246–248, p.298.
89. Ibid., v.253, p.299.
90. *Naradasmrti*, vv.2–4, p.165.
91. M.M. Patkar, *Narada, Brhaspati and Katyayana, A Comparative Study in Judicial Procedure*, p.153.
92. Buhler, *Laws of Manu*, Ch.IX, v.104, p.346.

93. Ibid., v.105, p.346.
94. Ibid., v.112, p.347.
95. Ibid., 116–117, p.348.
96. Buhler, *Laws of Manu*, Notes, p.349.
97. Ibid., v.120, p.348.
98. Ibid., v.125, p.351.
99. Ibid., v.126, p.351.
100. Ibid., v.209, p.376.
101. L.N.Rangarajan, Kautilya, The *Arthashastra* (3.7.40), p.414.
102. Ibid., (3.5.1).
103. Ibid., (3.5.16, 17)
104. Ibid., (3.5.3).
105. Buhler, *Laws of Manu*, 127, p.351.
106. Ibid., v.130, p.352.
107. Ibid., v.133, p.353.
108. Ibid., v.134, p.353.
109. Ibid., v.135, p.353.
110. L.N.Rangarajan, *Kautilya*, The *Arthashastra*, 3.5. 10–13.
111. Buhler, *Laws of Manu*, Ch.IX, v.151.
112. Vishnu has listed twelve kinds of sons. The Arthashastra adds one or more to Manu's text too, i.e., *putrikaputra* or son of a nominated daughter equal as *Aurasa*.
113. In all, Manu enumerated twelve kinds of sons
114. Buhler, *LOM*, v.191, p.369.
115. Ibid., v.192, p.370.
116. Ibid., v.193, p.370.
117. Ibid., v.196–197, p.371.
118. Ibid., v.210, p.376.
119. Ibid., v.211, p.376.
120. Ibid., v.213, p.377.
121. Buhler, *LOM*, v.189, p.367.
122. L.N. Rangarajan, p.415.
123. Ibid., p.421.
124. *Epigraphia Indica*, Vol.XXX, p.170.
125. B.S. Upadhyaya, *India in Kalidasa*, p.147.
126. B.S. Upadhyaya, *India in Kalidasa*, p.148 cites Shakuntala p.129

127. Kane, *Katyayanasmrti*, v.926, p.327.

128. Ibid., v.929, p.328.

129. Compare Yajnavalkya II, 121, Vishnu, 17.2, Brhaspati, p.370, v.3. The Mitakshara on Yajnavalkya II.121 explains that verses like Yajnavalkya II,114, Narada, p.191, V.12, which allows the father to make an unequal distribution among his sons refer to the father's self-acquired property.

130. Kane, *Katyayanasmrti*, Notes, p.303.

131. Kane, *Katyayanasmrti*, Notes, p.316.

132. Kane, *Katyayanasmrti*, Notes, p.318.

133. Ibid., Notes, p.318.

134. cf. Kautilya, III.2.p.153

CHAPTER V

Criminal Law and the Unique Charter of Vishnusena
The Relevance of Customary Law

When Green regarded the state as not just an end in itself but a means to fulfill the moral development of man, he probably implied a deeper belief in the worth and dignity of man. What he rightly emphasised on the part of an individual was the development of his moral nature—"the fulfillment of a moral capacity without which man would not be man". In the Indian tradition, in the context of the Dharma undercurrent, the aim was to develop a moral man and an ideal society too. The Dharmashastra enunciated a code of law that was based on a conception of morality derived from a preconceived notion of good and evil, virtues, and vices and that of sin. The *yoga* makes delusion *(moha)*, anger *(krodha)*, and greed *(lobha)* as the triple springs of vice.[1] *Nyaya* distinguishes vices into bodily *(sarira)* oral *(vak)* and mental *(manasa)*. The types of offences dealt with indicate an advanced stage of civilisation. Grave offences have been distinguished from common crimes. Modes of punishment have been studied in great detail. Most importantly, Hindu criminal law has been evolutionary and adaptive by nature, gradually humanising even the punishments.

In the Dharmashastra, the premise begins from the fact that *Sri* (prosperity) resides where virtue resides. To be evil or wicked means to be an offender, and misfortune alone could be their destiny. Virtues ought to be inculcated and vices ought to be purged from within oneselves. This was the plea of the Smrti writers. The virtues that are named by the smrtis are truth *(satyam)*, charity, compassion to all living beings, chastity, filial duty, gratitude, and piety.

Virtues, which are classified as *yama* (rules of restraint) and *niyama* (rules of obligation), indicate what should be done and what should not be done. Among the five *yama* specified, *ahimsa* (non-violence) comes first, because in the social relations, the earliest possibility is causing pain to one another.

- *satyam* comes after *ahimsa*
- *Asteyam*, i.e., avoidance of theft comes third
- Purity
- *Brahmacharya*, i.e., celibacy

On the other hand, in the Indian philosophical tradition, vices have also been mentioned inevitable and the approach is quite realistic. These vices are cited as the cause of crimes. Manu regards atheism as the first of the six vices to be avoided, the others being hatred (*dvesa*), ostentation (*dambha*), pride (*mana*), and violence (*taiksnya*). Crime owes its origin to these vices or state of mind. In the Indian tradition, crime was denoted by the term *sahasa*. It is graded into first, *prathama*, middle or *madhyama*, and the highest or *uttama*, with the graduated scale of fine for each class.

Sahasa, which again is an extension of the *himsa*, implies violence that causes pain. *Himsa*, as Aiyangar says, need not be physical. The torture of the mind might drive people to madness or suicide more readily than tormenting the body. Any kind of coercion, physical or mental was treated as *himsa*. *Prayopavesa* or fasting unto death to compel compliance with demand or *dharana* was *himsa*.[2]

Vishnu tells man has three most dangerous enemies called carnal desire, wrath and greed and householders are most vulnerable to fall prey to these as they have property (houses, wives and others).[3] Man, being overcome by these three enemies, commits crimes of highest degree as well as other categories or grades of crime. He warns of certain crimes such as loss of caste, degrading mixed castes, and caste defilements, etc.

Crimes, originating in *sahasa* or injury in ancient India, are divided into four categories by the Smrti writers like Manu, Narada, Brhaspati, and Katyayana.

- *Vakparusya* or abuse
- *Dandaparusya* or assault
- *Steya* or theft
- *Sahasa* or violence

Adultery is considered a great crime in the criminal category. Gambling and betting were crimes too.

In Kautilya's views, causing physical injury is the most serious offence, causing damage to property less serious and verbal injury the least serious (8.3 23–26) in 11.v. In general, the fines for verbal or physical injury against an equal in status were increased or decreased proportionately. It was to be double the fine in offences towards superiors in status, half towards those inferior in status, double in case towards wives of others, and halved if there was a case for diminished responsibility (mistake, intoxication, or temporary loss of sense) (3.18, 3.19.4).

However, it is very difficult to ascertain that rate of crime or the level of immorality that might have existed in actual ancient India. Laws were definitely stringent, punitive, and prohibitive; but the very fact that laws were spelt for the respective categories of crimes indicate the prevalence of such crimes. In Kalidasa's plays, the prevalence of a rigorous criminal code suggests of a time when probably crime of all sorts prevailed and was recognised as punishable. Theft and burglary are cited as prevalent. The prerogative of king to announce capital punishment for those accused of highest crimes suggests that criminal class might have necessitated a stringent code of criminal laws.

In the *Mrcchakatika* too, there are references to such crimes as theft, burglary, gambling, adultery, and political coups.

One interesting piece of evidence is delivered in the Chinese traveler Fahien's account of the character of the Indian people, He says,

"They are of hasty and irresolute temperaments, but of pure moral principles. They will not take anything wrongfully and they yield more than fairness requires. They fear the retribution for sins in other lives and make light of what conduct produces in this life. They do not practice deceit and they keep their sworn obligations."[4]

What Fahien asserts about the temperament of the Indian people may be purely subjective perception. But the fear for retribution of sins is visible as a decalogue to the concept of yama-niyama, by which certain vices lead to destruction of the person as well as the family (*kulanasanam*). Even though the belief that the sins of the father may be visited on the children is ancient, its utility lies as a restraint on the moral vagaries of an individual. It makes the entire family take up the moral responsibility for the conduct of each of its member.

Fahien remarked further that "as the government is honestly administered and the people live together on good terms, the criminal class is small".[5] However, neither the certainty of the first is proven now living together in good terms can be considered downward puller of crime rate. It may be that the criminal class was not very large.

Certain ideals with respect to criminal laws are discernible in the Charter of Vishnusena. For instance, achara 4 of this Charter ordains,

Sankaya grahanam n = asti.[6]

This implied that the royal officials should not go in for the apprehension of persons or for taking up a case against one or for seizing one's things through mere suspicion (*sanka*) of the crime. This may have been some sort of protection against false allegation or fabricated cases.

Likewise, achara 4 tells,

- *Purush – apradhe stri na grahya*[7] – this meant that the wife should not be apprehended for her husband's guilt or crime.

Likewise, when Kalidasa talks of the concept of *Yatha-apradha-dandanam*, (*Raghuvamsa 5.6*), the underlying emphasis is on maintaining a balance between or proportion between crime and the punishment for it. Kalidasa, on one hand, in fact, refers to a rather severe code of penal law; but at the same time, the system of punishment was a thorough and positive code of law in which punishment was graded according to the gravity of the offence.[8]

In Mrcchakatika, when the court reported the guilt of Charudatta to the king, there is a reference to Manu's laws by which a Brahmana could not be subjected to capital punishment *(vadhadanda)* and could only be banished. However, as an exception probably, the king overrules the decision of the court to impose capital punishment on the king.[9]

DEFAMATION (*Vakpanrushya*)

The term '*vakparushya*' or defamation literally implies violence by words. Manu propounded the laws for deciding cases of defamation while Yajnavalkya, Narada, Brhaspati, and Katyayana elaborated upon him consequently. Narada remarked that abuse, which is a title of law, arises when abusive language is offensive and bad terms is employed against another concerning the native country, caste, family, and so forth.[10]

Caste distinctions and biases are most visible in the laws for cases of defamation. Punishment for abusing one of the higher castes was severe, and Brahmanas enjoyed the most favoured position as in other social and legal matters. Manu tells that if a Kshatriya defamed a Brahmana, he was to be fined 100 panas, a Vaisya 150–200 panas, and a Shudra shall suffer corporal punishment for the same offence.[11] The disparity becomes even more obvious when there is a mention that a Brahmana shall be fined fifty panas for defaming a Kshatriya. In (the case of) a Vaishya, the fine was to be twenty-five panas and case of Shudra twelve panas.[12]

For offences, involving twice-born men against those of equal caste, the fine was to be twelve panas and for speeches not be uttered, double.[13]

For a Shudra, Manu ordains that he who insults a twice-born man with gross invective shall have his tongue cut just because he is of a low origin.[14] Not only this, if he mentions names and castes of the twice born with contumely, an iron nail ten fingers long, was to be thrust red hot into his mount.[15] If he originally teaches Brahmanas their duty, the king shall cause hot oil to be poured into his mouth and into his ears.[16] Rather than any connect with the wisdom of the law makers, these verses are indicative of the extent to which the law enunciating class was self centred, interested in claiming illegitimate superiority or oblivious to the idea of equitability in the area of law.

Manusmrti writes that one who through annoyance makes false statements about anybody shall pay a fine of 200 (*panas*) (V.273). If anybody calls another one eyed, lame, or like, he shall be fined at least one *Karshapana* (V.274). This punishment probably could not have referred to Shudra, for it is too light. Also, he who defames his mother, his father, his wife, his brother, his son, or his teacher—and he who gives not the way to his preceptor—shall be compelled to pay one hundred (panas) (V.275). When for any case of abuse, the text tells, the king is the discerning authority, he should impose lowest amercement for the Brahmana and middle for the Kshatriya. For Vaishyas and Shudras too, they should be punished according to their castes, but a Shudra's tongue cannot be cut off (V.276–277) in case he abuses a Vaishya.

Yajnavalkya provides the highest fine for him who abuses a Brahmana learned in the three Vedas, a king or the Gods. If the defamation is against a caste or a community, the fine is of middle amercement; and in case of a village or district, the fine is same as for a lower *sahasa*.

Kautilya distinguished three kinds of defamation: simple defamation, aggravated defamation, and intimidation (3.18.1). Simple defamation was when a person is disparaged about any of his qualities such as his body nature, character, learning, profession (3.18.2), etc. Defamation of physical characteristics could be true (such as you are one eyed when a person was actually blind in one eye), (ii) false (you are lame when a person was not), and (iii) sarcastic (what lovely eyes when a person was actually blind).

The punishment, however, depended on the caste of the defamed person. Aggravated defamation was when the defamation was in the form of taunting a person with being leprous, mad, or impotent or of low birth (3.18.4). A verbal intimidation was when a person threatens another with injury but is incapable of carrying it out or pleads diminished responsibility (anger, intoxication, or loss of sense). The fine shall be twelve panas.

Narada distinguishes among three kinds of defamation: (1) *nisthura*, (2) *aslila*, and (3) *tivra*. The first consists of abuse combined with reproaches, second when worded in insulting language, and third causing an expulsion from caste. Like Manu, Narada too could not dispense with the caste distinctions with regard to punishments. Brhaspati and Katyayana have more or less taken the line of Narada for rules regarding defamation. Katyayana, however, like Kautilya, tells that if the offence is committed due to ignorance, carelessness, rivalry, or familiarity and agrees that he would not repeat it, the fine should be reduced to half. Also, for those who spread false rumors, Katyayana enjoins severe punishments like mutilation of tongue (like Kautilya). In Arthashastra, it is told that if a prostitute abuses a client, the fine was twenty-four *panas*.

In all, some kind of limited immunity is visible in case of defamation against women. But overall, defamation rules are spelt mostly with regard to the caste hierarchy existent in the society rather than with respect to gender.

ASSAULT
(Dandaparusya)

Any attack that causes pain as well as blood, scars etc. in the skin by nails caused by a living thing to another has been declared by the Smrti writers as assault.[17] Manu, Narada, and Brhaspati, however, maintain that causing injury to lives of another person with foot, weapon, etc., constitute assault and are punishable. Narada and Brhaspati even talk of three levels of assault: light, middle, and heavy. Light assault is when the hand is raised for striking, middle when there is an unexpected attack, and heavy when a person suffers injury from the attack. Kautilya talks of three kinds of physical assault: touching (including pushing, kicking, throwing things, and bodily restraint), hurting, and wounding.[18]

Manu's laws of punishment for assault depict the caste differences at their maximum. The text says with whatever limb a man of law caste hurts one of the higher (castes), that limb shall be cut off.[19] Explaining further, it says if he raises his hand or stick, the hand will be cut off or who kicks with his foot, his foot be cut off. Not only this, if a low-caste man tried to place himself on the same seat as the high-caste one, he was to be branded on his hip and even banished, or (the king) shall cause his buttock to be gashed.[20] Such verses not only seem ridiculous but reflect the magnitude of the sting of the caste mind-set. For wounding others (where blood comes out), the offender, ordains Manu, shall be fined one hundred (panas), he who cuts a muscle, six niskas, while one who breaks a bone was to be banished.[21] If a blow was stuck against men or animals in order to give them pain, (the judge) should inflict a fine in proportion to the pain.[22] Also, in case of a wound inflicted, the assailant should pay not only the fine but the expenses of the cure too (to the king).[23]

For injuring trees, Manu has spelt that fine must be imposed according to the usefulness of the trees.[24] In case of leather or utensils of leather, of wood, or of clay, the fine was to be five times their value as also in case of damage to flowers, roots, and fruits.[25] For the failure of a driver, if a cart turns off the road, the owner shall be fined 200 panas if damage is done. If the driver is skilful, the occupants of the carriage too would pay a fine of one hundred panas each.[26]

If a man, says Manu, is killed, his guilt is same as a thief (i.e., he must pay the tightest amercement or 1,000 panas); for large animals, it is half of that for injuring small animals, the fine shall be 200 panas while that for birds about 50 panas, for donkey, sheep, goat, the fine shall be 5 masas but for killing a dog or pig, the fine was to be one masa. One who strikes from the back, his guilt is also like that of a thief.[27]

One verse of Manu, however, raises the big question related to gender equality. A wife, a son, a slave, a pupil, or a (younger brother) of the full blood who has committed faults may be beaten with a rope or a split bamboo. Here, what is the ground of pairing a wife as equal to son or a slave or a pupil or younger brother is not clear. The only commonality visible among them is that they are all subservient to the man to whom they belong. The sanction to beat or assault them is not only queer but absurd. Moreover, that the son, the pupil, and the brother who are deemed more independent than wife could be beaten seems illogical and improbable (unless they were too minor to retaliate).

Like Manu, Brhaspati and Katyayana (V.782) too assert that in certain assault, punishment should be in proportion to the pain caused. Brhaspati ordains that if assault results in death of the person hurt, capital punishment is awarded.[28] Like Manu, he too ordains that the assailant should be responsible for the expenses of the court. Narada provides that if a person through arrogance spits on a superior, the king should cause both the offender's lips to be cut off.[29] Another important provision in Narada says that no person than the perpetrator of the crime is liable to punishment unless he happens to be a party to the commission of the act.[30]

Kautilya is more meticulous with the monetary fines for assault. Fine was double or halved for assaults against person of superior or inferior *varnas* (3.19.4).

- For pushing with hand or throwing	-3 to 12 (depending on navel, above it or head) mud, ashes or dust
- For spitting, kicking, or throwing impure things	-6–12 (") panas
- Throwing vomit, etc.	- 12–48 panas (3.19,2,3)
-For holding and restraining	-6 panas (3.19, 5, 6)
- For hurting with hand	-3-12 panas
- For kicking with foot	-6-24 panas
- For wounding	- 24-28 panas
- While if the injury was to thigh	- Middle amercement cost of treatment. [31]

Neck or eye – affecting speech movement or eating

For striking anyone with weapons, if it was a crime of passion, the fine was to be 200 panas; when intoxicated, the fine was cutting of a hand; while assault resulting in death was to be punished with death (4.11,3–5). For injuring any organ, the fine was to cut off the same organ of the offender (4.11.25) while for making someone blind in both eyes, the punishment was that the offender too be blinded or 800 panas fine to be paid. In case a person of high *varna* beat or kicked a guru, the fine was to cut off a hand and a foot or 700 panas fine. In case of a prostitute causing physical injury to a client, the fine was 48 panas. For causing an abortion by physical blow, the fine was of the highest amercement while for arson or setting fire to pasture, field, house, or productive forest, the punishment was to be death by burning.

Katyayana provides that the ideal punishment for the untouchables, gamblers, slaves, *mlecchas* (those considered impure), or persistent sinners and for those who are born as a result of unions in reverse order of castes is whipping and not any monetary payment.[32] Katyayana does not exempt even a teacher who assaults a pupil with anything other than a creeper, causing pain. In such a case, the father may lodge a complaint against the teacher.

Brhaspati provides rules of procedure for determination of the offence or assault. If a person is beaten up in a lonely place or when no wound is visible, the offender is to be detected by circumstantial evidence of an oath.[33] Likewise, in case of injury or assault in the interior of a house or in a wood or at night blood is traced, witnesses shall not be examined.[34] The only lone case where the guilt of an assailant may be absolved is when the act is in self-defence.

The Charter of Vishnusena talks with reference to assault in more than a couple of its acharas. Achara 38 says,

Vakparushya – dandaparushyayoh vinaye rupakah shat = sa – padah.[35]

This means the fine for the offence of defamation and assault (or rough behavior) was $6^{1/4}$ silver coins. Here, the fine seems to be the same for defamation and light assault. In the very next achara (39), it says,

Kshata darsane rupakah ashtachatvarimsat

This means in the case of *danda—parushya*—involving visible injury or infliction of wounds, the fine was 48 silver coins. There is a similar reference in the Vishnusmrti (V.66–67).

Sonitena vina duhkham – utpadayita dvatrim – sat – panan, saha sonitene chatuhshasthina

The Charter, an achara 6, tells *Kshem – agni – samuthane chhalo na grahyah.*[36]

Chhala, which originally means pretext, may have meant 'a careless, declaration' in the smrti literature while '*kshemagni*' implies a sacred fire kindled on the occasion of marriage, etc. This achara may mean that no haphazard allegation should be entertained against one's neighbour for the burning of one's house when the accused says the conflagration resulted from the sacred fire. If any ordinary meaning of '*chhala*' is taken, the achara may refer to a case involving the burning of a neighbour's house in which such a plea that conflagration resulted out of the sacred fire was not acceptable.

On cutting of the ears, *karna trotana*, the charter, speaks in two acharas: no. 7 and no. 37. No. 7 says,

Swayam hrasita karne chhalo no grahyah.[37]

There was no pretext for a man who was himself responsible for cutting a bit from a neighbour's ear or that no careless declaration was acceptable from a man if he cut a bit from his own ears.

In Achara 37, it is mentioned thus:

Ullambane karnna trotana cha vinayo rupakah saptavimsat (satih)

The work '*ullambane*' is explained in the lexicon as 'leaping over someone', but Kautilya's Arthashastra (1 V, 8) uses it to indicate hanging, which could be applied to the present case. *Karna trotana*, i.e., "cutting off a bit from some one's ear was a crime and the fine was 27 silver coins.

The Charter also talks about the offence involving *taundika* (biting of crops by mouth) by the cows. The fine for such offence was five *vimsopakas*.[38] However, for an offence of *aundika* by a she-buffalo, the fine was ten *vimsopakas*, i.e., one-half silver coin. Yajnavalkya prescribed four masas for the offence.[39]

THEFT *(Steya)*

By punishing the thieves, Manu ordains the attainment of fame by the king and the prosperity of his kingdom. The text of Manu says, "A king who (duly) protects (his subjects), receives firm each and all the sixth part of their spiritual merit, if he does not protect them, the sixth part of their demerit also (will fall on him).[40] The task of protection endowed on the king has been detailed by Manu and has been compared as equal in merit to that obtained from reading the Veda by sacrificing by charitable gifts (or by) worshipping (Gurus and gods) when the king, says Manu protects the kingdom according to sacred laws, it is a great sacrifice on the part of the king while if he does not afford protection and takes his share, he sinks into hell.[41] Also, if the king does not punish the thief, he incurs the guilt of the thief upon himself.[42]

Manu advises three modes of punishment for the wicked (wicked here means thieves for Manu is dwelling here on the topic of theft): by sending them to prison, by putting them in fetters, and by meting various (kinds of) corporal punishments. The king could pardon one in pain, and thus, he exalted in heaven, says Manu. But he should never be arrogant of his kingly state and not pardon those who deserve. Manu says he should forgive the litigants, infants, aged, and sick people.

In Yajnavalkyasmrti, there is reference to a more developed penal code and interesting rules of procedure for dealing with thieves, actual and suspected. He advised the king to restitute the stone property and punish the thieves by different modes of corporal punishment.

In Arthashastra, robbery is dealt with in Book 3 and punishment for theft in Book 4. L.N. Rangarajan mentions that two important aspects of theft (investigation of reported theft and a graded set of punishment for theft) are covered in (4.6) on arresting suspects and (9.10) on payment of redemption money in lieu of mutilation.[43] The text describes robbery with violence on seizing forcibly a person or property in the presence of the owner. If the owner is absent or if the seizure is indirect (e.g. by fraud), it shall be considered theft (3.17.1.2).

The text elucidates that the school of Manu holds the fine, in case of precious objects, articles of high or low value and forest produce shall be equal to the value of the goods seized. Kautilya propounds that punishment must be commensurate with the offence and agrees with the scale recommended by other teachers (3.17.3–5).

The school of Brhaspati advocates increasing the fines for one who instigates another to commit robbery with violence. Kautilya agrees subject to the condition that only the basic fine shall be levied if the instigation was done in a moment of diminished responsibility such as anger, intoxication, or passion[44] (3.17.11–14). The text also tells that when a territory is newly acquired by conquest, thieves shall be removed from their usual places of residence and dispersed.

Narada's text (as preserved in the commentary of *Ashaya*) does not deal with the topic of theft.[45]

Brhaspati considers theft as among the few species of *sahasa*. According to him and Katyayana, thieves are of two kinds: (1) open and (2) concealed. Brhaspati, whose list is more elaborate, includes traders, quacks, gamblers, corruptible judges, cheats, perjured witnesses, etc. Open thieves,[46] house breakers, highwaymen, robbers, and thieves of clothes are considered secret or concealed thieves.[47] Brhaspati ordains that judges who pass unjust sentence, persons living by bribe, and such other persons as betray confidence on them are as good as thieves and deserve punishment.

Vishnu speaks that he who has stolen a goat or a sheep shall have one hand (cut off).[48] A stealer of thread cotton, cow dung, sugar, butter milk, grass, salt, clay, ashes, birds, fish, clarified butter, oil, meat, honey, basket work, canes of bamboo, earthenware, or iron pots shall pay three times their value as a fine (V.83). Thieves should be compelled to restore all stolen goods to the owners and after that shall suffer the punishment ordained for them (V.89–90).

Manu speaks about the guilt of theft with reference to caste distinction. In case of thefts the guilt of Shudra shall be eightfold that of a Vaisya sixteenfold and that of Kshatriya two- and thirtyfold that of a Brahmana, he says shall be sixty-four-fold or hundredfold or even twice four- and sixtyfold. So to say, the guilt of the Brahmana is highest in case of a theft. In other words, the higher in hierarchy of caste, a higher character was expected and deviations or failings in character were serious offence. Guilt here implied that the offender had to pay fine in proportion. Some specific punishments entailed in Manusmrti are as follows. One who steals more than two kumbhas of grain shall be inflicted with corporal punishment (V.320). So also it was for stealing over a hundred (palas) of articles sold by weight (i.e.) of gold, silver, and so forth and of most excellent clothes (V.321). For stealing more than fifty cases, a fine of eleven times the value was to be imposed (V.322). For stealing men of noble family and especially women, ordains Manu, of their precious gems, the offender deserved corporal (or capital) punishment (V.323). For the theft of large animals, weapons, or medicines, the king could fix the punishment after considering time and the purpose (for which they were destined) (V.324).

Likewise, for stealing cows belonging to Brahmanas, piercing the nostril of a barren cow, and for stealing cattle (belonging to Brahmanas), the offender was to lose half his feet. Kautilya differs here and prescribes a monetary fine worth the value of animal add to the equal amount as fine for stealing cattle, deer, birds etc (4.10.3). Further, for stealing thread cotton, cow dung, molasses, bamboo vessels, salts, oil, fish, birds, honey, or cooked food, the fine was to be twice the value (of the stolen article) (V.326–329). For agricultural produce, vegetables, fruits, etc., the fine was to be one hundred panas. Kautilya, however, proposed a fine of 200 panas for the theft of agricultural produce (4.10.6).

Manu mentions two more interesting assertions: One that neither a father nor a teacher, nor a friend, nor a mother, nor a wife, nor a son, nor a priest must be left unpunished by a king if they do not keep within their duty (V.335). Also, where another common man would be fined 1 *karshapana*, the king shall be fined 1,000 (V.336). In other words, considerations of relations should not be allowed to interfere with punishments when the king meted out punishments for theft, no matter if they were the parents, children, or priest. The highest responsibility, however, was of the king, where common man's crime was equivalent to one that of king was to be one thousand times more. It was the king who had the highest responsibility to ensure justice and morality, and any breach by him was uncalled for.

In Kautilya's Arthashastra, it is mentioned that for robbing a prostitute of her belongings or ornaments, a fine eight times the stolen amount was to be prescribed (2.27.23). If a soldier stole weapon or armour, highest punishment was ordained (4.11.23). Also, for theft in holy place, mutilation was ordained by the text (4.10.1). For concealment or embezzlement of temple property, the fine was blinding of both the eyes along with a monetary fine of 800 panas (4.10.13). Also, for theft of temple property such as images, cattle, persons, field, house, and gems, etc., the punishment was nothing less than death. Death punishment was also prescribed for stealing a herd, weapons, or armour by one who was not a soldier, theft by breaking into treasury, etc. (4.11.15, 4.11.22, and 4.9.7). As for helping a thief (or adulterer), the fine was cutting of the nose and an ear or a fine of 500 panas. For hiding a thief, the fine was same as that for the theft (4.8.6).

Katyayana too mentions that "those who supply food to thieves, those who give them fire and water, those who purchase (stolen) goods from them and receive (stolen) property from them and those who hide them—these are all declared to be liable to the same punishment (as the thieves themselves)."[49]

Katyayana also emphasises on the procedure to be adopted in case of theft. Whenever anything is stolen of a person in one's kingdom, the king must restore it back (Vishnu (III,65, 66 also has a similar provision). The king should search the thing lost, and if found (after the price is paid to the owner), he should retain it himself. In the absence of the article, the king should pay the price; otherwise, the king incurs sin even if the king was to restore the thing or he could make the thief pay as per his (king's) pleasure.[50] Also, if anything was stolen from the houses in a village, (the king) was to make the thief catchers pay it (to the owner). He could make the guarding officers and warden pay the price of the stolen article if the thief was not found. The property stolen in a village was to be restored by the village headman come to that stolen in the forest by the king, but if the theft occurred at a place other than the forest, the officer appointed to catch thieves was to restore the property or its price.[51] These thief catchers were the officers appointed to trace and catch the thieves. In the inscriptions, the office who matches the description is called "*chauroddaranika*" (mentioned in the inscription of Dharasena II of Valabhi).

Likewise, *Nagarika*, of *Abhijnanshakuntalam* was perhaps like the *koshtapala* of later time, the head of the establishment of the guards of the city. We come across this official in the Shakuntala leading a criminal to the court of justice with the help of his guards (*rakshinah*). In the Vikramorvashi, he seems to be connected with the city administration. There again, he is entrusted with the work of police by the king who commands him to hunt after the winged offender (a bird that had flown away with a gold chain of the king) when, at evening, it goes to its resting place.[52]

B.S. Upadhaya, who has studied India in Kalidasa, remarks that despite the severity of the criminal law, thieves (*pataccara*) and burglars (*gandabhedakah*) and waylayers were not unknown; and the poet's assertion that theft, not being in practice was to be found, in books alone (*Raghuvamsa*, 1–27) is sadly exposed to criticism unless it be supposed to refer to an ancient regime (or earlier times) which it does.[53]

Kalidasa does refer to a severe code of penal law. As evidenced in the poet's writings, the offence of theft was punishable with death.[54]

The fisherman of the Shakuntala was accused of theft alone of the royal jewel for which he was considered doomed to destruction by snake, dogs, or vultures. (This seems similar to Manu's provision of capital punishment for theft.)[55]

In *Mrcchakatika* too, there is reference to an episode of theft. Vasantasena, the courtesan, intentionally deposits her ornaments at Charudatta's house in order to take ahead their love story. The ornaments are stolen from Charudatta's house, which was once opulent but now poor. The thief is no other than Sarvilaka, the brother-in-law of Charudatta who is also lovelorn for Vasantasena. Charudatta is afraid that people may not believe in theft and will suspect him on account of his property. He even sends his wife's percious *ratnavali* (jewellery) to Vasantasena. He had entrusted the responsibility of ornaments on friend Maitreya, but when the latter told him to place the ornaments in the inner apartments, Charudatta refused on the grounds that it was the jewellery of a public woman. The theft, however, over here is a dramatic interlude to shed light on the characters of Charudatta, his wife, Sarvilaka, and Vasantasena rather than as a reference to a crime as such. There is no explicit mention of the punishment, although the handing over of '*Ratnavali*' suggests the compensation for the theft.

VIOLENCE *(Sahasa)*

Manu opined that the king in whose town lives no thief, no adulterer, no defamer, no women guilty of violence, and no committer of assaults attains the world of *Sakra* Indra.[56] The text tells that he who commits violence must be considered as the worst offender (more wicked) than a defamer than a thief and than he who injures (another) with a staff.[57] *Sahasa*, violence, comprises, according to Medhalithi, robbery, rape, arson, cutting of clothes, or forcible destruction of property.[58]

Narada gives a more conclusive elaboration of the term. He defines '*sahasa*' as an act of force performed by persons inflamed. Heinous crimes are of four kinds—man slaughter, robbery, and indecent assault on taking another man's wife—and the two types of insult: abuse and assault.[59] Offences could be of first middle or highest degree. For not very serious offences of first degree, such as damage to crops, water, or agricultural implements, fine was up to a hundred panas. For offences of middle degree, such as spoiling clothes, food, or drink of others, the fine was up to 500 panas while fine for highest type of offences causing injury to human life or property was up to 1,000 panas along with corporal punishment, confiscation of property, banishment from the country, and even mutilation.[60]

Brhaspati prescribes caution in arriving at decision about proof in heinous crimes, especially manslaughter. Vishnu regards the killing of Brahmana with the offence of drinking the killing of Brahmana with the offence of drinking spirituous liquor, stealing the gold of a Brahmana and sexual connection with a Guru's wife as high crimes.[61] Vishnu says that killing a Kshatriya or Vaishya engaged in sacrifice or a woman in her courses or a pregnant woman or a woman of the Brahmana caste who bathed after temporary uncleanness or killing an embryo of an unknown sex or one who comes for protection was equivalent to the crime of killing a Brahmana. Likewise, he enunciates that giving fake evidence and killing a friend were crimes equal to drinking of spirituous liquor.[62]

Katyayana has described *sahasa* as an act of dare with force.[63] A person charged with violence should establish his innocence by oaths (and ordeals).[64] If several men violently beat one man to death, the one who strikes the fatal blow is held as the murderer.[65] No blame attaches to him who kills a wicked man ready to kill another.[66] Katyayana describes an *atatayin* as a desperate fellow and entails that if the *atatayin* belongs to a higher caste, killing him is not proper; killing is prescribed for a sinner of a lower class. This is also the view of Bhrgu, one of the great sages and first compiler of text on predictive astrology.

He explains an *atatayin* as one who is about to use his sword, poison, or fire; whose hands wield a drawn bow; who kills by incantations as per the Atharvaveda; who is a backbiter conveying to the king; who assaults another's wife; and who is bent on fault finding (V.802–803). These wicked men rob a person of his fame and character and deprive one of Dharma and Artha (V.80). Even one who kills animals having sharp claws, horned animals are called *atatayin* (V.805).

Katyayana makes a deviation in assertion about crimes committed by a Brahmana when he tells that "even a Brahman deserves to be killed if he be guilty of abortion, if he be a thief (of gold), of if he strikes as Brahmana with a sharp weapon or if he kills an innocent woman."[67] Otherwise, elsewhere, a Brahmana has overall been exempted from capital punishment of death; even for the highest crimes, he could at most be banished or exiled according to the Smrti jurists.

Killing a woman (*strihatya*) was considered at great sin. In the Ramayana, Rama, the lord and hero of he text who epitomises an ideal man by Dharma standards, himself tells Laksmana (Bala Kanda, 26–12).[68]

Nahyenamutsahe hantum strisvabhavena raksitam. Being protected by her feminine nature, I have no heart to kill her (Ayodhya Kanda, 7821). Likewise, Bharata tells Shatrughna,

Avardhyah sarva bhutanam pramadah, meaning women ought not to be slain by any creature. Likewise, Hanuman refers to the special hell reserved for the slayer of a woman reiterating the concept of blissful *karma* as guarantor of entry to heaven:

Ye ca stnghatinam loka vadhyaisca kutsitah (Yuddha Kanda), 81–23)

However, Rama, following the behest of Vishvamitra, killed Tataka. This act of Rama is defended by scholars in the light of relatively pragmatic Valmikian Dharma. Three arguments are advanced. First, Tataka was a murderess who had murdered a number of holy persons (Bala kanda, 25–16, 19), and it was the duty of the king to protect his subject. Second, Vishvamitra tells Rama that Indra too killed a woman, and he should not consider for a woman who is a murderess, and third, Rama must obey the behest of his father as Parasurama killed his mother on receiving order from his father.

Moreover, Rama's act was an act of self-defense and, hence, fully justified.

In Manu and Vishnu too, it is entailed that "by killing an assassin, the slayer incurs no guilt, whether (he does it) publicly or secretly, in that case fury recoils upon furty."[69]

In the Mrcchakatika too, the murder of women is regarded as a heinous crime. However, the law that made an exception, if the murderer was Brahmana as ordained by Manu was not applied here. Here, we have a deviation from the established norms. The king puts aside the request of judge to exile Carudatta and confirms the death sentence to set an example.

ADULTERY *(Strisamgrahana)*

The state was presumed to be a protector of the people against all sorts of crimes. All the smrti writers have extolled and emphasised upon the role of the king in preventing the crime. One such verse in Vishnu tells, "A king in whose dominion, there exists neither thief nor adulterer, nor calumniator, nor robber nor murderer, attains the world of Indra."[70]

Adultery has been deplored by all the Smrti writers unanimously. It was seen as great sin strictly punishable and requiring penances. Various possible relationships have been examined, and rules forbidding them hence had been laid down. The scope of the term itself was very elaborately deliberated upon as also the punishments for it.

Manu's harsh verses on adulterer begin with this verse: 'Men who commit adultery with the wives of others, the king shall cause to be marked by punishments which cause terror and afterwards banish.[71] In the very next verse, Manu puts forward his logic for such pronouncement when he says, "For by (adultery) is caused a mixture of the castes (varna) among men, thence (follows) sin, which cuts up even the roots and causes the destruction of everything."[72]

Manu's definition of adultery *(samgrahana)* is wide and elaborate. If a man is formerly accused of such offences with another man's wife, he is liable to be fined with the lowest amercement. But if he is an unaccused person, then no guilt is incurred.[73] If one addresses a wife of another at a tirtha, outside the village, in a forest, or at the confluence of rivers, he is taken as an adulterer, offering presents (to a woman) romping, touching invalidly or with mutual consent, these are all considered adulterers acts by Manu.[74] Except for the wives of actors and singers, who Manu believes live in their wives intrigues, let no man converse with wives of theirs lest he be fined one *suvarna*.[75]

Manu seems markedly harsh in pronouncing punishments for adulterers, representing an aspiration for a higher ideal of moral code. The text of Manu says that a man who is not a Brahmana ought to suffer death for adultery (*samgrahana*)—that is to say that punishments for adultery should be death, except for the Brahmanas. In this very verse, he tells that wives of all four castes should be carefully guarded.[76]

For violating an unwilling maiden, the adulterer should suffer corporal punishment instantly; but if he enjoys a willing maiden, he may not suffer corporal punishment if both were of the same caste.[77] In another caste-tainted verse, Manu tells that if a maiden makes advances to a (man of) high caste, he shall not take any fine; but if she courts a man of low (caste), let him force to live confined in her house (V.365). On the other hand, if a man of low caste indulges with a maiden of the highest caste, he shall suffer corporal punishment (V.366). If this person addresses a maiden of equal caste, he shall pay nuptial fee, if her father desires. If a man defiles a willing maiden of equal caste, he would pay fine of 200 panas in order to deter a repetition (V.368). But if a man forcibly defiles a maiden, he would not only pay a fine of 600 panas but two of his fingers should be chopped off (V.367). Likewise, if a woman violates a damsel, her head shall be shaved off, two fingers cut, and she should be made to ride on a donkey through the town.

The harshness of punishment for a wife adulterer is not less pronounced. Manu says, "If a wife, proud of the greatness of her relatives or (her own) excellence, violates the duty which she owes to her lord, the king shall cause her to be devoured by dogs in a place frequented by many." As for the male offender, the punishment seems to be the most stringent: "Let him cause the male offender to be burnt on a red hot iron bed, they shall put legs under it (until) the sinner is burned (to death). "Rules and punishments were more vigorous for Brahmana offenders. If the offence was with the lowest caste female, fine imposed on Brahmana was one thousand (V.385). The latter provision appears to be in tune with the expected behavioual norms and high morality expected from the highest class in society as ordained in the caste structure.

Manu ordains tonsure (of the head) for a Brahmana offender instead of capital punishment, but for the same crime, men of other castes were to suffer capital punishment. Taking that further, he forbids the king to ever slay a brahmana even for all possible crimes. He could at most be banished. In fact, he pronounces the killing of a Brahmana as the highest crime in the context and continuation of above verses (V.381).

Kautilya's Arthashastra mentions that a kinsman or a servant of husband who is away on a long journey shall keep an adulterous wife under guard till the husband returns. If, on return, the husband does not raise any objections, neither the woman nor her lover shall be prosecuted; otherwise, the wife shall suffer mutilation and the lover death.[78] Anybody who conceals adultery or catches an adulterer and declares him to be thief (to save him of the punishment of adultery) shall himself be punished. No one should take bribe to allow an adulterer to escape. Kautilya also mentions gradation of monetary punishments for misconduct on the part of man or woman. If a wife was caught in adultery, the punishment, which Kautilya ordains, is mutilation by cutting of nose and an ear or 500 panas; same mutilation for the lover was also prescribed with a fine of 1000 panas. For helping an adulteress, the fine was 900 panas or mutilation by cutting off both feet and a hand.

Kautilya has dealt with other sexual offences and punishments for them elaborately. Mainly the punishments pertain to defloration of a virgin, rape, prohibited relationships. Defloration was considered a serious offence and especially of a minor (4.12.1-7.20-29). Even a prostitute was not to be enjoyed against her will, which was classed as rape. The list of prohibited relationships was explicitly mentioned. For instance, sexual relations with wife of a teacher were prohibited, as well as relations between ascetics or relations with kin like aunt, daughter, sister, a daughter-in-law. The rigorousness is especially noticeable in the enunciation that if any woman permits such a relationship, she should be sentenced to death (4.13.31). Person of lower caste was prohibited to have incest relation with women of higher caste.

If a person had such relation with the queen, he should be boiled alive (4.13.33). The punishment for rape varied in monetary terms except in case of an Arya minor when the punishment declared was death. For those who violated caste norms in having incest relations, punishments like branding, mutilation, or death were prescribed.

Narada (V.91) says when a woman commits adultery, her hair shall be shaven, she shall have to lie on a low bed and shall receive bad food and clothing, and her occupation shall be the removal of sweepings of her husband's house. Dr. Kane has interpreted the adultery laws of Smrti with comparisons from the English law. He tells under the English law that if the wife commits adultery, the husband's obligation to maintain her ceases altogether unless he had connived at it or condoned it.[79] Kane studies that the human character of the legislation of the Indian sages is seen by the fact that even for adultery, they do not allow the husband to drive the wife out of the house and to abandon her. Kane asserts that the husband possessed some kind of correction power over the wife as those possessed by a teacher over pupil or a father over son. He could administer beating with a rope or thin piece of bamboo on the back but never on the head. Kane considers this as comparable to the common law of England.

However, what appears from the entire study is that punishment for adultery and rape varied according to the caste of the man or the woman, was different for men and women and variation was also considering the fact whether the women was a maiden or married. If a Shudra committed this offence with the Brahmani (wife of a Brahman), it was the highest offence of adultery. A Brahmana committing such offence was banished while a Shudra in the same place was prescribed death. Violating a maiden was greater sin than relation with a married woman. If a woman was guilty, she was not to be exempted or shown any mercy. Both Manu and Katyayana prescribed her devouring by dogs. The paramour was, however, to be killed. Rules and punishments are most elaborately and rigorously dealt with in the Arthashastra rather than the Smrtis. Smrtis underline the seriousness of the offence by all means. Punishments were rigorous both for men and women, and no preference is exhibited in the favour of any particular gender. Caste however was a major determinant in the prescription of punishments.

GAMBLING AND BETTING

Recognised as a criminal offence, gambling and betting seem to have been widely prevented in early India, as can be gathered from the instances in epic, plays, or the Arthashastra. Manu entailed that gambling and betting amount to open theft. The king shall always exert himself in suppressing both (of them).[80]

Manu explains that "when inanimate (things) are used (for staking money on them), that is called among men gambling (*dyuta*), when animate beings are used (for the same purpose), one must know that to be betting.[81] He further says that "in a former, *kalpa* (indicating time-single period of Universe) this (vice of) gambling has been seen to cause great enmity, a wise man, therefore, should not practice it even for amusement".[82] He advises the king to corporally punish all those (persons) who either gamble and bet or afford (an opportunity for it), likewise Shudras who assume the distinctive marks of twice-born (men).

In the Arthashastra, or discussion is there on the seriousness of vices springing from excessive desire such as addiction to hunting, gambling, women and drink. Pisuna considers hunting a worse vice than gambling, for anything can happen in a hunting while in gambling, experts like Jayatsena or Duryodhona wins (8.e.39–41).[83] Kautilya disagrees and remarks that in gambling, one party has to lose as is known from the stories of Nala and Yudhisthira. It becomes a source of enmity. A gambler never knows how much wealth he has got, tries to enjoy wealth that he has not got, and loses it before he can enjoy it.

Kautilya says that a gambler can be reformed but not so a man who lusts after women. Gambling is worse than addiction to drink. Gambling with one's property and betting on animal races leads to a win for one and loss to the other. Gambling promotes factionalism, and it is the most evil of the vices because it destroys the ruling class by depriving them of their ability to govern.[84]

From the play Mrcchakatika, it appears that gambling was a well-organised and somewhat approved social pastime. There were gambling houses, chief of which was called *sabhika*. There used to be association of gamblers (*dyutakara mandali*), which promulgated its own laws and gamblers were bound by them. It also seems to have had royal sanction, for the chief was not only the king's messenger but also an independent power who could punish the defaulters. It was a game for the rich but nearly always lured the poor to try their luck. As Samvahaka says in the play, "the sound of the dice throw *(kattasabda)* sways a penniless heart as the sound of the drum stirs the heart of a king fallen from his throne. Gambling is a steep fall from a precipice and I know, I shall not play, but the rattle of dice is as sweet as cuckoo's voice and draws my mind."[85]

Vasantasena had the entire equipment at her house, and Charudatta did not hesitate to state that the deposited ornaments were lost by him in gambling.[86]

The play mentions that for failure in paying the gambling debt, the debtor had to face harsh treatment. Samvahaka ran for his life, did every possible trick to dupe the master of the gambling house, but he was pursued and persecuted. Act II (12) mentions that a defaulter was suspended with his head down for a whole day or dragged along the street or wild dogs let loose on him. These cruel tortures a defaulter was likely to face suggest the severity of the punishment entailed for an offender of gambling debt.

In the Yajnavalkya smrti, it is mentioned that persons gambling with false dice or other instruments shall be fined and banished by the king.[87]

MISCELLANEOUS CRIMES

Manu has listed some thirty verses spelling miscellaneous rules in Chapter VIII. Many of them are worth bringing to study. Verse 389 says, "Neither a mother, nor a father nor wife, nor a son shall be cast off; he who casts them off unless guilty of a crime causing loss of caste shall be fined by the king 600 (panas)." Here, to cast off implies to deny the due maintenance to these relations, and the rule does not apply to a person who has already committed a crime that led to his being ostracised from the particular caste.

A high code of behavior was expected of the Brahmanas. Manu says Brahmana should entertain his neighbors or pay a fine of one masa (V.392). If dispute occurs between them, the king should amicably mediate. Especially, a *srotriya* was expected to be more virtuous.

For the traders, Manu says, let the king confiscate the whole property (of a trader) who out of greed exports goods of which the king has monopoly or (the export of which is) forbidden.[88] Also, he who avoids a custom house (or a toll), he who brings or sells at an improper time, or he who makes a false statement in enumerating (his goods) shall be fined eight times (the amount of duty he tried to evade).

One verse tells that a Brahmana could employ a Kshatriya or Vaishya if distressed for livelihood (V.111), but he should not employ men of twice-born castes against their will to do the work of slaves; otherwise, he will be fined by the king 600 panas. A Shudra was, however, deemed to have been created by the self-existent (*svayambhu*) to be slave of a Brahmana.

Another verse puts the wife, son, and slave on the same plane and says, "These three are declared to have no property; the wealth which they earn is (acquired) for him to whom they belong." Probably what was implied was that these three had no rights to dispose of their property independently. Manu concludes the legal provisions by telling that a king who brings all these legal business and removes all sin reaches the highest state (of bliss), the king however, remaining the upholder of the laws ordained or prevalent.

The Charter of Vishnushena has references to certain miscellaneous rules. Achara 2 of the charter says,

unmaro-bhedo na karaniyo raja – purushena.[89]

The royal officials were asked not to break open or violate the *unmara*, the exact meaning of which is not known. It may be related to Gujarati *umbro*, which means 'threshold' or door of a house. Vishnu (V.116) prescribes a fine of 100 panas for a '*sa-mudra-griha-bhedeka*' (one who breaks open the sealed door of a house). Kautilya prescribes 48 panas as the fine for same offence (Arthashastra, III 20).

Achara 11 of the Charter tells a rule that '*samant – amatya = dutanam = anyesham ch = abhyupagama sayaniy – asana – siddhannam na dapayet,*[90]

Whenever a subordinate chief, an officer, or an army of the king came to a village, the inhabitants there should not be compelled to supply beds or couches, seats, and boiled rice(it could mean unboiled rice was to be supplied)

Some rules were laid down for guilds in this Charter. Acara 12 says, 'Members of different guilds should not be allowed to flock to the same market (*sarva – sreninam = ek apanako na deyah*). The idea was probably to see that different guilds did not occupy the same markets. The next acara says all the guilds should not be compelled to pay '*khova*', which may have meant 'share' of the lord of the market (*atta pati - bhaga*)

Achara 20 says,

Prapapuraka – go palah raja – grahena na grahyah.[91]

Prapa-puraka is a person entrusted with filling the cisterns with water in a place for watering cattle or supplying water to travellers. Such persons or milkmen were not to be apprehended or recruited for free labour on the king's behalf. Likewise, achara 24 says, *varshasu sva-vishayat ley artham – agataka – karshakah svamina na grahyah*—i.e.[92] cultivators coming out of areas for sowing seeds during rainy season were not be apprehended or engaged by the king as free labour.

Achara 32 tells that in case of fraud in delivery of raj— argghika (periodical offering made to the king)—the officers engaged were liable to a fine of three and one-fourth silver coins, and the fine could not be reduced even when there was a reasonable excuse.[93]

Achara 33 says an important provision. It says,

'*Mudr – apachare vinaye rupakah shat = sa padah saha dharmmikena.*[94]

Mudr-apachara is the crime of using counterfeit coins or misuse of official seals, the fine for which was six and one-fourth silver coins and no excuse for reduction was allowed.[95]

Another achara 34 says,

'*sthavara*' *– tya (vya) vahare samantaih avasitasya vinayo rupaka – satam – asht – ottaram*'[96]—i.e., if a *samanta* (or subordinate ruler) disposed of a case involving landed property without informing his overlord, he was liable to pay a fine of 108 silver coins.

Likewise, if somebody was found with a vessel full of wine distilled illegally, his fine was five silver coins (*madya-bhajan syavalokya rupakah pancha*). If, however, it was the first offence, fine was reduced to 21/2 silver coins. If he was caught a second time, the fine was doubled.[97]

On the other hand, an achara tells that the blacksmiths, carpenter, barbers, potters, and others could be recruited for forced labour under the supervision of *varikas* or officers.

(*Lohakara – rathakara – napita – kumbhakara – prabhritinam varikena vishtih karaniya*)[98]

The Madhuban C.P. of Harsha (632 AD) talks of a grant of a village *Somakundika* to learned Brahmana. The village had been formerly enjoyed by one Vamarthaya on the basis of a forged *shasana (kutasashasana)*. It shows that rules of Smrti to settle the punishment of forgers of royal edicts were not superfluous or unnecessary and that ancient forgeries did exist.

LAWS OF ARREST

Law of arrests, which is plain in itself, has been enunciated by Narada. A plaintiff should arrest a defendant who absconds when the cause is about to be tried, and one disregards the plaintiff's words until the legal summons has been issued. Confinement to a place, arrest for a limited time, restrictions regarding travelling, and prohibition from a specific act—this is the fourfold division of arrests.[99]

Kautilya's Arthashastra too dwells on them quite at length. In Chapter VIII, it deals possession and for a crime such as murder. Also, an investigating officer was liable to be punished if he held under restraint anyone who was clearly not guilty.[100] No one should falsely accuse another of being a thief. Doing so was a punishable offence. Protesting a thief (by hiding him) was also a punishable offence. If the ground was adequate, a person could be arrested on suspicion of having committed murder or theft or having a secret income from misappropriation or fraud or spying the enemy. Anybody with a suspicious behavior or disposition could be arrested. Because interrogation after some days was inadmissible, no one was to be arrested on suspicion of having committed theft or burglary if three nights elapsed since the crime unless caught with the tools of crime.

However, here we have an interesting variation in the inscription of Vishnusena, which denies arrest on ground of suspicion. Achara 4 in the Charter speaks,

'*sankaya grahanam n = asti*'—i.e., the royal officials should not go in for the apprehension of the persons, for taking up a case against one, or for seizing one's things through mere suspicion (*sanka*) of a crime.

PUNISHMENTS

The Indian philosophical tradition based on the concept of '*papa*' and '*punya*' presupposes on expiation of sins for any wrongs committed. Every action has a visible or invisible result or spiritual implications. Crime must be expiated, and in Hindu belief, expiation occurs in the form of punishment and repentance. K.V. Rangaswami Aiyangar rightly analyses punishment in the Hindu context and tells, "A crime has the feature of sin and sin is a crime against God." This is the ground for the collocation of both expiation and a secular penalty for crimes punishable by the state. The Hindu theory of punishment has the aim of deterrence and correction. Several times, the Smrti writers do not appear practical in some of the rigorous punishments prescribed. This is because the aim was to announce such punishments that deter the occurrence of the crimes.

The Indian belief, in other words distinguishes between expiation of sins and punishment for crime. Expiation was supposedly a moral act in order to evince the wrong done in the form of sin, which was against the God. Punishment was the visible penalty imposed at the behest of the king and enforceable by the state. In other words, as the idea of Dharma was evidently intertwined with law, any crime was perceived as violation of the stipulated Dharma norms as envisaged by law texts and law of the land in practice. Hence, it was seen as offence to divine (as law is religion based) and needed to be punished strongly to bring back moralities.

In the ancient tradition, the highly centralised Kautilyan state prescribed a classic example of a state regulated by an elaborate system of penalties.

Among the Smrtis, Manu has dwelled on what is punishment in detail in Chapter VII. He tells for the sake of the king, God formerly created his own son, Punishment, the protector of all creatures as an incarnation of law.[101] He advises the king to consider all time, place, strength and knowledge (of the offender) before inflicting just punishment on me who act unjustly. He tells that it is punishment which is the king, the manager of affairs and the surety for the four orders (social classes) obedience to the law.[102] It is punishment that governs all created being, protects them, watches over them while they sleep, and hence the wise declares punishment to be identical with the law.[103] If inflicted after due consideration, it makes all happy; but if inflicted without consideration, it destroys everything. It is the fear of punishment that yields the world enjoyment.[104]

The ancient Indian theory of punishment also puts up the ideal that the sinner if punished justly by the king. is absolved of the sin. Narada observes that offenders punished by the king attain heaven and they are absolved of sin if they were virtuous men.[105] Narada further advocates that if the accused such as thief is not punished by the king, the crime falls on the king.[106]

As far as rigorousness is concerned, it is generally accepted that the tone of punishment in the Dharmashastras and early Smrtis was more severe than the latter ones. Dr. Kane rightly remarked that "from Yajnavalkya, Narada and Brhaspati, the rigor of punishment was lessened and softened and fines came to be the ordinary punishment for many crimes".[107]

Katyayana has detailed the rules of punishment (he has devoted eighteen verses to it). Some of them are worth bringing to notice over here. In verse 481, he says, "Punishment is not at all prescribed (by sacred texts) for the preceptor, the father, the mother and also the relatives, when these are guilty of offences.[108] There was to be no punishment for an offence committed when one's life was in danger. Toeing the line of early Smrtis, Katyayana enunciates that a Brahmana could not be awarded death punishment even though he may be guilty of such offence. The king could banish him from the kingdom with all his wealth and without any bodily injury to him.[109] All the *varnas* were to follow the rules of *prayaschitta* (expiation for offences committed), or the king should prescribe proper punishment like fine or corporal injury.[110]

Further, if a Shudra was liable to be punished for a crime, the punishment would be double for the Kshatriyas and and double of it for Brahmanas.[111] The idea seems to be that a Kshatriya should receive double the punishment, which a Shudra would be awarded for the same offence and a Brahmana four times as much as of Shudra In other words, the social responsibility of maintaining law and order was greater on the upper two varnas than the lower orders. Rigourness of caste is also seen in the enunciation that if a Shudra was caught forsaking the order of *sanyasins* or practising '*japa*' (extent muttering of prayers) or home, he was to submit to death or corporal punishment or was liable to be punished with double fine.[112] The monopoly to offer such religious rituals or method of worship, as *japa* or chanting of verses were again caste tained and ironically limited to the uppermost class.

In the next three verses, Katyayana talks about punishment rules for women, all of which highlight the concern for women. First, women should pay half of the fine in money prescribed for a male; when the punishment is death in case of males that for women should be mutilation of a limb.[113]

Second, if women are not independent, they should not be arrested. It is the male (on whom they are dependent) who should be held the offender. The women should be punished by their lord, but the king should take away (for punishment) the male.[114] Third, even if a woman whose lord has gone on a journey be consigned to jail, she should be kept in confinement only till her lord returns.[115]

This assertion that women should not be arrested and that men whom they are dependent should be does not find any corroboration in secular literature. However, the Charter of Vishnusena mentions that for a crime committed by the husband, the wife should not be arrested (*Purusa apradhe stri na grahya*).[116]

Hiuen Tsang has mentioned about crime and punishment in his travelogue ((629–645 AD). He says, "As the government is honestly administered and the people live together on good terms, the criminal class is small. The statute law is sometimes violated and plots made against the sovereign, when the crime is brought to light the offender is imprisoned for life, he does not suffer any corporal punishment, but alive and dead, he is not treated as the member of the community (lit, as a man). For offences against social morality and disloyal and unfilial conduct, the punishment is to cut off the nose, or an ear, or a hand or a foot, or to banish the offender to another country or into the wildness. Other offences can be atoned for by a money payment."[117]

From his account, it appears that mutilation, banishing, imprisonment, or capital punishment was the prevalent modes of punishing the offender. Fahien[118] also informs that in mid-India, the criminals were fined according to the gravity of the offence committed, which might suggest that caste or Varna alone was not the lone basis of punishment. But Legge's translation of passages from Fahien suggests that criminals were fined according to circumstances of each caste, which may refer to caste variations.[119]

Torture existed as a method of punishment to extract the truth. In the *Dashakumaracarita*, in one instance, a jailor tells Apparavarman, who was put in jail on account of being drunk, "If you refuse to return Dhanamitra's magic purse or if you fail to restore your picking and stealing to the citizen, you will face eighteen tortures one after another."[120] Likewise, the Junagadh rock inscription of Skandagupta (AD 456) mentions that in his reign, a person discerning punishment was not subjected to such torture.[121] Probably, the suggestion was that in Skanadagupta's reign, though torture existed as a mode of punishment, it was not taken to extremes.

In *Dashakumaracharita*, Kampala, the King's minister, having his eyes on the kingdom, poisoned his sovereign Chandrasimha and heir apparent Chandaghosh, and so his eyes were taken away.

Banishment was quite a prevalent mode of punishment. This was the highest punishment a Brahmana offender could be subjected (for he was excused of death punishment, being the highest in the social order). Hiuen Tsang had mentioned as to how once a person dared to make an attempt on the life of Harsa and everybody demanded that he be put to death. The king, however, enquired into the matter, punished the main culprit, and pardoned the rest. He banished 500 Brahmanas to the frontier and then had returned to his capital.[122] Probably, under the influence of Buddhism, Harsha did not take up capital punishment and substituted it with banishment.

In a number of cases, property of the criminal was confiscated, but that was after the due permission from the town council and the king. A person could be exempted from death, and instead his property could be confiscated and he could be exited. There is a mention of such a plea in the Dashakumaracharita where the king condemned a merchant to death, accused of theft and Dhanamitra on his fellow's behalf pleads – "Oh! Sir, royal tradition graciously grants exemption from the death penalty to merchant's guilty of such felonies. If you feel furious confiscate the criminal's property and exile him."[123]

Death punishment was the severe form of punishment. It is mentioned in Ashokan inscription as that the king granted the accused 'three days respite' in one such case, being trampled by elephant was considered the most agonising. *Dashakumaracharita* also mentions one Arthapala as condemned to death for theft.[124]

Royal amnesty could be granted to the accused. Kalidasa has this practice to have prevailed in Gupta times. Bana has also mentioned that on Harsha's birth, all prisoners were set free by Prabhakarvardana. Most of these punishments seem to have prevailed in South India too.

The penal system then that emerges from the Smrti provisions seems to be a harsh one. Monier Williams gave a critical analysis when he pointed out the three most conspicuous features of Manu's penal laws as marking those which represent the earliest forms of criminal legislation—severity, inconsistency and a belief in the supposed justice of the lex talionis, the latter leading to punishments which in later times would be considered unjustifiably disproportionate to the offences committed and sometimes barbaric.

More or less, nearly all the Smrti writers exhibit a tough stand with respect to punishments although the punishments mildened by the time of Katyayana. Mutilation, death sentence, and imprisonment indicate that punishments were in the nature of deterrents. It was aimed to create a fear psychosis that would deter people from committing such crimes. However, the singlemost conspicuous feature of the entire system of punishments was the legal privileges enjoyed by the Brahmana offender. He is treated only leniently but evidently excused from the purview of harsh punishments owning just this birth in the highest social strata. The offenders are punished, but there seems to be a graduated scale of punishments according to their social class. Punishments were brutal for all the lesser socials, except the privileged Brahmanas.

One could question the prevalence of such a society where death penalty had a distinctly marked space. Given the debates in today's context when Law

Commission has been urging to restrict the use of death penalty to only the cases of terrorism, a question that eludes us still is which is the most human way of punishing a heinous crime as human annihilation. A very paradoxical fact is whether a death sentence can be human? The truth is that there is no humane way to implement death sentence, which is simply an act of revenge, a tit for tat. The death sentence is simply the society's revenge on the individual and this cannot form the basis of a civilized polity. Indeed by sanctioning violence, death penalty brutalises society as a whole. Moreover. there is no certainty whether justice has been done or undone.

On the other hand, it is also not fair to permit the murderers or serial killers back into the society. Principles of justice demand that a person should be punished according to the gravity of the offence and most important should be held accountable for his irrational actions. If there would be no capital punishment, life imprisonment would be the other option. But this is neither economically viable nor a hope for a person who knows that he is going to spend the rest of his life in the prison. As a journalist once wrote (TOI), 'his life is already over. It's just his desire that has been indefinitely delayed. In such a case, he would rather prefer to die once than every day. In this light perhaps, it's time to initiate a debate as to how to put such prisoners to death humanely than by hanging. Lethal injection, as the talk goes on, could be one option that could minimise suffering.

NOTES AND REFERENCES

1.   K.V. Rangaswami Aiyangar, *Some Aspects of the Hindu View of Life according to Dharmashastra*, p.160.
2.   Ibid., p.161.
3.   Vishnu, Ch.XXXIII, v.1, 2; p.131–132.
4.   Thomas Watters, *On Yuan Chwang's Travels in India*, p.171–172.
5.   Ibid., p.172.
6.   *Epigraphia Indica*, Vol.XXX, p.170.
7.   Ibid.
8.   B.S. Upadhyaya, *India in Kalidasa*, p.144.
9.   *Proceedings of Indian History Congress*, 1959, p.150.
10.   cf. Naradasmrti, v.1, p.201

11. Buhler, *Laws of Manu*, v.267, p.301.
12. Ibid., v.268, p.301.
13. Ibid., v.269, p.301.
14. Ibid., v.270, p.301–302.
15. Ibid., v.271, p.302.
16. Ibid., v.272, p.303.
17. cf. *Smrti Chandrika*, II, p.328.
18. L.N. Rangarajan, *Kautilya: The Arthashastra*, p.472.
19. Buhler, *Laws of Manu*, v.279–280, p.303.
20. Ibid., v.281, p.303.
21. Ibid., v.284, p.304.
22. Ibid., v.286, p.304.
23. Ibid., v.287, p.304.
24. Ibid., v.285, p.304.
25. Ibid., v.289, p.305.
26. Ibid., v.293–294, p.305.
27. Ibid., v.296–298, 300, p.306.
28. cf. *Brhaspatismrti*, v.11, p.175.
29. cf. *Naradasmrti*, v.27, p.213.
30. Ibid., v.32, p.213.
31. L.N. Rangarajan, *Kautilya: The Arthashastra*, pp.474–475.
32. cf. *Katyayanasmrti*, v.783, p.281.
33. cf. *Brhaspatismrti*, v.16, p.176.
34. Ibid., v.17, p.176.
35. *Epigraphia Indica*, Vol.XXX, p.175.
36. Ibid., p.170.
37. Ibid., p.170.
38. Achara 40, Ibid., p.175
    5 vimsopaka = 1/4 of the silver coin.
    1 vimsopaka = 1/20 of the standard silver coin.
39. cf. *Yajnavalkyasmrti*, II, 159.
40. Buhler, *Laws of Manu*, v.304, p.307.
41. Ibid., v.306–307, p.307
42. Ibid., v.316, p.309.
    v.317 tells, "The killer of a learned Brahmana throws his guilt on him who eats his food, an adulterous wife on her (negligent) husband, a

(sinning) pupil or sacrifice on (their negligent) teacher (or priest), a thief on the king (who pardons him)."

43. L.N. Rangarajan, *The Arthashastra*, p.478.
44. Ibid., p.479.
45. It is, however, found as an additional section in a Nepali manuscript discovered by Jolly. *Cf. Sacred Books of the East* XXXIII, pp.223–32.
46. cf. *Brhaspatismrti*, v.2–3, p.178.
47. cf. Ibid., v.4, p.178.
48. cf. *Vishnusmrti*, v.78, p.32.
49. cf. *Katyayanasmrti*, v.827, p.291.
50. Ibid., v.815–817, p.288.
51. Ibid., v.813–814, p.288.
52. B.S. Upadhyaya, *India in Kalidasa*, p.142.
     cf. Vikramorvashi, p.124 –
53. Ibid., p.146.
54. Ibid., cf. *Shakuntala*, p.186.
55. Ibid., cf. I *Shakuntala*, p.187
56. Ibid., v.797, p.283.
57. Ibid., v.345, p.314.
58. Ibid., Notes.
59. cf. *Naradasmrti*, v.2, p.204.
60. cf. *Vishnusmrti*, Ch.XXXV, v.1, pp.132–133.
61. Ibid., Ch.XXXVI, v.102.
62. cf. *Katyayanasmrti*, v.795, p.283.
63. Ibid., v.797, p.283.
64. Ibid., v.798, p.284.
65. Ibid., v.800, p.284.
66. Katyayana on Vyavahara, v.806, p.286. There is a similar verse in Yajnavalkya, II.277.
67. Benjamin Khan, *Concept of Dharma in Valmiki Ramayana*, p.137.
68. Buhler, *Laws of Manu*, Ch VIII, v.351, p.315.
69. Visnu, Ch.V, v.190, p.41
70. Visnu, Ch.V, v.196, p.41, vide Manu. Ch.VIII, v.386, p.321.
71. Buhler, *Laws of Manu*, Ch VIII, v.352, p.315.
72. Ibid., Ch.VIII, v.353.
73. Ibid., Ch.VIII, v.354. 355, p.315.
74. Ibid., Ch.VIII, v.356. 358, p.316.

75. Ibid., v.361, p.317.
76. Ibid., v. 359, p.316.
77. Ibid., v. 364, p.317.
78. L.N. Rangarajan, *Kautilya, The Arthashastra*, p.405.
79. P.V. Kane, *History of Dharmashastra*, p.572–573.
80. Buhler, *Laws of Manu*, Ch. IX, V.222, p.387.
81. Ibid., v.223.
82. Ibid., v.227.
83. L.N. Rangarajan, *Kautilya, The Arthashastra*, p.139.
84. Ibid., p.139–140.
85. G.K. Bhat, Preface to *Mrcchakatika*, cf, II, 5,6.
86. cf. Act III.
87. cf. *Yajnavalkyasmrti*, v.202, p.341.
88. Buhler, *Laws of Manu*, Ch.VIII, v.222, p.387.
89. *Epigraphia Indica*, Vol.XXX, p.170.
90. Ibid., p.171.
91. Ibid., p.172.
92. Ibid., p.173.
93. Ibid., p.174.
94. Ibid., p.174.
95. Vide. *Yajnavalkyasmrti*, p.268 (v.240).
96. *Epigraphia Indica*, Vol.XXX, p.174.
97. Ibid., p.175.
98. Ibid., p.178
99. cf. *Naradasmrti*, I, 47–54, quoted by J.R. Gharpure in *Yajnavalkyasmrti*, Book II, p.8.
100. L.N. Rangarajan, *Kautilya, The Arthashastra*, (4.8.8) in VI.Iv.
101. Buhler, *Laws of Manu*, Ch. VII, v.14, p.218.
102. Ibid., Ch.VII, v.17, p.219.
103. Ibid., v.18, p.219.
104. Ibid., Ch.VII, v.22, p.219.
105. Cf. *Naradasmrti*, v.48, p.228.
106. Ibid., v.49, p.228.
107. P.V. Kane, *History of Dharmashastra*, 3.390.
108. P.V. Kane, *Katyayana on Vyavahara*, v.481, p.210–211.
109. Ibid., v.483, p.211.
110. Ibid., v.484, p.211.

111. Ibid., v.485, p.211.
112. Ibid., v.486, p.212.
113. Ibid., v.487, p.212.
114. Ibid., v.488, p.212.
115. Ibid., v.489, p.212.
116. *Epigraphia Indica*, Vol.XXX, p.170.
117. Thomas Watters, *On Yuan Chwang's Travels in India*, pp.171–172.
118. S. Beal, *Travels of Fahsien*, pp.54–55.
119. Legge, *A Record of Buddhist Kingdom*, p.43.
120. cf. *Dashakumaracharita*, p.78.
121. *Corpus Inscriptionum Indicarum*, III, No.14, p.62.
122. Watters, op cit., I, p.172.
123. *cf. Dashakumaracharita*, p.137.
124. Ibid. p.101.

CHAPTER VI

Law and the Gender Discourse
Understanding Legal Injunctions
for Men and Women

One of the prime concerns of women's movement in the history of Indian law has been the concern for equality and gender justice. Law plays an important role in shaping the gender status in the society and more so where unequal status may be rooted in prevailing patriarchal discourses through religion. Under a male dominated society, whether in a religion based society or in a modern state, law becomes a terrain where the discourse of patriarchy could not only be mooted but could also be perpetuated. It could even turn out to be a site for contestation of power for each in terms of legal priviliges and obligations. Early India provides a picture of female exclusion from the arena of education, political representation, economy and law and hence, provides a pertinent area for study. The struggle for women became an accentuated struggle in early India as gender was complicated further by other stratifiers such as race, caste, rural, urban or class differences. One could study the gender status of men or women with reference to primarily issues such as the access or ease to legal recourse, protections available, responsibilities endorsed on each one of them by laws, their role in law making if the political environment was so conducive or with regard to the punishments- whether they were gendered. A parallel search in gender status in law could be to study the legal texts or available codes and analyse if there were any distinct efforts to mute or overlook women's voices, as the society was engineered by ruling male elite as well as to look for gender consciousness in particular.

In an interesting article titled *"Total liberation: No place for Gender"* by Andrew Cohen, who analysed the concept of gender consciousness, a question was raised whether the path for liberation, which implies doing away with ego, fundamentally the same for both sexes? If the goal is enlightenment, Cohen says, the path is one and the same. Total liberation means transcendence of all differences to discover the true self. He remarks, "Our true self is free from any notion of gender, from any sense of difference, whatsoever. And, in order to discover that self, which is our 'natural state or already liberated condition, the intense attachment to and identification with being a separate personality, including its maleness or femaleness, has to be transcended." Very truly, men and women may be physically separate identities but what is required for total freedom is doing away with the investment, both emotional and psychological in being male and female. Only then gender consciousness would be free from the ego's unsavory motives—desire to dominate, control and seduce.

But doing away with this gender consciousness at the emotional and psychological level is very difficult in a preconditioned, patriarch-driven society where gender plays an important role. A society may be patriarchal or matrilineal or egalitarian, but what is nearly always pervasive as a constitutive element in the society is the consciousness of gender—the awareness of the maleness or femaleness of oneself. It is this consciousness, then, that lends to a framework of society that defines the place of men and women over there. In this way, in connecting with the past, gender becomes not only an important and useful tool of analysis but also an essential category for historical understanding. What appears paradoxical is that despite an innate consciousness about the existence of gender thoughts, there is a deliberate attempt to mute these voices of gender especially of women on the part of earlier historians. The history that we have then becomes the history with respect to primarily one half of the society and hardly any women to talk of.

Prof. Alice Kessler Harris has analysed that considering a gendered perspective would involve the study of social relations of sexes as a source of change and power. It would then enable us to acknowledge men and women as gendered identities and explain their behavior towards the social responsibility. Gender is an axis that we need to understand in consonance with other axes such as class, race, ethnicity, political structures, or economic institutions. Gender is embedded in these axes[1]

Alice goes on to explain appropriately that the focus of post -modern theory, not merely on identity but on multiple identities introduces gender into the formula for assessing consciousness, turning masculinity and femininity into the central tropes through which interpretation is rendered. In such a situation, there is better comprehension of the past, for gender then comes as a beacon light on the dark corners of the history. Moreover, he emphasises on two important aspects of gender: One that gender is fluid. It is a process, changing over time, and its participation varies with historical circumstance; and like class, it is identical and normative, conditioning both individual futures and views of the world. Second, because it constitutes the ground on which identity is built and consciousness formed, it is more pervasive than class and becomes a constitutive element of it. More simply, the influence of gender varies from society to society. The consciousness of gender is more far reaching than the consciousness of class, and both have a conditioning role in society parallel to each other.

Gender consciousness in a patriarchal lineage society, such as in India, can be analysed at two levels. One can understand this consciousness from the theoretical point of view and the perceived consciousness with regards to male and female in the society while the other could be at the level of everyday experience in different stratas or set of people spread over a geographical area. In the Vedic conception, there seems to be a unity of perception and a unitary approach (embodied in the concept of ultimate Brahmana who is gender neutral). While at the societal level, there prevailed distinct gender preferences, at the consciousness level, the soul was supposed to be form less and without any attributes and in unity.

In the Indian context, where the patriarchal society defined the norms of social and ethical living in ancient society, gender comes forth as an influence that not only determined the larger framework of society but dictated even the minutest details in various institutional structures. The consciousness of masculinity and femininity seems to be the case on the minds of the Smrti writers so much that nearly every injunction is with respect to men and women separately rather than treating them as a single identity. These gendered identities define the respective status of men and women in society. The all-pervasive masculinity relegates women to a secondary position in society and from there builds up her position as one in need of special legal protection.

Historically seen, the earliest gods, which is the Vedic gods, were genderless. Vedic society too was deemed to be fairer towards women than the society of the *Dharmashastra* period. The Vedic texts do not forbid women from performing any rituals either. In other words, the masculine and the feminine components of the society were more or less equally important even though the logic for it was derived from the argument that no religious action was complete without the participation of the better half. Even the *Upanishads* do not speak of discrimination based on gender. The *atma* by itself is believed to be genderless.

Then how did gender differences originate? Probably the only explanation lies in the fact that it's human constructions or barriers of thinking that brought forth these discriminations based on gender.

It was a post-Vedic phenomenon and legitimised by the *Dharmasutras* period. More specifically, the patriarchal elements, by means of their rising superior positions continuously idealised and imposed a society with explicit gender differences. A schemed and biased consciousness created such texts and enunciations that ensured that women were systematically relegated to a subjugated status, and by attaching divine sanctions or venerable status to the law writers, the same was strengthened in the society. Subsequently, these gender discriminations were given the veil of customs and further perpetrated. A going back at any point was neither aimed nor desired, for it ensured the male superiority position as well as the Brahmana's privileged status and upper hand in the society. The casualty however was the society, for gender differences dictated first the social norms and then entered in law itself.

Law seems to be the most appropriate area that needs to be focused under the auspices of gender. Law not only defines or determines the gender boundaries but also gets affected. It sets the pace for development of men and women in society. It also gets affected in turn by the status of gender in society. Law and gender are somewhat in a symbiotic relationship. An understanding about this dynamics will help us in understanding both law and gender.

In early India, conjugal togetherness was seen as the converging point of gender holisticism. Any balanced approach would begin from the premise that in Indian thinking, the concept of 'eternal companionship', i.e., the union of *'Purusha'* and *'Prakriti'* was the essence of eternal peace and perpetuation in the society. Any deviation from it was considered gender imbalance as envisioned by seers. Quite naturally then, nearly all the Smrtis, peace, and dramas extolled the men and more so women within the familial context rather than in isolation from this basic social unit. Both men and women were bestowed with privileges of varying gradient but not without obligations and disabilities. Law was not equal, for both the genders for the social status was not of parity. The social status in turn brought the gender prejudices in law, which not only restricted the evolutionary nature of law but marred it with such weaknesses that led to further deterioration of women's position in society as such and their subserviation to the patriarchal elite in early India.

Law in ancient India considered men as invested with a juristic personality and women as a dependent on him. She was deemed to have no juristic individuality although she was punishable for her offences. Whether we study the celestial or terrestrial, divine or semi-divine, characters, princesses, hermit girls, or courtesans, the predominant conception of women is in the capacity of daughter, sister, mother, or wife. The man, however, could stand outside these relations as well. Both were expected to adhere to the laws of Dharma introduced in the concept of *rta* or the Smrti laws. Any breach or deviation from it was a crime committed by them in person that called for punishment. Women, however, being assumed into a subjugated status, for crimes committed by her, it was the male relation to whom she obeyed that was called for owning the responsibility. For her crimes, it was the feminine character that was deemed despicable and was considered the reason. For men, however, no definition or limits of male character were laid down. Hence, he could commit crimes under the influence of vices laid down in the *shastras*, which probably would be treated more a matter of circumstance than the inherent nature of the masculine sex!

Equality before law was a far cry from the gender point of view. Along with gender prejudices, the caste distinctions accentuated, the rigors of punishment for the legally and socially less privileged men and women in society. A Brahmana male enjoyed far better immunities in law than a Shudra male. Similarly, Shudra woman, who was considered despicable by birth, got far less legal protection than a *Brahmani* or a *Ksatriyani*. For the same crime that a Shudra man was to be hanged, the Brahmana offender was not to be punished more than banishment. Likewise, for a similar crime that man was to be put to death, a female was to be either mutilated for publicly ostracised (adultery). The husband seems to have been holding some kind of correcting powers over the wife (with law permitting a certain degree of violence for this sake). She could act as witness but to her group alone. Male witnesses were, however, not bound by any such gender rules.

Here, we undertake a review of the legal provisions as laid down by the Smrtis, epics, and seen in the dramas with respect to men and women with respect to various social segments. Although at some places, moral and social injunctions have also been cited along with legal injunctions, the purpose is to give a complete perspective to the place of gender prevalent in law as seen in early India.

The Smrtis, as a whole, have devoted long sections dwelling upon the duties of husband and wife. That is because marriage was considered the ultimate need of society for the sake of continuance of peace and perpetuation. Nearly all the Smrtis have given much importance to the *'grhastha' asrama*, which is considered the most important Dharma of a person. For women, especially, marriage was seen as essential sacrament without which she was not only incomplete but also devoid of any respect in the society. As Manu put it, "between wives *(striyah)* who are destined) to bear children, who secure many blessings, who are worthy of worship and irradiate (their dwellings) and between goddesses of fortune *(striyah* who reside) in the houses (of men), there is no difference whatsoever".[2] The *Arthashastra* succinctly states that "the aim of taking a wife is to beget sons" (3.2.4.2). From this followed the principle of partition of the family line through sons[3] and the basis of discrimination between sons and daughters. Also, within the class of women, it distinguished between women who were blessed with children and those who for some reason failed to beget offsprings.

For the men, all the *ashramas* were important. As a *'snataka'* or student, he was expected to follow the rules of brahmacharya while, when married, the husband held an authority over his wife and was emphasised upon the role of wife. Manu writes, "Offsprings, religious rites, faithful service, highest conjugal happiness and heavenly bliss for the ancestors and oneself depend on one's wife alone."[4] Women were to be honoured if they were wives, daughters, sisters, and mothers. Some moral injunctions even coaxed the men to take care of women in relation if they desired their own welfare. In verse 57, Manu says,

"Where the female relations, live in grief the family soon wholly perishes, but that family where they are not unhappy ever prosperous.[5]

Viewed from the legal eye, marriage was a compulsion for women and a matter of choice for men. The legal tie of marriage was stronger for the weaker sex in the society. It was a lifelong contract between the husband and the wife, considered sacred and above law. As Manu puts it, neither by sale nor by repudiation is a wife released from her husband, such we know the law to be which the Lord of creatures (*Prajapati*) made of old.[6] However, permission was there to supersede women if they failed in begetting the offsprings. Manu quite blatantly puts it that "a barren wife may be superseded in the eighth year, she whose children all die in the tenth, she who bears only daughters in the eleventh but she who is quarrelsome without delay."[7] However, for a sick but virtuous wife, Manu tells she may be superseded only with her consent and must never be disgraced! The text of Manusmrti has hence been very controversial as though it extolls women at times, at other times completely appears to be utterly biased against women. These discrepancies or heterogeneities could be attributed to the text being authored by several Manu (s) instead of one single author.

For the wife, Manu spells that if the husband went abroad for some sacred duty, (she) must wait for him eight years; if to acquire leaning or fame, six years; if for pleasures, three years.[8] However, she was not to be considered independent at any time. Her father protects (her) in childhood, her husband protects (her) in youth, and her sons protect (her) in old age; a woman is never fit for independence.[9] Moreover, she who controls her thoughts, speech, and acts violates not her duty towards the lord, dwells with him in the heaven, and in this world is called virtuous. Manu enjoins that a virtuous wife should serve her husband as if he were a god, whether he was of evil character or lustful or devoid of good qualities (V.154).

Likewise, Yajnavalkya (1.77) opines that for women, this is the highest duty that they obey their husband's words.

Kane quotes the Ramayana (Ayodhya Kanda 24, 26–27), which says, "The husband is the God and the master of the wife, while she is alive and she obtains the highest heaven by serving her husband."[10]

Marriage was considered so important that if the father did not fulfill the duty, the maiden could select the bridegroom by choice without incurring any guilt (Ch.IX, V.91). In fact, there is a beckoning for the male relations if they fail in this duty. As Manu put it, "Reprehensible is the father who gives not (his daughter in marriage) at a proper times, reprehensible is the husband who approaches not (his wife in due season) and reprehensible is the son who does not protect his mother after her husband has died" (Ch.IX V.24). Wife was essential for the performance of religious sacraments in the Hindu household; hence, religious rites were to be performed by the husband together with wife (Manu, Ch.IX, V. 96). The father was condemned if he accepted a gratuity for his daughter's marriage. Manu says, "Even a Shudra ought not to take a nuptial fee, when he gives away his daughter, for he who takes a fee sells his daughter, covering (the transaction by another name)" (Manu, Ch.IX V.96).

Much has been said despicable about the feminine character in the Smrtis. Husbands were supposed to guard their wives against evil inclinations, which were supposed to be the second nature of women. Manu puts it quite distastefully that "women must particularly be guarded against evil inclinations, however trifling, for if they are not guarded they will be sorrow on two families" (Chi, V.5). However, no such assertion in any of the smrtis is made about the character of men who often exhibited such inclinations. Manu has even discussed the causes of ruin of women, not of men. It is difficult to imagine that women who were already relegated to a weaker position and made dependent, did they dare to follow any such inclinations? He says, "Drinking (spirituous liquor) associating with wicked people, separation from the husband, gambling abroad, sleeping (at unreasonable hours) and dwelling in other men's houses are the six causes of the ruin of women. The texts, however, do not speak anything on causes of ruin for men as such.

On the other hand, a virtuous wife is extolled to immense heights. All the smrtis and digests speak about the duties of wife and that she should not only obey but be devoted to her husband. Rewards were there for such faithful women Pativrata as being called virtuous in this world and securing place in the heaven. If, however, she was faithless to her husband, she could incur censure in this world and may be lean as a female jackal in the next life or could be afflicted with bad diseases (Ch.IX, V.165)! Likewise, Yajnavalkya (1.75 and 87) too praised a faithful wife. She attains glory in this world and begets heaven. Nearly all the epics, Puranas speak of the powers of faithful wife. However, here again faithfulness is an attribute that is expected more from the women than from men. Why the smritis and other texts do not talk of bestowing heaven on faithful husbands falls in line with the argument of patriarchal preceptors of the society!

However, a wife had the legal right to reside in her husband's house. She was further entitled to be maintained in the house by the husband. As Manu puts it (XI.10), 'one must maintain one's aged parents a virtuous wife and a minor son by doing even a hundred bad acts. "They can never be cast off as such." Narada (*Stripumsa* V.95) suggests that the king should bring to the proper path by inflicting heavy fines a husband who abandons his wife that is obedient, not harsh of tongue, vigilant, chaste, and endowed with sons. Maintenance was an essential element of the husband duties. Manu tells that a man must never leave his wife without maintenance: "A man who has business may depart after securing maintenance for his wife, for a wife even though virtuous may be corrupted if she be distressed by want of subsistence." Hence, for the wife (who was expected to be faithful), maintenance by husband was her legal right and privilege, which could not be neglected.

Yajnavalkya, 1.76, Narada (Stripumsa, V.95) says that the husband is liable to pay one-third of his estate or a fine for deserting a virtuous wife. Also, in number of instances, the king had the right to interfere to ensure justice.

Manu and other Smrti writers have emphasised mutual fidelity as the highest law of the dharma of husband and wife. Both were to consciously avoid venturing outside the marriage, although the prevalence of instances of polygamy and an organised class of courtesans suggests that men had the option to look beyond the legally wedded wife. However, punishments for adultery were severe for both the sexes (as discussed under adultery section).

Men had certain legal protections against deception in marriage agreements. Giving a damsel without having told the defect was a punishable offence (only Kautilya explicitly mentions that arranging the marriage of a man married without mentioning a sexual defect is also an offence punishable with a fine double that for a girl) (VIII 3.15).However, there is no instance of a verse that speaks vice-versa.

Narada (Stripumsa, V.89) prohibits the husband or wife to lodge a complaint against each other with their relations or with the king. Yajnavalkya (11.294—Mitakshara) tells that a judicial proceeding between husband and wife as plaintiff and defendant before the king is forbidden. However, if the king gets to know personally or individually of the wrong done by one to the other, the king must bring round the husband or the wife to the path of duty by appropriate punishment or it is the king who incurs the sin.[11] Kane has listed certain matters of which the king could take cognisance without anybody's complaint: the murder of a woman, *varnasankara* (admixture of castes), adultery, pregnancy of a widow from a person other than the husband, abortion, etc.

Marriage was further an insoluble tie for both men and women. In Manu (IX. 46), dissolution of marriage was not legally permissible. Mutual fidelity was the law for the husband and wife until death. There is nothing in the smrtis, epics, or digests to suggest that a legal divorce kind of thing existed in early India. In fact, as Kane puts it, "divorce in the ordinary sense of the word has been unknown to the Dharmashastras and to the Hindu Society for about 2000 years (except on ground of custom among lower castes). Even when the husband was allowed to abandon the wife for her lapses, still she in most cases was entitled to at least a starving maintenance." The word '*punarbhu*' might suggest a remarriage of widow, but divorce does not appear to be in vogue from any instance.

Marriage was emphasised as the most important *samskara* or sacrament by all Smrtis. Stripumdharma or the section in Manusmrti (Ch IX) discusses the respective duties of husband and wife as one of the eighteen titles of *Vyavahara*. This section was meant to regulate the marriages and it deterred both from initiating any legal proceedings against each other.

The right to supercession in marriage, under certain circumstances, led to practices like polyandry. Instances of polyandry are very meagre, except for the glaring example of Draupadi in the epic Mahabharata. Likewise, suggesting a period of waiting for women when her husband had gone abroad, the Smrti writers also suggests a possibility of remarriage of women. Dr. Kane cites the story of Damayanti, which suggests that when the husband was not heard of for many years, a wife could remarry again. Damayanti is said to have sent a message to Rtuparna that Nala was not heard for many years. Damayanti was going to celebrate svayamvara (process of choosing bridegroom by self choice), and Rtuparna hurried for it without thinking it as a strange thing (vanaparva 70.24).[12] However, remarriage was more an idealistic alternative than a practical option for chastity of women, especially as the wife was emphasised not only till the husband was alive but even after his death. Nowhere is a second husband recommended for virtuous women. (Manu says IX.47, "A maiden can be given only once.") A husband could, however, take another wife in practical life. Kane has written that Haradatta quotes Manu 111.174 and says that a son procreated on another's wife is called '*kunda*' if the husband is living and '*golaka*' if the husband is dead.[13] Narada prescribes a fine for taking a second wife without reason, but it is doubtful whether it was enforced. Kautilya (3.241) writes a man may marry any number of wives (subject to conditions spelt out) provided that he pays (each of) the wives their dowry, their property, and adequate maintenance (instance of polyandry is seen in Mahabharata epic).

Moreover, in suggesting the maintaining of chastity, the smrti writers were harsh on the widows. Sati was advocated for the chaste wives after the death of the husband. However, none of the smrtis actually talk of sati, except for a reference about it in Vishnu. The Manusmrti is silent on it. The Vishnu Dharmasutra says that "on her husband's death, the widow should observe celibacy or should ascend the funeral pyre after him.[14] Kane has studied that. Strabo (DV,1.30 and 62), a Greek write on early India, mentions that Greeks under Alexander found sati being practised among the Cathais in the Punjab, and the practice arose from the apprehension that wives would desert or poison their husbands.[15] However, sati was a social practice with no legal sanction. However, the state showed no special initiative to mitigate this evil, which continued illegally till much after.

After the death of the spouse, it was woman who suffered the stigma as a widow, and nowhere the Smrti writers talk of a widower. Remarriage being an easier option for men, it was the women who suffered the social abuse after the death of the husband. Widows were referred as having dishevelled hair, in despair, and inauspicious. There were no special laws for the protection of widows except that she got few rights in the property (discussed later). Nonetheless, a host of duties have been ascribed to the widows.

Niyoga (practice of getting married to the appointed person when the husband was either incapable of fatherhood or died without having a child) permitted within certain limits. Manu first suggested it and then condemned it in strongest possible terms. Manu (IX 59–61) and Narada (Stripumsa, 80-83) allow a woman to go for *niyoga* or secure a son from her brother-in law if her husband is dead and she desired to have an offspring (Gautama 18, 4–8). If the child was begotten at the request of a living husband, the child belonged to the husband. The focus was so much on begetting a 'son' or a 'legal heir' that woman's wishes were neglected to a secondary position. More often than not, niyoga was a matter of compulsion than choice. Narada, however, providing certain immunities, says that if a widow or a male acts contrary to the stringent provision about *niyoga*, he or she should be severely punished by the king in order to avoid confusion. Yajnavalkya (11.234) makes such a person liable to be sentenced to a fine of one hundred panas. These restrictions must have made the prevalence of such practices on large scale impossible.

The Hindu Law of inheritance has its origins in the Vedic school of thought in the thought that son is the one who libertes the soul or helps in achieving salvation. According to Manu, the moment a son was born, he was freed from his debts towards ancestors and hence, entitled for receiving the whole estate. Jimutavahana says that Smrti does not presume any property rights for sons or daughters while the parents are alive. For the sons, however, the law of primogeniture applied, and the eldest son succeeded to the property, taking care of the youngsters, giving them respective shares. A daughter, however, had no direct legal right in the property of her father. To maiden sisters, as the Smrti writer envisaged, the brothers were expected to give a share (one-fourth each of his share); and if anybody refused, he was to be considered an outcaste (there was no legal punishment for him but a social one). In short, the brothers were expected to arrange the dowry of their sisters (as referred earlier in chapter on civil law). An appointed daughter's (*putrika*) son, however, could be taken as an heir. Kautilya allows the daughters to succeed if there are no sons. Among wives of different castes, however, a son of a Brahmana wife was allowed three shares; a son of a Kshatriya, two; a son of a Vaishya, a share and a half; and a son of Shudra, one share (Ch.IX.V.157—Manu).

A wife had the right to maintenance, but no explicit legal share in the property of her husband is spelt out. Manu and other writers recognise the limited separate property of women (*stridhana*) that was for the unmarried daughters alone. Manu and Narada do not allow the widow of a sonless male to succeed as heir (Gautama contemplates that she could be the heir along with other sapindas-which means till third generation from mother's side and fifth generation from father's side and sagotra-same clan lineage). Yanjavalkya (II.85) mentions the widow as the first heir to the property of a sonless husband. Brhaspati declared that the wife was to be the successor to the wealth of her husband in such situation and in her default, the daughter. But Katyayana puts across a hedging and says a widow could take the wealth of her husband provided she was chaste (and, in her default, the unmarried daughter) (V.926). But a wife who is full of evil deeds, is immodest, wastes her property, or is given to adultery does not (deserve) to inherit the wealth of her husband (V.929). The fact that widowers actually enjoyed very meager rights and no practical right to succeed becomes clear from Shakuntala (Act VI) where the minister writes to the king that the estate of a merchant dying at sea will escheat to the crown and will not go to his widow.[16]

Women were given the legal right over her property called *stridhana*. Katyayana, who is the most advanced in the treatment of the topic, recognised six types of stridhana,[17] (mentioned in chapter on Civil Law) This right was not over the immovable property. But Katyayana tells that if any property was brought by her labour, the wife's ownership was recognised over it, but the right of alienation was subject to the husband's writers. Katyayana says that where basic maintenance was denied, the wife had full right to demand her *stridhana* and also her share (that would have been her husband's on partition) from the coparceners. She had the perpetual legal right to reside in her husband's house (V.910) except when afflicted with deadly disease. None of the male members were deemed to have any right over this woman's own property, and if anybody would forcibly take it away, he was to be fined along with interest. Another verse (V.916) makes it binding for the sons to pay the stridhana promised to a woman by her husband as seriously as a debit.

Here, as Kane pointed out, the instance from Smrtichandrika (III.P.656) that when a wife got married, she had some kind of dominion over her husband's property, though always subordinate to him but the man did not even enjoy any kind of dominion over his wife's *stridhana*. *Stridhana*, hence was then the only area in which women enjoyed absolute legal right without any interference from men's side. Even when the *stridhana* devolved in the absence of daughters, it went to the sons in their absence to relatives (who gave this wealth) and only as a last option to the husband (Kautilya 111.2 p.153).

Among the epics, especially if we focus on gender picturisation, we get a picture of society where Dharma was considered the supreme goal of human life, the 'Summum bonum of life', and both. Sita and Ram come forth as the epitomes of ideal 'womanhood' or 'manhood'. It is so much a glorious illustration of the ideal 'women' perceived by the Brahamana preceptors that her purity of moral character and her devotion to her husband in prosperity and poverty have become proverbial. Likewise, Rama is picturised as the ideal son, ideal brother, and ideal husband. Valmiki, in fact, finds an obedient wife synonymous with *Dharma* in which *Artha* (material prosperity) and *Kama* (desire) fully reside.

He says righteousness, *kama*, and *artha* combine in one as a virtuous woman. If obedient and dutiful, she helps a man to acquire *Dharma* by her charm and beauty. She satisfies *kama*, and by giving birth to a son, she brings profit. In short, Sita is the representative of the typical stereotype of a subservient woman as would be picturised by the Brahmanical patriarchs. No wonder, it is she who is chosen as the ideal than the women characters from Mahabharata who seem to be more independent and assertive.

Rama, fulfilling the roles as ideal son and brother, also appears as an ideal husband (in vow of ekapatni-one wife). His love and devotion towards his wife depicts a society where husband respected the wife. Valmiki describes the relationship between husband and wife and says, "The lute without strings does no sound, and the car without wheels does not move, so although having a hundred sons, a woman without her husband cannot attain happiness" (Ayodhya Kanda, 39–39, 30).The life of wife in other words, envisioned a centricty around husband and a non independence for women as desired by the men who wrote these epics and law books. However, the epics do not reflect much upon the legal rights of men and women. The only allusion to law is probably with the reference to *'strihatya'*.

When Rama killed Tataka, a woman *rakshasi* (demoness), his act is defended on the grounds that she was a murderer, so the act was an act of self-defence. It is cited that even Parasurama (a sixth incarnation of Vishnu and one of the famous sage mentioned in epics) had killed his mother at the instance of his father. *Strihatya*, killing a woman was a condemned crime, but it is told that if it was need of the hour in one's defence or if the woman was a murderer, same could be permitted.

The Smrti writers offer a great variety of thoughts on women. Right from her character to the set of duties prescribed for her, there seems to be a 'gender suffering' on the part of the women. Either she has been elevated to the pedestal of a goddess or plunged into the throes of critical remarks against her. Women are declared to be the incarnations of falsehood (*Maitranyaya*, S. I, 10–11). The *Satapatha Brahmana* (a prose text describing Vedic rituals) declares that women were not worthy of friendship, for they have hearts of hyenas. Manu not only denies them an independent existence at any stage of life but stresses their continual dependence on male relations. Whether it is the epics or the plays, all have mostly remarked strongly against the women and their character. The Mahabharata compared women with the edge of a razor, prison, snake, and fire in one (Anushasana 38.12 and 29). The Ramayana sees women as the 'renegades from Dharma, fickle, cruel and create estrangement' (Aranyakanda 45.29–30) Women's character is a subject to not only deep analysis by men, which not only seems imbalanced but even appears presumptuous, reflecting the societal biases of the time.

The ideal characterisation of women begins from her familial context and lies within it only. The idea of the whole and sole submission of woman to her one lord or husband is the predominant stereotype image envisioned by the Brahmana preceptors. She was acceptable neither as an individual of own identity nor with an identity of an ascetic (shunning the prescribed duties). The society permitted the courtesans to practise their profession and men were privileged to use licence to enjoy them. But the courtesans themselves were given a low-grade status.

If one cites the dicta in favour of woman, the defence seems incomplete. Whatsoever good or appreciative has been said about women, it is most vividly about the women who are dutiful or chaste wives, mothers, daughters, or sisters.

The gender quest would bring us the question as to the characterisation of men. Men per se, as a gender, have not been remarked in favour or against.

But the verses that came forth depict an explicit tilt in the favour of men, giving them an upper hand with respect to legally permissible rights. Where then duties and liabilities have been imposed, they seem to be more in the nature of assertion, reminding them of their responsibilities. But nowhere these obligations erode or undermine the privileges they were bestowed upon by the Brahmana Smrti writers.

Hence, within the legal arena, this gender divide was even more visible. The discriminations against women are discernible both in civil and criminal law. Women have been treated as of secondary status right from the beginning of legal history. She has, therefore, been awarded same special protections with respect to punishment or been treated as a class different from men. Within the sphere of procedural law, women had negligible roles. Women judges were unheard of, and even for writers, she was deemed unfit except for her own category.

According to Yanjavalkya (11.70), Narada (*Rnadana* 178, 190,191), a woman was unfit to be a witness in the court of law. But Manu, VIII. 68, 70, Yajnavalkya 11.72, and Narada (*Rnadana*, 155) allow women to be witnesses in disputes between women or in such cases where witnesses other than herself was unavailable. She could also be witness in cases of theft, adultery, or other offences in which there was an element of force or where to gather witness was difficult. Yajnavalkya considered a transaction with women as invalid.

In the field of civil laws, women enjoyed a host of legal protections starting from the premise that she had not enjoyed a status independent of men. A woman was not compelled to pay the debt of her husband or son (Yaj. III. 46, Vishnu, VUI. 31). However, if the wife contracted the debt and husband went away without providing for her, the husband would be responsible (Kautilya 3.11-21-24). Moreover, the debt of the wife of a herdsman, vintner, dancer, washerman, or hunter should be paid by the husband since their livelihood depends on them (Yaj Ch.VII, V.48, Vishnu, VI.37)

As far as property rights are concerned, we have already seen (in early part of this chapter) that women per se had no legally sanctioned property rights as daughter, wife, mother, or sister. They were deemed to have no property of their own. This probably referred to movable property. The only rights legally permitted were the right to maintenance and an absolute right of control over her movable property called *stridhana*.

As mentioned earlier, in the field of practice, in Vishnusena's Charter, we come across a gender-related ideal with respect to accusation of crime. It says, *'purusa apradhe stri na grahyam.'* (for a crime committed by her husband, wife could not be apprehended. This is probably the singlemost assertion that saves her from becoming a convict for a crime committed by her husband. It also puts forward the premise that crimes are committed individually and each should be held responsible singly for the wrong committed by him or her. However, if any wrong is committed by women, the indirect responsibility, the Smrti writers say, lies with her male relation on whom she may be dependent. The Mahabharata even says that it is not the woman who is at fault but it is the man who is at fault (when the woman goes astray) (Santiparva 267.38).

Among the plays, those of Kalidasa and few others reflect nearly similar views upon the status of women. One does not came across any gender defence with respect to women but only an affirmation of the stereotype of conventionally subjugated womanhood envisioned by the Smrti writers.

If we make a survey of the historical plays that fall in the period of the study, the gender consciousness seems no less pervasive. There is a predominance of male characters while female characters surface in various forms such as celestial and terrestrial women, women of noble descent, princesses, affectionate mothers, hermit girls, or courtesans. The picturisation of women is mostly with respect to her familial identity, and where courtesans are discussed, their status was deemed to be secondary to those with family links. It is a story of continuous deterioration of women's position with changing positions of male superiority.

The dutiful wife Sita is depicted by most poets as the highest ideal of womanhood. From Bhasa to Kalidasa, the stereotype of Sita is considered to be the ideal meant to be emulated by the female section in the society. Her wifely duties are more emphasised than her rights. Bhavabhuti asserted a slightly different image of Sita, for the poet wished to uphold the society that respected women's honor. However, lawgivers as much as the play writers (especially, Shaktibhadra, the author of Ascaryacudamani) talked about the character of women (*strisvabhava*), more often denouncing Sita. A representative of the Arya family is portrayed by most poets with same traits such as simple, obedient, soft-hearted, and completely dependent on husband. Women of so called Dravidian races—Surpanakha, Sramana, and other were depicted as having an emotional individuality of their own. Ratnamayidevi Dikshit has remarked after surveying the plays that "perhaps it may not be wrong to conclude that while in the North, which was the birth place of the Dharmasutras, the Smrti etc, the women were being pushed down, the South, which was kept safely apart from those influences due to geographical, historical and political reasons, had its women continuing more or less in the same old way, enjoying equal rights with the men."[18]

In the Mrcchakatika of Shudraka, the married women were held with great respect compared to any courtesan. In the play, the wife of hero Charudatta, Vasantsena, who was a courtesan was desperate to become respectable. However, Sarvilaka, brother –in- law of hero says that it was not easy to secure the position as the first wife. A polygamous society (Charudatta takes Vasantasena as his wife when his first wife is living) definitely implied the woman as having a secondary position. He, the hero, however had the freedom of extra-marital relation (for which no objections were raised). The existence of the class of courtesans by itself was indicative of their legal right to entertain as also the testimony to relationships being promoted outside the marriage.

The play has snide remarks on women's character, which is reminiscent of Manu's strictures on the nature of women such as where Sarvilaka says, "Only fools can put faith in women and in riches; both wriggle like serpents. Women do not deserve deep attachment; they are apt to insult a man who is attached to them. They should be enjoyed as long as they are themselves in love; otherwise, they deserve to be abandoned."

The first inscriptional evidence of Sati is mentioned in the Eran pillar inscription (510 AD).The first reference of Sati was for wife of Shiva God who immolated as mark of protest when her father did not accord her husband the respect she thought he deserved from him. Another mythological reference is with regards to Savitri and Satyavana (in *Satyuga* which was a mythological era when truth prevailed all around) where she symbolised the fidelity and devotion of a virtuous wife who was willing to follow her dead husband to heaven. The divine figure associated with death (Yama) then decided to allow her a wish and she asked for children, which in turn led to Yama giving back life to her husband.

The mythologies and social thought patterns directed women into certain ideal behavior modes to be adopted, as in any patriarchal society one would see. This social status and normative lessons filtrated even unto law where she was once again secondary by rights and privileges. Enunciations clearly exhibited the biases against gender existent at those times and sanctified by religion. On one hand between 250 BC to 650 AD, there was a deterioration of the social condition of women and on the other, law reflected the subordinating instinct towards women grew a little milder with regard to firming her control over moveable property and protecting her maintenance rights. All types of marriage were within the purview of the civil law. *Stridhana* was a permanent asset for her and an insurance. Law protected *stridhana* against misappropriation and misuse. This right was best protected under Brahma form of marriage where the bridegroom became the protector of the bride as commitment made to father at the time of *kanyadaan* (gifting of daughter after due rituals).Thisi form of marriage provided her the best legal and social protection.

Law, in ultimate analysis, is a pervasive institution. It can have lasting impact on people's lives in terms of their potential to accumulate endowments, access to resources or socio-economic status. If women or men have greater control over property, the gender balance in terms of economic productivity might be affected in any set up. Similarly, greater emphasis on position of son may both be a cause and result of differential status in the society as well as in law, particularly if inheritance rights would favour anyone group. Legal strengths would fortify men's position compared to women or within the caste structure of the upper classes men against the so called lower classes.

In early India, the position of women in law was distinctly one of subordination to the interests of male counterpart. Though in the society, she had an important role to play as a daughter, wife or mother, as an independent entity, she lacked an empowerment which would be the edifice for an identity that could be strong or consistent. Even though she may have enjoyed certain immunities as a dependent, her position and status in property rights was largely limited, more so with regard to immoveable property.

The unequal legal provisions in area of family, property, inheritance and status could define women's access to justice. And so it was in the early India. The emphasis on roles envisioned for her such as as an ideal daughter, mother or wife further may have discouraged the women to seek legal recourse of any kind without the explicit consent and support of any male support. The educational and social marginalisation too seems would have limited her access to seeking her rights. Legal consciousness was lesser in women as she had limited access to education, information or control.

The debate about the rights of women in law was addressed only under the colonial masters much later, although the struggle for gender justice continues even in free India. As Dr. Chitra writes in her introduction, the need to reform the Hindu legal system became very clear to the British by the end of the eighteenth century, when the British policy of non-interference with customary laws met with difficulties in implementation at ground level. She rightly points out that two factors, the national movement and the women's movement necessitated a reconfiguration in terms of legal rights and family laws.[19]

NOTES AND REFERENCES

1. An article, "What is Gender History Now?" by Alice Kessler Harris in the book *What is History Now?* authored by David Cannadine, p.99
2. Buhler, *Laws of Manu*, Ch.IX, v.26, p.332
3. Manu explains, '*putra*' as the 'deliverer from hell', who alone could do the '*pinda*' for the ancestors.
4. Buhler, *Laws of Manu*, Ch.IX, v.28, p.332.
5. Ibid., Ch.III, v.57, p.85
6. Ibid., Ch.IX, v.46.
7. Ibid., Ch.IX, v.81, p.342.
8. Ibid., Ch.IX, v.74, 76, p.340–41.
9. Ibid., Ch.IX, v.3, p.328.
10. P.V. Kane, *History of Dharmashastra*, p.562, quotes *Mahabharata* and *Kamasutra*, too.
11. Ibid., p.574.
12. Ibid., p.613.
13. Ibid., p.612.

14. Quoted by *Mitakshara* or 1.86
15. Kane, *History of Dharmashastra*, p.626.
16. Ibid., p.581.
17. Mentioned in Chapter on Civil Laws.
18. Ratnamayidevi Dikshit, *"Women in Sanskrit Dramas"*, *p.482*, Delhi
19. Chitra Sinha, *Debating Patriarchy, The Hindu Code Bill Controversy in India* (1941-56) Introduction, pp-xvi-xvii, OUP, 2012

CONCLUSION

Jurisprudentially, Positivists have overlooked the relation between law and morality while thinkers like Rawls, speaking on the sense of justice emphasised on both, the behavior code as well as the infrastructure of justice. Since Justice could also be interpretative, some scholars consider prime responsibility as on courts while others emphasise on the state role. Early India had a combination of emphasis on an ideal society and its norms on the one hand and the administration of justice on the other hand. An analysis of early Indian jurisprudence exhibits the prevalence of an intertwined law and Dharma and intersections of caste and gender in the society, proliferating in the area of law as well. The Smrti outlook towards law was to set a norm for society through the religious and legal injunctions. The presumption was that in society, standards of morality set by the intelligentsia would serve as a plea to the people to follow the ethical code without any challenges. State being the enforcer of Dharma laws had a special role, particularly as part of king's prime duties. Laws continued to evolve under these norms and customary laws and especially under visionary rulers. Historically, law saw an evolution through several milieu in the chosen period. One could take recourse to the approach of legal history in order to understand as to what constituted law, what served as its sources and also what purpose it served in such a society at different times.

Legal history is not merely a study of the theoretical or the idealistic aspects, but by incorporating the elements of legal practice, it comes off as a study of great practical value too. The various insights that we gain by close analysis of purely legal injunctions or instances in secular literature, throw welcome light on various aspects of the legal process that existed then. Further, the epigraphic instance of Vishnusena's Charter and the readings from secular literature reveal that law was a living entity shaped by community usages and king's intervention through the interpretation of the Dharma clauses.

Hindu Law in India, was an organic phenomenon, a vibrant social process, and a dynamic concept, filtered by creativity and deep thinking, keeping in mind the goal of social order or equilibrium. Law largely remained in the shadow of religion and when religious heterodoxies challenged established religions, law too underwent changes. Except under Ashoka, it may not have been egalitarian by approach or as secular as law of today's times in India; but it was a rich legal tradition that spoke on nearly all the aspects of law as in civil, criminal, and procedural components, evolving from rudiments to considerable requirements. However, it was a legal system where race, caste and gender were not only all pervasive but almost determined its course of development. Yet, the moral code emphasised a tone of conscientiousness and state clearly had to enforce these Dharma based enunciations judiciously. Dharma, in short formed the basis of the foundation for the emergence of law as a definite institution.

It is in the textual sources, in the form of the Dharmashastras that the basic concept of law originated and, combined with customary law and in some cases the royal edicts, it evolved into mature law. The nature of Indian law was cumulative, in the sense that rescensionary layers kept on being added to a core of legal thought and ideas on ideal or righteous society, depending upon the wisdom and seers of that social milieu as exemplified in the Smrti texts.

In the works of early *Smrti* writers, there seems to be an overlapping of the legal and moral injunctions with the dividing line between them being very thin. Religion and law were not clearly separated and often the abundance of verses related to norms overpowered the systematic enunciations of law. It is only in the later *Smrti* works that law emerged somewhat as a pure science with laws that seems to separate elements of law from religion. Religion, in other words was quite inseparable from the realm of law. Until the works of Narada, Brhaspati and Katyayana emerge, *Smritis* focus on cultivating a righteous conduct rather than being focused on pure legal injunctions. Hence, to classify them as pure legal texts would be overdrawn.

In fact, three stages are discernible in the growth and evolution of early Indian Law. The first stage was the Vedic and post-Vedic period, which talked of law as '*rta*' or the governing principle somewhat similar to Natural law. The principle of truth came to be added to it in the second stage when the concept of *Dharma*, the idea of righteousness, was developed. Some Smrtis such as Manu and Yajnavalkya belong to this category. The third stage is represented by the *Smrti* writers such as Narada, Brhaspati and Katyayana, in whose texts, are visible the crystallisation of pure legal injunctions and the idea of law acquiring proportions towards the form of law that we see today. It is remarkable that without having a notion of positive law in the beginning, it not only evolved but attained the status of a science and methodology gradually. The role of customs and practical wisdom cannot be undermined too as those too presumably, continually evolved. In the context of libertarian theories, which stress on autonomous or state founded laws, the early Indian scene provides an example of rich legal traditions with multiple sources.

Further, there are certain interesting features of the Hindu law that emerge from this study. First, in the study of legal history of India, the conscience of individual seems to have a centric role, especially in the texts of Manu and Yajnavalkya. The aim of law was ultimately to preserve the righteousness that could preserve the then social structure, as envisioned by those who had voice or were dominant in the society. The idea of Dharma was meant for a society where each would be conscientious of their duties and responsibilities in order to ensure harmony in the society.

Second, the need to preserve justice and fairness in judgement based on existent norms was spelt out in very strong words. If justice was neglected, it was continuously being emphasised, that it could lead to destruction of social order. The king, the state and the entire legal administrative set up had an immense responsibility in preserving the society through ensuring the prevalence and preservation of justice. It emphasised the need of impeccability of judicial decisions. In other words, it underlined the quality of justice system prevalent and the fairness of decisions thereof. Justice was treated like a virtue to be sought after.

Third, external factors like caste and gender determined the legal status of people or decided the immunities and punishments. The idea of equality before law was marred as some classes and castes had special status in the area of law and justice by virtue of being declared superior in the social ladder. Even though equal access may have been there, the punishments and penance differed for different castes and even gender. In other words, law was supportive of the social cleavages and hierarchy, instead of being an instrument to do away with these differences as would have been under a positive liberal state. The legal status of an individual was compounded due to these simultaneous limitations of class, caste, gender and race.

Fourth feature that is evident is that from the Dharmashastra stage, there is vertical development in role of the king in the concept of law. In early Indian Jurisprudence, the king was seen to assume wider powers, and he was deemed as the fountainhead of law and justice. He had no independent authority to make laws, but he was given the responsibility to uphold and maintain the laws existent, thereby giving protection to subjects and maintaining the status quo with respect to varnas (castes) and *ashramas* (stages of life). It became one of his primary duties to punish the wrongdoer and provide justice. Heavenly rewards were spelt out for a righteous king or who protected his subjects justly. He was expected to be learned in legal matters and was to attend personally to the administration of justice. In doing so, the *Varna* (caste) basis was not to be tampered with or the advice of legal advisors be ignored. He had a special role, in deciding the capital punishment. He was supposed to take opinion of the Brahmanical jury though, who were presumed to be knowledgeable and men with sense of fair judgement. Through Vishnusens's Charter, we even see that king had a role in legitimising popular demands in law through royal decree.

Fifth, there is a great deal of emphasis on the administration of justice and the precision to be followed in its delivery. The King was an essential part of the judicial procedure set up. As an apex of law, he was supposed to ensure that law was justly administered. He could initiate certain suits. He had the right to information through separate personages (appointed as *Suchaka* or *Stobhaka* as told by Katyayana). Vishnusena's Charter and the nature of the document suggest that the king was expected to incorporate the elements of prevalent customary laws in practice. The detailed specifications and requirements about the calibre of judges and their ability to distinguish between right and wrong indicate the need to choose such people who would have adequate legal acumen and sweet temper or patience.

The pro active role of king is seen asserted in King Ashoka's concern for justice in his empire and its administration through able functionaries. That the king had little role in creating fresh norms is visible in the laws preserved and implemented by various ancient India rulers and even in the case of Ashoka, who despite having professed ahimsa, did not abolish capital punishment. However, he makes the provision of retrial, *punar- nyaya*, which underlines the concept of appeal once again. He stands out in the comity of ancient kings as he voices out the need to enforce a certain amount of uniformity of procedure and uniformity of decisions on the part of judicial administration. Similarly, another instance of ideal in the realm of law and justice is visible in the advice to the king as laid down in Kalidasa's play in the term "*Yathapradhadanda*", as referred too earlier. He was expected to administer punishments in proportion to the crime committed. Ashoka was an exception as a king as through his edicts, he proclaimed laws which laid the basis of a state committed to welfare, secularism and uniformity of law and procedure.

Sixth noticeable feature of Indian legal system was the set of privileges extended to the special class of Brahmanas, the intellectual elites in early India as well as the upper three classes in the social ladder. Brahmanas enjoyed the supreme position with respect to law. As advisor and assistant to the king, the Brahmana's position remained unequalled. The king was expected to abide by the advice of this court of Brahmanas. However, Brahmanas who dealt with the legal matters were expected to be men well versed in the science of law and man of character, sweet tempered, and not greedy. If such Brahmanas were unavailable, Kshatriyas and Vaishyas (Katyayana added *Vanij* or merchant too) could take their place but never a Shudra (lowest in the caste hierarchy). As preceptors of society, however, the class of Brahmanas imposed its biases on the general fabric of the society.

As perpetuators of the caste-based hierarchical society, the intellectual elites practised and enforced these divisions in the realm of law. Their perception of the patriarchal supremacy and subjugation of the womenfolk to the men on whom they were dependent, determined the levels of gender pervasion in the area of law. Quite naturally, they enjoyed special protection in penal laws. A Brahmana offender was excluded from the purview of capital or death punishment. Since he was fortified by being born into the higher caste, he was expected to be of the least criminal temperament (by birth and social place). Hence, he could at best be banished or branded but never be hanged, for that itself (*Brahmanahatya*) was considered to be a grave offence.

Among the other classes, the Kshatriyas and Vaishyas enjoyed the middle position in society as in law. With respect to offence, guilt and punishment, they represented the middle layer. However, it was the Shudra who was as vulnerably placed in society as in law. For a similar offence, a Shudra was to be awarded death or capital punishment while a Brahmana was to be banished. Social hierarchy hence, created way for legal inequalities with the general position of Varnas remaining same in law as well as in society. This systemic social discrimination and marginalisation of Shudras practised over a long period of time sowed the seeds for the rise of dalit consciousness and led to the movement to oppose Brahmanism, symbolised in the Mahad Satyagraha where Ambedkar, the tallest leader among the dalits, set the Manusmrti on fire. Subsequently, the Dalit Movement has been carried forward.

Seventh, early Indian law exhibited idealistic concerns not only in the Smrti texts but even in some inscriptions that came within the purview of the study. For instance, the unique charter of Vishnusena serves a landmark document which underlines the importance of customary traditions of people as well as the earnestness of people to take their aspirations to royal authorities. This was in order to ensure that the same concerns may be embodied in the laws which may be finally enlisted for practice. It highlights the role of a legal remembrancer or an Ombudsman, who facilitated communication as well as depicted concern for welfare of the community. It even highlighted the role of state in the field of customary law.

The document stands out in such clauses, which mentioned norms, which were both indicative of a justice conscious society and a society where laws had seen significant growth of procedural aspects. Some of these clauses as follows substantiate thus-

1) *"purushapradhe strinagrahyam"*- This was a maxim that implied two things—that every individual was accountable for an offence committed by him or her; secondly, since women had no independent status with respect to law, she was not to be apprehended for an offence committed by her husband. However, the same is not spelt out vice versa. This could suggest that for a crime committed by her, it was the husband (or the male on whom she was dependent) who could be held responsible, directly or indirectly. Also, this could suggest that offence

by male was considered more grave and inexcusable. It offers some kind of legal immunity to wives from the ills or the wrongs committed by their husbands. While on all aspects, the wife is expected to be supportive or complementary to her husband, in matters of crime she has been given exemption. She is presumed to be secondary in household status and thus, also in law.

2) "*Aputrakamnagrahyam*"- It forbids the confiscation of property of one who died without leaving a son. It asserts that state could not confiscate at the cost of any legal heir other than the son. It is a strong assertion on role and responsibility of state in ensuring safety of people's property.

3) "*Sankayagrahanam n-asti*"- It referred to avoiding a situation where a royal official could apprehend a person or seize his things merely on the basis of suspicion. This called for a more professional and thorough approach to be adopted by the state with regard to arrests or confiscation.

4) "*arthi-pratyarthinavinavyavhaharanagrahya*" –It underlined the discipline of legal procedure that a suit could only be taken up for disposal if both complainant and defendant present and never in their absence. This aspect highlights the discipline of procedure to be followed.

5) "*kshem-agnisamutthanechhalonagrahya*"–*chhala* meaning pretext, it implied that no haphazard allegation should be entertained (against one's accusing neighbour for burning one's house when the conflagration may have occurred by fire originating in one's own house).

The Smrti texts lay a great deal of stress both in theory and in practice on the integrity and conduct of judges. If they performed any extra legal act, there were liable to double punishment. Further, they were not only expected to be just but also prevent the king from being unjust. Ashoka's edicts lay great deal of stress in the integrity of judicial officers too.

However, the ideal of '*Yathapradhadandanam*', however, seems to be an idealistic principle which may have been put in practice, as substantiated by Mudrarakshasa. In fact, early India represents a society where law was morality ridden while punishments were severe, even for crimes like thefts. Punishments, more often than not (until the later law writers), were out of proportion to the offence committed. Punishments were harsh, brutal and inhuman for a civilised society. Punishments varied from incapacitation to fines to physical or monetary punishments to admonition. Punishments were meant not only to prevent crimes and act as deterrent but also were reformative by approach as the purpose of punishments was also envisioned as to bring the culprit back to the path of ideal behavior.

Nearly all the Smrti writers exhibit a tough stand with respect to punishments. However, compared to Manu, the later writers are more reasonable with respect to punishments. The single most conspicuous feature of criminal legislation was the immunities enjoyed by the Brahmana class who were not only treated leniently but excused from death punishment for any serious offence for which the other castes could be hanged. There seems to be a graduated scale of punishment according to the social classes.

Criminal laws were based on the notions of good and evil, virtues and vices and rewards and sins. Abuse, assault, theft, and betting were considered as major crimes. The prevalence of stringent criminal code suggests that crimes such as these must have prevailed and therefore, necessitated such rules. Punishments varied from monetary payment to mutilation to capital punishment for these range of crimes. Theft and burglary especially, were seen as serious offences. With respect to theft, a maxim of Manu holds Brahmana more responsible than Shudra, with respect to guilt incurred. (Shudra's guilt as eightfold, that of Vaishya as sixteenfold, that of Kshatriya thirty-two-fold, and that of Brahmana as sixty-four-fold). Killing a Brahmana and killing of women were considered great sins. Adultery and forced abortion were deplored by nearly all the *Smrti* writers.

Judicial procedure or *Vyavahara* came to be dealt more scientifically by the later Smrti writers like Narada, Brhaspati and Katyayana. *Vyavahara* summed up the theoretical and practical aspects of judicial procedure. The Chief judge or *Pradvivaka* conducted the judicial trial under the auspices of the king. Trial began only when the plaintiff and defendant were present. Cases could be civil or criminal. Although a clear-cut distinction on modern lines is not discernible, elements like summons, evidence, witnesses and documents were all there. There are rules negating retrial or *punar-nyaya* as well. The titles or topics of Procedural law were organised into eighteen heads. The Chief judge was supposed to be a learned man who had the capacity to differentiate right and wrong and would be bold enough to even take on the head of the state if need be for the sake of justice. King remained the highest court of appeal.

Civil law, encompassing the property law, law of debt, inheritance, pledges, surety, ownership, deposits and partnerships, gifts, nonpayment of wages, and boundary disputes have also been dealt with at great length by the *Smrti* writers. That the patriarch or the head of the family had a complete control over the property is undisputed. The daughter had no power of control over the property while the parents were alive. There seems to be an absence of testamentary power as well. Wife was co-owner of the husband's property except that she had no right to dispose it off on her own. She was entitled to a right of maintenance and control over her *stridhana* (movable property acquired as gifts). After the father, the eldest son was supposed to shoulder the responsibility with respect to property and family and others were deemed dependent on him (Debt was a responsibility of the son too). In the absence of sons, one could appoint a daughter and allow her son to inherit all property. There were no clear-cut rights for women as wife or daughter or mother. Although it was a sin and offence to cast them off, the wife or daughter or mother had a theoretical say in the property of male dependents and a right to maintenance, dowry or *stridhana*.

The consciousness of gender is even more pervasive than the awareness of caste, both however playing a conditioning role in the society. As mentioned in the chapter on gender, it is a fluid concept that is normative and it conditions both the individual futures and the world view. The awareness as to the masculinity or femininity of oneself leads to particular types of behavior in the same society. This then influences the minds of both those who lead and those who are led. Gender identities define the respective status of men and women and their relationships in society. In the context of law, gender gets affected as well as affects the tone of law. Ancient India presents a classic example where gender consciousness was exhibited in nearly all socio-legal relationships.

Law in early India accorded an independent, high and a privileged status to men and a weaker, subjugated and vulnerable status to women. Equality before law was a far cry from gender viewpoint. Law treated women as weak and one in need of protection. She was deemed dependent on her male relations;

hence, it was the responsibility of the male relations to take care of her legal status. She was not secure even as a legally wedded wife as she had no control over husband taking more than one wife. However, with only a theoretical ownership in husband's property, she was entitled to no more powers than mere maintenance. Even in this, the legal tie of marriage was stronger for the lower classes. Likewise, women of lower classes were more miserably placed than the higher ones vis-à-vis the law. Familial ties, chastity and devotion to husband were extolled as feminine virtues, which secured her position in the heaven. Feminine character, however, was seen more often than not as despicable and in need to be guarded by men on whom she depended.

For men, the concept and perception of masculinity created through scriptural writings demanded that they consider the women as dependent on them. To provide protection and maintenance was his supreme obligation. As father, brother, husband, and son, he was to take care of his female relations by keeping them under restraint and allowing them only as much as the Brahmana law writers permitted. One virtue that was emphasised was fidelity towards wife. The punishment for adultery was tough for men (more than women). However, by permitting him to take another wife legally on grounds such as infertility or disease, etc., of first wife, it seems men were not bound to carry on the marriage contract. Remarriage was an easier option for men than women, for once he paid the maintenance to the first wife, there was no legal compulsion of divorce before taking another wife. Women, however enjoyed absolute right as far the *stridhana* (moveable assets) was concerned.

In punishments, the treatment of women is more liberal compared to men. Pregnant women, daughters and mothers had some special protection. Laws for abortion and adultery were strict for both sexes. Hence, in theory as well as in practice, law was overall more favourably placed towards men but certain immunities do come forth in favour of women.

The evolution of Indian law has continued uninterrupted except with some slowing down in medieval times. As while civil law in India is largely religion based, the pluralities continue even in modern India and have invited lot of attention. Criminal laws were reformed under inspiration of secular laws and the concept of 'Rule of law' from the West. The precepts of the Smrti period were argued and interpreted by the later commentators and this gave rise to various digests and commentaries on the Smrti texts, which embody the elements of pure law better. Two schools of law which emerged from the corpus of legal literature of early India were the thoughts of the Dayabhaga and Mitakshara schools, as mentioned earlier in the chapter on sources. While Dayabhaga was based on commentary of Jimutavahana, Mitakshara was based on the commentary written by Vijnaneswar on the Code of Yajnavalkya, the central difference being along the line of inheritance. The latter recognised the right of son over father's property, as soon as he was born while the former did not give the son the right to inheritance until the death of the father (or if he took to ascetism).The first was generally followed in West Bengal and Assam, while the latter was applied in co-parcenary rights as rule in rest of India and embodied in law in 1956. These commentaries form are relevant legacies of early Indian Jurisprudence.

The varieties of legal thought in one single period point that the idea and need for a study of jurisprudence, essentially stems from the fact that all laws emanate in some context and are shaped by structural as well as functional factors. By analysing through the approach of sociological jurisprudence, one not only appreciates the transition from the ancient to the modern in the historical and societal context, but also gains valuable insights into the current legal dilemmas stemming from certain legacies. Since, traditionally, the terms 'morality' and 'law' were used interchangeably, the same is indicative of the fact that morality had an unprecedented place in the thought process of such a society while pure law, as understood today, though co-existed, may have existed only in its rudiments. As traditional societies, including that in India, were based on foundational myths and on the idea to carry forward what the ancestors did, the growth in the concept of law was also limited correspondingly.

The core objective, which was to stress on cooperative and enduring relationships in a society where kin relationships and interdependencies were significant was to shape the ideas pertaining to both, morality as well as law in early India. Social relationships, which were based on scriptural foundational myths, laid the basis of emergence of power groups in the society. However, these were also a way of promoting social harmony or occupational order. What was essentially questionable was the hierarchy that was justified citing references in sacred texts, which were a product of the intellectual elites.

Law was largely supplementing these myths and the moralities emphasised in scriptures. Since it was religion based, people easily accepted these laws and codes. This was owing to the fact that in that milieu, rationality was secondary to religious beliefs. Yet, there is no doubt that these laws ensured the peaceful continuance and prevented the breakdown of society, despite political upheavals. Law not only emerged out of but also fostered these needs arising out of socio-economic relationships, transactions and partnerships, in the context of a distinct worldview. And while conflict resolution may have been one of the goals, law had a deeper role and that was to set a standard and tone of morality for society and sustain the social order. Though hierarchies and hegemonies existed, essentially, law served as a binder and the basis of a stable and perpetuating society. Justice was the goal to be achieved, through deliberations by the law functionaries and the king as it was a conjunct of welfare of all. Particular worldview had led to a unique design of law, guided by morality and an aspiration to create an ideal society.

It is important to note that in traditional societies such as in India, where kin was a prime factor and Sacred texts held a sway, morality played a larger role as compared to law. The context in which morality received greater primacy than rules thrived, as the situation was very different from modern liberal democracy, where people have greater say over law-making and greater awareness to defend individual and collective rights. Morality, was linked to the idea of subjective evolution as well as to that of social sustenance, as it was envisioned in a society, which laid immense emphasis on concept of salvation. It seems ironical though that while Dharma aimed for welfare of all, laws were discriminatory according to caste and gender. This was because the idea of social order itself was hierarchical. As interactions became multiple in a culturally diverse society, law gradually evolved. As more alternative ways of thought emerged in and outside Hinduism, Hindu law had to adapt for better. Under enlightened rulers like Ashoka, it had become more logical and universal while owing to the needs arising out of change in social and economic relations and under the impact of Upanishadic Hinduism, it became more tolerant, accommodative and milder in punishments than before.

Modern democratic societies, which are based on notion of equality and a non-hierarchical social base coupled with concern for individual and group rights, often present a challenge to law-makers. Law either becomes an instrument at the hands of governing elite or provides as an instrument to foster change in the light of positive liberal philosophy. Religion and law get segregated and divorced, except where personal laws may be allowed to prevail, based on religion as means to guard multiculturalism. As democracy becomes the preferred form of government and best guarantee for rights, several groups and aspirations start showing up the urge for legitimisation and this throws a big challenge to law and order. Various interest groups struggle to establish or constitute laws upholding their viewpoint.

Another dilemma and debate which emerges in multicultural societies with diversities is whether legal universalism would be a better guarantor of rights or legal pluralism. Should community law be allowed to evolve at the community level or should a positive liberal state seeking rule of law intervene and standardise the civil laws? In the case of India, as the colonial masters did not want to interfere with the different religious groups, religion based laws were not only continued but somewhat legitimised by the Britishers. This has clearly further accentuated the debate between universalism and pluralism in law in contemporary India. The colonial state's mediation to seek or standardise the texts, which could be the basis of dispensation of law for communities in civil arena exhibited an initiative of state to reconcile tradition in modern law with the help of religious scholars of each community. Should these trends be further carried forward or should the voice of Father of the Indian Constitution, Dr. Ambedkar be considered when he commented that state had power to intervene and usher in a Uniform Civil Code and act in favour of achieving social justice?

While in early India, the king epitomized the executive and judicial powers, in modern contemporary societies, this has undergone a transformation as all the three functions of government are segregated. Judiciary is expected to be independent, responsible, largely neutral as upholder of laws and act as a watchdog to the legislature and executive. The implication is that today the responsibility of justice is more of the Judiciary than the executive. Legislature ought to make laws as required by the changes in society but Judiciary must keep a check on its intentions and actions. If public welfare is overlooked or pertinent demands overlooked by the legislature due to ideological alignments of governing parties, Judiciary has to become the agency through which public welfare could be effected. This is exactly what happened in India. As the conscience keeper of the state, when the welfare state could not make justice accessible to all, Judiciary, deeming its accountability in imparting justice started with the idea of Public Interest Litigation or Social legislation. If legislature fails to provide adequate laws for public welfare, Judiciary could serve as an instrument for law creation. It has the potential to be the instrument in social change if so desired or need be in a democracy. Judiciary, hence in modern India is also caught in the debate of how to draw the line and not be too interfering with the legislature. It is a challenge for Indian Judiciary to combine the roles of independence, accountability as well as purposeful activism.

In the context of early India, wherein there were only few statutory laws under occasional rulers, it was largely great deal of legal scholarship and philosophy that shaped societal norms, morality and law. This legal scholarship and meaningful argumentation needs to be revived today. There appears to be an aspiration in early India to usher in an ideal moral code along with the set of laws. We may not impose moralities but we need to think, grow, evolve and adapt to the changes in society, which demand change in the laws. While the legal identity of a person in such a society was the product of caste and gender, where religion and law were interlinked, there was simultaneous existence of the ethical code that reminded individuals, the need to incorporate social obligations while on path of individual salvation. It is true that though in comparison to modern laws, the Smrti laws fall short on the touchstone of equality, their importance in forming the legal traditions of the country cannot be undervalued. They do provide the rudiments of the later emergence of pure legal system with greater clarity in subsequent commentaries.

The legacies of older social structure continue to pose a question whether religion should be allowed to prevail in the discourse of law today. Democracies essentially function on the principle of rule of law and the Constitution chosen. Law in such a set up is meant to strengthen human rights, though sometimes the legislators may fall short of expectations. In a heterogeneous society, laws should be consciously chosen and both, the lawmakers and the protectors would have immense responsibility in maintaining a progressive social order. Particularly, in today's pluralist world, where assertions of identities are permitted and continually keep emerging, law becomes a site and a means to achieve legitimacy to one's right to experience freedom. If good governance is to combine individual freedom with social harmony, the law making body would require to be benevolent and passionate about the quality of laws, while the judiciary must necessarily ensure that justice is not violated owing to individual or systemic failures. The solution does not lie merely in increasing the number of courts but rather in allowing laws to continually evolve at community level and through public debates. Justice cannot be mechanically implemented, it requires a soul to understand and a conscience to guard.

In Modern India, the personal laws constitute a challenge to the democratisation and equal development of all people across all religious groups. At the same time, as certain laws are age old and were largely the result of the challenges faced during the time of its making lead to situations of deadlock. Legal wisdom lies in sensitiveness to the discerning use of these laws and appropriate interpretation of the same in the present context in a careful manner. At the same time, those which have become effete, should be phased out or eliminated after ascertaining through public debates and by substitution with improved laws.

Law must qualitatively evolve in order to provision for a society, which is less fragile in terms of stability as well as is able to withstand dissent in a multicultural set up where multiple identities constantly compete for assertion and legitimisation. The emphasis of earlier legal system was on achieving Justice, emanating from effective interpretation of laws and dialogue based on qualitative argument by judges. Justice was seen as the primary test of the greatness of a ruler or state. Laws, elaborate yet far from being equitable, were to be applied using judgement by the capable and carefully nominated. The evidence of acceptance of inputs from the people or governed themselves in the form of representations indicates a system which was alive to the aspirations of people. On the part of civil society, there is seen an urge to legitimising such demands through the institution and apparatus of state. We need to revist the same.

If legal fairness and justice have to prevail and become the basis of an equitable society, the structures of power that prevail in various law making discourses today, will have to be carefully altered or reoriented. The responsibities of judiciary will have to be conscientiously carried forward in order to usher in a completely inclusive legal system. The intellectual civil society must involve itself and participate in public debates related to law and become the watchdog and the propeller of a fair system.

LEGAL GLOSSARY

A

Achara, (I E 8-5, E I), a custom or customary law.

Abhikara, cf krt-abhikara (CII I), probably means one who has committed an offence under the instigation of others.

Abhilekhitaka, clerks who wrote down the statement of cases in the law

Achara – patra (EK, 30), or sthiti-patra, acara-sthiti –patra; a document relating to customary laws.

Achara sthiti patra (IE, 8-5, EK, Vol.XXX, p.169), a code of customary laws; *sthiti patra* or a charter of customary laws. Vishnusena's charter is in the nature of charter. It is given the name acara sthiti patra.

Adeya (EI 7, 12, 15, CII III) implies what is to be taken or levied or dues (EI, Vol.XXV, p.237)

Adhikarana (EI 8-1, 8-8, EI 28, EI, Vol.XXX, p.173) implies a law court.

Adhikaranika (Mrcchakatika), IX.5) implied a judge.

Ahikaranamandapa, the Mrcchakatika mentions the court building thus.

Ashedha (Mar 1.4,47-54, Kat., 103-110) means arrest.

Adhikarana-danda (SITI) fine imposed by adhikarana or law court.

Adhikarana-lekhaka (EI, Vol.XXX), a scribe in a law court or office.

Adhikarika (IE 8-3, EI 2, 23, 28, HD), an officer same as adhikarin, Niyogika, Adhyaksha implying a minister, magistrate, superintendent or governor.

Adhipatra, (PL), a mortgage bond.

Adhisthana, (CII I), cf dharm-adhisthana, or the establishment of morality.

Akshatin, (EI, 29, HD) explained as an officer in charge of the gambling hall.

Angamani (SITI), property owned by a woman or dowry.

Anugraha-Sthiti patra is same as sthiti patra or achara sthiti patra (EI, Vol. XXX, p.169).

Anupratipatti, of dharma anupratipatti (CII, I), the practice of morality.

Anuttara (EI, 18), penance.

Apagratha (CII, I), same as upaghata, injury

Apada-dharma (EI, 15), custom regarding inalienable gift land.

Araksha adhikrta (ie, 8-3), cf, a police officer; a magistrate looking after the maintenance of law and order or the chief of the king's body-guards; same as araksika.

Adhilekhya, a kind of document mentioned by Brhaspati and Katyayana.

Angamabhukti means possession without title.

Arthasamudbhava (Brhaspati) implied suits originating in wealth.

Aputrakam (EI, Vol.XXX, p.170) means 'property belong to a person who dies without leaving a son 'Acara 1 of Visnusena say *'aputrakam na grahyam'*– that is to say that such property should not be confiscated by royal officials disregarding the claim of any legal heir other than the son.

Apradhe IEK, Vol.XXX, p.170) means guilt or offence.

Arthi (ei, Vol.XXX, p.170) implied a complainant.

Avedanakena, (EI, Vol.XXX, p.172) may indicate a formal complaint in court.

Ahvanam (EI, Vol.XXX, p.172) or being summoned to court.

Artha may refer to artha mula or civil suits (not himsa mula or criminal suit.)

Abhiyuktanam,(EL, Vol.XXX, 172) or the one against whom charges have been brought into the court.

Abhilekhita (IEL, Vol.XXX, p.172) or a written complaint.

Abhilekhitaka (EL, Vol.XXX, 174) or the clerks who wrote down the statements of cases in the law court.

Apachare (EL, Vol.XXX, p.174) used in the context of mudra apachare context.

Avalokya, (EL, Vol.XXX, p.175) derived from avaloka seems to indicate detection.

Anaprishtave (ch chhya), (EL, Vol.XXX, p.175) or a person let off for the first offence.

Adanam (MS, Ch.VIII, v.4), means non payment used with reference to debts. (masya adanam).

Artham (MS, Ch.VIII, v.45), or the object of the dispute, i.e., if it be not too insignificant in which case the plaint must not be accepted.

Anyavadi, (Narada) implies a person who after lodging a complaint abandons or puts forward a different one.

Abhishastas, (MS, Ch.VIII, v.64) meant "those accused of mortal crimes or offences (used in the context of witness; that Abhisastas could not be made witnesses).

Angasa, (MS, Ch. VIII, v.101) mean 'truly' or 'quickly'.

Anumana or proof. (MS, Ch. VIII, v.109).

Anubandham (MS, Ch.VIII, v.126) or the 'motive' or the frequency of the offence (used in the context that let the king ascertain the motive of the offence or anubandham.

Atisamvatsarim (Narada, v.151) means that (interest) which after the lapse of one year only is redundant, i.e., exceeds that which has been doubled.

Asteya or theft.

Adrishtam, or unapproved in the law books.

Alakshitah, (MS, Ch.VIII, v.162) the commentators explained it 'if a surety who received be not found.' (has died or disappeared, etc.)

Adhyadhinah, (MS, Ch.viii, v.167) or a person wholly dependent, i.e., a servant, a slave or the youngest brother or one in similar position.

Aksharayati, (MS, Ch.VIII, v.275) means 'defames' or 'accuses one of a mortan sin'.

Adhyagni, (Katyayana, v.895) that which a woman receives at the time of marriage before the (nuptial) fire.

Adhyavahanika, (Katyayana, v.896) that which she receives when being taken (in a procession) from her father's house (at the time of vidai or dwiragmana).

Anvadheya, (Katyayana, v.900) whatever is obtained by a woman from the family of her husband and family of her kinsmen.

Akshapatala - the Nalanda Spurious Copper Plate inscription of Samudragupta mentions *Aksapataladhikrta* as the keeper of records. Sircar explains Aksapatala as the court of law, a depository of legal documents.

Asvamivikraya, sale without ownership.

Atatayin, (Vasistha Dh-Sutra, III.15) could mean an incendiary, a poisoner, a man armed with weapon, a robber, one who wrested a field or carried away other's wife.

B

Bandhadanda, (IE, 8-5, EI, 12, 33), probably ransom or fine in lieu of imprisonment.

Brahmahatya, (CITD), killing a Brahmana, considered to be a great sin.

Bhedo, (EI, Vol.XXX, p.170) means break open or violate.

Bhrti, (Katyayana) defined as wages.

Bhogya, (Narada, v.124-125) to be enjoyed on pledges

C

Cara, (EK, XXVI, p.199) was a simple spy.

Chauroddharana, (EK XXXIII; HRS) was the right to punish or levy fines from thieves; probably, the right to recover the stolen property; recovery of stolen property; of sa – cauroddharana, (IE VIII-V, EI XXIII).

Carua-varjam, (CII III; HRS) 'with immunity from the police tax according to some; may imply without any right to inflict punishment on thieves and persons committing the crime of treason or to levy fines from them; may also be connected with a-bhata-praversa so as to indicate that the bhatas should not enter except for catching thieves and persons committing the crime of treason.

Chaurodharanika (IE 8-3, EI 23; G 13) – an officer incharge of the recovery of stolen property; a police officer; same as corodharanika (HD; CII, Vol.III, p.216) (mentioned in the inscription of Dharasena II of Valabhi).

Cirika (EI XXVI), a document, of kraya-cirika, 'a deed of purchasse', i.e., a sale deed.

Chauroddhartr (Yaj, II, 271, Katyayana as quoted by Apararka) was another denomination for a thief catcher.

Cora-drohaka-varja (CII III) a fiscal term which is similar to Coradandavraja. The work drohaka means one committing a crime against the king.

Coragraha (HD) a thief catcher (of Narada, Katyayana as quoted by Apararka, p.844).

Corarajjuka (HD) probably the same as dandapasika, an officer whose duty was to secure robbers with ropes (of Arthashastra, IV.13).

Cakravrddhi or compound interest.

Coravarjam, coradandavarjam implying fine imposed on thieves (Khoh CP grant of maharaja hastin and Jayanatha dated 496-97 AD (CII, III, p.124).

Chorpalli meant well protected robber settlements in which notorious robbers resided mentioned in Jain canonical literature (Uttaradhyayana sutra, 9.28).

Chhalam or a 'pretext'; in smrti literature it is used in the sense of a careless declaration' (EI, Vol. XXX, p.170).

D

Dharmasasana, (EI DXIII, XXII), an edict relating to dharma.

Dharmasthana IN Chammak Copper Plate grant of Maharaja Pravarasena (II, III, p.245-249).

Dharmamahamatras (Asokan Edicts) were those who looked after religious matters.

Dandanayaka (SI) probably indicated some sort of hereditary title of nobility rather than just an official connected with law and judiciary.

Dandapasika mentioned in Basarh seal and Valabhi grant of Dharasena mentions dandapasika as officer incharge of punishment and criminal justice. (IA, VV, p.187).

Dharmasava, Narada mentions it as the king's court of justice.

Danalekhya, (Brhaspati, v.16) was a deed of gift made when any property was given as gift.

Dasapatra was a deed of bondage or contract for labor (Brhaspati, v.16)

Dandaparushya or assault mentioned in Narada, Brhaspati and Katyayana.

Danda, (IE 8-5;EI 12) fine or tax mentioned along with sunks, (CII I), punishment.

Danda dasapradha (CII), fines including those imposed for the ten offences.

Dandaka (EI,30), probably a regulation.

Danda sulka (EK,23), income from fines and tolls.

Desa maryada, custom prevalent in a locality.

Dharmadhikarana (EI, 18, 23, 25, CII.4), a law court or a court of justice.

Dharmadhikaranim (HD), a judge.

Dharma adhikarin (IE 8-3, EI,33), an officer incharge of civil and criminal justice as well as charitable institutions.

Duhsadhya IEI 2), a criminal.

Dyuta (HRS), gambling, the king's dues collected by the superintendent of gambling.

Dyutasabhapati or the superintendent of the gambling hall.

Dutaka, a messenger witness.

Dattapradanika or resumption of gifts.

Dashapradha, or the ten offences or crims (of which murder occupied the foremost position. (CII, 3, pp.189, 218).

Dashapradhika was the designation of a class of officers who were incharge of
    ten specified kinds of criminal offences or apradhas. It occurs in several
    inscriptions (EI, 17, p.321, IA, 15, P.304).

G

Gandabhedakah, (kalidasa, Raghuvamsa) means burglars.
Gudhasaksin (one of Brhaspati's list of 12 witnesses), a secret witness, who stays
    concealed at the time of occurrence of the offence.
Granthibhedaka meant cut – purses who carried away things by loosening or
    cutting the knot (Yajnavalkya, II, 274).
Gudanta patra (Journal of the Bihar research Society, Vol.XL, Part.2, pp.96-
    97) meant a type of document, the exact nature of which is doubtful. It
    is a kind of lease deed.
Grahyam, (EI, 30, p.170) means to confiscate or take up.
Grihapana, (EI, Vol.30, p.172) implies persons engaged in work at home or
    shops (in the context that they should not be summoned to the court by
    means of a seal ring or a letter or messenger involved in acriminal case.
Gudhapurusa, EI, 4, p.250) was a secret service man.

H

Hastochhaya, the expression probably implies the raising of hand of a person
    engaged in making any kind of gifts.
Hinavadin, the defeated party. Katyayana calls such a person cast out in their
    pending suit as hinavadin.
Hrtapgrahah-amatya (EI 31), an officer incharge of the recovery of stolen
    property.
Hrasita (EI, 8-3), cf.svayam brasita karne, party cut off.
Himsamula or criminal suits, Yajnavalkya, p.125).

J

Jayapatra, (Brhaspati, VIII,19, Katyayana, 259, 260), the document of victory
    to be given to winners by the losing party.

K

Kantaka shodhana, (SITI) implied criminal justice.

Karana, (IE, 8-1, 8-8) same as or shortened form of *adhikarana.*

Kovera (IE, 8-5) cf. *karana koveram* was some levy at the court of law.

Kuta sasana (EI.7; IA, 30), a forged charter.

Karanapratyavasakandana, (Brhaspati, III.4, IV.9) was a type of answer (by the accused).

Kartta Kritika is unknown, but it may have indicated a royal agent or a, judge of a superior court or an officer, like the present day legal Remembrancer

L

Lekhaka or scribe write down the judgements delivered and was acquainted with various methods of writing.

M

Mahadharmadhikaranika, (CII,4) implied the Chief Justice. cf., Epigraphia Indica, (Vol.II, p.209).

Mahadharmadhyaksa, (IE 8-3;EI 12,21,26,33) explained as Chief Judge, officer incharge of charities.

Maha-dosa, cf mahadeva-vivarjita, EI 23) as an epithet of gift Village; probably fines for great crimes.

Matsyanyaya or the strong devouring the weak in the absence of proper punishment.

Mudrita, (Brhaspati, 1.3) meant furnished with royal seal (it was the court of Chief Judge who carries the seal of the king.)

Mudra, (Yajnavalkya, II.32; Katyayana, 88) was a sealed warrant by which the judge summoned the accused.

Mudraapachare, (El, Vol.XXX, p. 174) is the crime of using counterfeit coins (or the misuse of official seal.)

N

Nagavarika, Monier Williams calls him the chief person in a court or assembly.

Nirnaya or the decision was a part of the trial, the final stage of judicial trial, the verdict.

Nirarthaka, (Brhaspati as quoted in Smrti Candrika) complaint was one where injury or monetary value was negligible and could be rejected by king.

P

Pratyarthina (El, Vol.XXX, p. 170) or defendant.

Pratisthita (Brhaspati, I.3) were stationary courts.

Purvanyaya or *prannyaya*, (Brhaspati, III.4, IV.9) meant an answer by the accused with reference to a previous verdict in a similar sense.

Purusa apradhe or husband's guilt (El, Vol.XXX, p. 170)

R

Rta used in Rgveda meant the divine cosmic order by which the universe and even the gods were governed.

S

Sabhyas, (Manu, VIII, 10-11, Yaj, II.3, Narada, I, III.4) or assessors appointed by the king to assist the Chief Judge.

Sadhyapala or *sapurusa*, (Brhaspati, I.15) was the bailiff who was selected by the king from honest and obedient persons to summon and to keep in custody the witness, plaintiff and the defendant.

Sasita, (Brhaspati, I.3) or court directly presided over the king. *Sodhanaka*, (Mrcchakatika, IX) was a servant whose duty was to sweep the court hall and arrange seats.

Sreni was the corporation of persons practicing same kind of craft or profession though of different castes. They had their own executives committees and must have functioned as courts tosettle disputes among the members of the guild.

Sampratipatti or satya, (Brhaspati, III.4, IV.9) was a confession by the accused, a category of answer.

Sapatha, (Manu, VIII.109) or oath was a type of mode applied for the search of truth.

Sodhya, (Narada, II.95, 276) was a person who was to perform an ordeal.

Swahasta or signature, Katyayana recommended that king and his judicial members should affix their svahasta on the jayapatra (Katyayana, as quoted in Smrti Candrika, II, p.130). *Sasacara* or good custom or practice was regarded as a source of law.

Svayam hrasite, (El, Vol.XXX, p.170), a man who cut a bit of his own ears.

Sankaya grhanam n=asti, EI, Vol.XXX. P.170) or on the basis of sanka of a crime, the royal officials should not got on apprehending the persons (EI, Vol.XXX, p.170)

Sakshitve or witness (EI, Vol.XXX, p.172).

T

Tirtam (Manu, IX. 223) means on whom the sentence of imprisonment has been decided or adjudicated.

U

Uttarakulika varikaih, like the petavika meant a class of varikas or official associated with the law court.

V

Vakaparusya (EI, Vol. XXX, p.175) or defamation.

Vailabdhika may have been the custodian of recovered stolen property

BIBLIOGRAPHY

PRIMARY SOURCES

Textual

1. *The Bhagavadgita*, Eng.Tr. by Shakuntala Rao Shastri, New York, East West Institute, 1959.
2. *The Harshacharita of Bana*, Eng Tr by E.B. Cowell and F.W. Thomas, London, 1961.
3. *The Kautilya Arthashastra*, Ed. And Tr. by R.P. Kangle, 3 vols (reprint), Delhi, Motilal Banarsidass, 1992.
4. *Kautilya, The Arthashastra*, Ed. And Tr. by L. N. Rangarajan, Penguin Books, 1992.
5. *Katyayanasmrti on Vyavahara*, Ed. and Tr. by P.V. Kane, reprint from Hindu Law Quarterly, Bombay, 1933.
6. *The Manusmrti*, Ed. And Tr. By George Buhler, The Laws of Manu, S.B.E., Vol.XXV, Oxford, Clarendon Press, 1886.
7. *The Manusmrti* Ed. and Tr. by Narayana Ram Acharya, Bombay. Nirnaya Sagar Press, 1946.
8. *The Mahabharata*, Ed. and Tr. by V.S. Sukthankar, Poona, 1927-33.
9. *The Mahabharata*, Hindi translation by J.D. Goenka, Gorakhpur, Geeta Press.
10. *Narada Brhaspati smrti*, Ed. and Tr. by J. Jolly, S.B.E., Vol.XXXIII, Oxford 1889.
11. *The Ramayana*, Hindi Tr. by hanuman Prasad Potdar, 1994.
12. *Vishnu Dharmashastra*, Ed. by A.A. Fuhrer, Poona, Bombay Sanskrit and Prakrit series, Govt, Book Depot, 1914.

13.   *Yajnavalkyasmrti, (With the commentary of Vijnanesvara known as the Mitaksara and notes from the floss of Balambhatta),* Book I, *Achara Adhyaya,* Tr. by Srisa Chandra Vidyarnava, Allahabad, 1918.

14.   *Yajnavalkyasmrti,* Book II, ED. by J.R. Gharpure.

Epigraphic

1.   Burgess, J.ED, *Epigraphia Indica, Vols. I to XI.II.*

2.   Bhandarkar, D.R. (Revised and Ed.), *Corpus Insciptionum Indicarum,* Vol.III.

3.   Basak, Radhagovind, Ed. and Tr., by *Asokan Inscriptions,* Calcutta, Progressive Publishers, 1959.

4.   Diskalkar, D.B., Ed., *Selectinos from Sanskrit Inscriptions,* Vol.I, Part II, Madras.

5.   Devasthali, G.V., *Introduction to the Study of Mudra Rakshasa,* Keshav Bhikaji Dhavale, Bombai, 1948.

6.   Hultzsch, E,ed., *Corpus Inscriptionum Indicarum,* Vol I, *Inscriptions of Asoka* (reprint, New Delhi, Archaeological Survey of India, 1991.

7.   Mirashi, V.V.ed., *Corpus Inscriptionum Indicarum,* Vol.IV, *Inscriptions of the Kalchuri-Chedi Era,* Ootacaumund, Govt. Epigraphis for India, 1955.

8.   Sen, Amulyachandra, ed., *Ashoka's Edicts,* Published for the Institute of Indology by the Indian Publicity Society, Calcutta, Institute of Indology series, No.7,1956.

9.   Sircar, D.C., *Select Inscriptions Bearing on Indian History and Civilisation,* Vol.I, Calcutta, 1965.

SECONDARY SOURCE

1.   Aiyangar, K.V. Rangaswami, *Some Aspects of the Hindu View of Life According to Dharmasastras(*Baroda Oriental Institute, 1952)

2.   Altekar, A.S., *State and Government in Ancient India,* Delhi, 1962.

3.   Altekar, A.S., *Position of Women in Hindu Civilisation,* Motilal Banarsidass, 1962.

4.   Basham, A.L., *Wonder That Was India,* London 1954.

5.   Barder, C, *Women in Ancient India,* Varanasi, Chowkhamba series, 1964.

6.   Burke, Peter, *history and Theory,* Cambridge, 1992.

7.   Bhat, G.R., *Preface to mrcchakatika,* Ahmedabad, 1953.

8. Banerjee, Suresh Chandra, *A Companion to Dharmasastra*, D.K. Printworld Ltd., New Delhi, 1998.

9. Bhattacharjee, Sukumari, *History of Classical Sanskrit Literature*, Calcutta, Orient Longman, 1983.

10. Choudhary, R.L., *Hindu Women's Right to Property*, Calcutta, 1961.

11. Chandra, Moti, *The World of Courtesans*, New Delhi, Vikas, 1973.

12. Chitnis, K.N., Research Methodology in History, Delhi, 1990.

13. Derret, J.D.M., *Hindu law: Past and Present*, Calcutta, 1957.

14. Drekmeir, Charles, K*ingship and Communities in Early India*, Stanford University Press, California, 1962 (87).

15. Dikshit, Ratnamayidevi, *Women in Sanskrit Dramas*, Delhi, Meharchand Lachman Das, 1964.

16. Dikshitar, V.R.R., *Gupta Polity*, Madras, 1952.

17. Das, R.M., *Women in Manu and his Seven Commentators*, Varanasi, 1962.

18. Ghoshal, U.N., *History of Indian Political Ideas*, Oxford, 1959.

19. Jolly.J, *Hindu Law and Custom*, Calcutta, 1925.

20. Jha, Ganganath, *Hindu Law in its Sources*, Vol.I.

21. Jayaswal, K.P, *Manu and Yajnavalkya: A Basic Study in Hindu Law*, Calcutta, 1930.

22. Jain, M.P, *Outlines of Indian Legal History*, Bombay, 1966.

23. Kane, P.V, *History of Dharmashastra*, Vol.I-IV, Poona, 1946.

24. Kurundkar, Narhar, *Manusmrti – Contemporary Thoughts*, Tr. from Marathi by Madhukar Deshpande, Bombay, Popular Prakashan, 1993.

25. Kosambi, D.D, *The Culture and Civilisation of Ancient India in Historical Outline*, London, 1965.

26. Khan, Benjamin, *The Concept of Dharma in Valmiki Ramayana*, Delhi, Munshi Ram Manohar Lal, 1965.

27. Ketkar, Sridhar V, *Hindu Law and Methods and Procedure of Historical Study Thereof.*

28. Law, N.N, *Studies in Ancient Hindu Polity*, Vol.I, New York, 1914.

29. Majumdar, R.C, *Classical Age*, Bharatiya Vidya Bhavan, Bombay, 1954.

30. Mulla, D.F, *Principles of Hindu Law*, Bombay, 1962.

31. Mayne, J.D, *Treatise on Hindu Law*, Bombay, 1963.

32. Moghe, S.G, *Studies in the Dharmashastra*, Delhi, Ajanta Publications, 1991.

33. Pal, R.B., *History of Hindu Law in the Vedic Age*, Calcutta, 1958.

34. Patkar, Madhukar M, *Narada, Brhaspati and Katyayana, A Comparative Study in Judicial Procedure,* Delhi, Munshiram Manohar Lal, 1979.

35. Prasad, Beni, *The State in Ancient India,* Allahabad, 1928.

36. Sharma, R.S. *Aspects of Political Ideas and Institutions in Ancient India,* Delhi, Motilal Banarsidass, 1962.

37. Sengupta, N.C., *Sources of Law and Society in Ancient India,* Calcutta, 1930.

38. Spellman, J.W., Political *Theory of Ancient India,* Oxford, 1964.

39. Sircar, D.C., *Political and Administrative Systems of Ancient and Medieval India,* Delhi, Motilal Banarsidass, 1974.

40. Shastri, Shakuntala Rao, *Women in the Vedic Age,* Bombay, 1969.

41. Shastri, V.S. Srinivasa, *Lectures on the Ramayana,* Madras, 1994.

42. Sinha, G.P., *Post-Gupta Polity (A.D.500-750),* Punthi Pustak, Calcutta, 1972.

43. Thapar, Romila, *Ancient Indian Social History: Some Interpretations,* Delhi, Orient Longman, 1984.

44. Upadhyaya, B.S., *India in Kalidasa,* Delhi, Sultan Chand and Company, 1968.

45. Varadachariar, S. *The Hindu Judicial System,* Lucknow, 1949.

46. Watters, Thomas, *On Yuan Chwang's Travels in India* (A.D.-629-645), Munshiram Manoharlal Publisher's Pvt. Ltd.

JOURNALS AND ARTICLES

1. Journal of Ancient Indian History, Vol.I, Parts I and II, 1967-68.

2. Proceedings of Indian History Congress.

3. Indian Antiquary.

4. Journal of Indian History.

5. *"In Search of our Past: A Review of the Limitations and Possibilities of the Historiography of Women in early India",* in Economic and Political Weekly, April 30, 1988.

6. *"Beyond the Altekarian Paradigm: Towards a new Understanding of Gender Relations, in Early Indian History",* In Social Scientist, Vol.16, No.8, 1988.

NEW READINGS

1. Justice M.Rama Jois, *Legal, Judicial and Constitutional History of India*, Universal Law Publishing Company,1984
2. Kumkum Roy, *The Power of Gender and the Gender of Power*, OUP
3. Chitra Sinha, *Debating Patriarchy, The Hindu Code Bill Controversy in India* (1941-56)